BARRON'S BUSINESS LIBRARY

Financial
and Business
Statements

Second Edition

George T. Friedlob
Clemson University

Franklin J. Plewa, Jr.
Idaho State University

BARRON'S

All inquiries should be addressed to:
Barron's Educational Series, Inc.
250 Wireless Boulevard
Hauppauge, NY 11788
http://www.barronseduc.com

Library of Congress Catalog Card Number 99-57924

International Standard Book Number 0-7641-1339-9

Library of Congress Cataloging-in-Publication Data

Friedlob, G. Thomas.
    Financial and business statements / George T. Friedlob, Franklin J. Plewa, Jr. –
2nd ed.
        p. cm. — (Barron's business library)
    Includes index.
    ISBN 0-7641-1339-9
        1. Financial statements. I. Plewa, Franklin James, 1949- II. Title. III. Series.
HF5681.B2F7725   2000
657'.3—dc21   99-57924
                                                                               CIP

PRINTED IN THE UNITED STATES OF AMERICA
9 8 7 6 5 4 3 2 1

Contents

Introduction to Reports and Basic Accounting

INTRODUCTION AND MAIN POINTS

Almost all measures of business activity involve numbers and are presented in accounting reports. Dollars earned last quarter, labor variances at a new plant, production scheduled for next month—all sorts of reports are prepared and presented to managers, owners, regulatory agencies, and other interested parties on a regular basis. Other reports, such as those analyzing capital acquisitions or reporting the results of special management studies, are prepared on an as-needed basis. Regularly prepared reports help the reader make routine decisions; they might be consulted by stockholders considering whether to buy or sell stock, managers adjusting production techniques, and purchasing agents ordering raw materials, for instance. Other reports provide information for nonroutine decisions, helping managers select a merger candidate or react to a change in market conditions, for example.

After studying the material in this chapter:

■ You will appreciate the many forms accounting reports can take.
■ You will realize that all accounting reports are created for a particular end use and that understanding that use can help you begin to understand the report.
■ You will understand the basic mechanics of the double-entry system of accounting.
■ You will understand the principles that underlie all accounting reports.

HOW THIS BOOK IS ARRANGED

Learning to understand accounting reports is a formidable objective. Accountants produce reports for many different end uses; some reports go to stockholders, creditors, and others outside the company, while others are targeted for managers and employees inside. The Securities and Exchange Commission (SEC), the Financial Accounting Standards Board, and various committees of the American Institute of

Certified Public Accountants have promulgated volumes of formal principles, standards, and rules to organize and regiment reporting to individuals outside the company. Reporting inside the company is less structured but is often confusing to the uninitiated.

Regardless of their appearance, accountants' reports are created to meet an objective and to satisfy a need. If you understand the objective and know what is necessary to satisfy the need, you can learn to understand the report. This book contains 20 chapters, each of which offers a practical guide to understanding some aspect of a particular report and is designed to be read either straight through or in random order. If you are puzzled, for example, over the significance of earnings per share, you can consult the chapter on earnings and read the section that discusses that topic. Similarly, if you do not understand the mechanics of budgeting or performance reporting, you can turn directly to those particular chapters for help.

Financial and Business Statements is divided into sections, each focusing on one type of report—the annual report, other public reports, financial-statement analysis, budgeted reports, performance reports, government reports, personal financial statements, and prospectuses of mutual funds.

Section One introduces the reader to the contents of an annual report; each of its eight chapters covers one component of a typical statement. Management's presentation, financial statements, notes, supplementary schedules—all are discussed in practical, down-to-earth language so you can begin to understand and interpret published annual reports. Section Two covers other public reports, including quarterly reports, compilations and reviews, and filings with the SEC. Section Three consists of two chapters on financial-statement analysis. These chapters contain the ratios, techniques, and tips needed to analyze and understand the content of the reports discussed in the first 12 chapters.

Section Four covers budgeted reports, including standard costs and variances for control, and the business plans required by many bankers. The use of budgets (and other tools) for performance appraisal and the reports of company internal auditors are discussed in Section Five. The material in these two sections should arm you with the basics necessary for understanding the ways accounting reports are used to evaluate and control performance. Whether you are an employee evaluated by a system of accounting reports or a manager using reports to assess and control the behavior of others, a knowledge of the process and games involved is invaluable.

Finally, Section Six discusses government reports, personal financial statements, and prospectuses of mutual funds. The discussion of government reports includes governmental budgets and encumbrances (quite different from profit-oriented budgeting), funds, and the government-wide financial report. The chapter on personal financial statements includes a how-to discussion on preparing the type of personal financial statement required by lenders. And, the chapter on the mutual fund prospectus will teach you how to locate and interpret the information you need to select the funds for your investments.

ACCOUNTING STRUCTURE AND PRINCIPLES

In order to understand many accounting reports, you must have at least a rudimentary understanding of basic accounting. This is particularly true for understanding annual reports or budget schedules that culminate in forecasted statements. The accounting you will need is not that difficult. We will introduce you first to the basic structure of accounting and then to the accounting principles that govern annual reports, the subject of the next seven chapters.

The Basic Structure of Accounting

Accounting is based on a simple relationship that explains both the different types of accounts and the way events are recorded and that can be understood by thinking of a business or government entity in terms of resources and sources.

All the economic resources that a company owns came from somewhere—their source. The dollar amount of resources must equal the dollar amount of sources. The basic accounting relationship (called the accounting equation) can be stated as:

$$\text{Resources Owned} = \text{Sources of the Resources}$$

The accounting term for the resources owned by the company is *assets*. The two sources of a company's assets are borrowing (debt) and owner investment. The dollar amount of assets must equal the dollar amount of debts and owners' investment.

$$\text{Assets} = \text{Debts} + \text{Owners' Investment}$$

The accounting term for debts is *liabilities;* another name for owners' investment is *owners' equity.* Owners' equity includes both the owners' initial investment and reinvestment of company earnings not distributed to owners. In its final form, the *accounting equation,* sometimes called the *balance-sheet equation,* is as follows:

$$\text{Assets} = \text{Liabilities} + \text{Owners' Equity}$$

Understanding the balance-sheet equation is fundamental to understanding accounting. The construction of the balance sheet provides a system of checks on the accuracy of the accounting system. This system of checks is called the *double-entry system,* so called because each economic event must affect the balance-sheet equation in two ways in order to keep the equation in balance. For instance, if a company is formed by an investment in stock of $5,000, two components of the equation must be increased to show the effect of this transaction: assets (cash) and owners' equity (owners' investment). If either assets or owners' equity is not increased, the equation will not balance.

$$\text{Assets} = \text{Liabilities} + \text{Owners' Equity}$$
$$+ \$5,000 = 0 \qquad + \$5,000$$

If the company then borrows another $15,000, two more effects must be recorded: Assets are increased by the cash received, and the property rights of the bank are recorded.

	Assets	=	Liabilities	+	Owners' Equity
	+ $5,000	=	$0	+	$5,000
	+ 15,000	=	+ 15,000	+	0
Total	$20,000	=	$15,000	+	$5,000

If the company buys a building for $4,000, the asset "cash" must be decreased and the asset "building" increased. In this example, one asset is traded for another of equal value, and the equation still balances. When a loan is repaid, cash (an asset) is decreased and a liability is decreased. When one account is increased, another must be decreased to keep the equation in balance.

Revenues are increases in owners' equity produced by inflows of assets as a result of doing business. As cash or accounts receivable increase, owners' equity also increases. *Expenses* are decreases in owners' equity produced by outflows of assets (or inflows of liabilities) from doing business. Expenses result when the company consumes the benefit of its assets. The assets are decreased, and the owners' equity is also decreased.

Revenues and expenses, like assets, liabilities, and owners' equity, are types of accounts. The accounting equation, expanded to include revenues and expenses, is as follows:

$$\text{Assets} = \text{Liabilities} + \text{Owners' Equity} + \text{Revenues} - \text{Expenses}$$

This equation contains all the types of accounts that accountants use; there are no others.

Basic Accounting Principles

Basic accounting principles are the rules and assumptions that under-lie financial reporting in published annual reports, quarterly reports, and reports to the SEC. The same principles also guide accountants in the preparation of budgets and other reports for use inside the organization. These principles tell accountants what items to measure and when and how to measure them. Basic accounting principles include

1. The accounting entity
2. Measurement of resources and obligations
3. Periodicity
4. Going concern
5. Historical cost and unit of measure
6. Accrual accounting
7. Substance versus form
8. Conservatism
9. Materiality

Each of these concepts is defined and discussed in the remaining sections of this chapter.

Accounting Entity. The *accounting entity* is the business unit for which financial statements are being prepared. Legal form does not determine the accounting entity. For example, only corporations and trusts are granted legal existence separate from their owners; a proprietor's business is legally an extension of his personal affairs. Accountants do, however, account for the personal affairs of the proprietor as separate from the business affairs of the proprietorship. Unless the proprietorship affairs are accounted for separately, it is not possible to determine if the business activity has been profitable. An accounting entity may also be composed of a parent company and its majority-owned subsidiaries—legally separate entities but in substance a single economic entity.

Measurement of Resources and Obligations. *Business resources* (assets) are those items of value that the business possesses and can use to produce a profit. *Obligations (liabilities) are amounts owed to nonowners of the business. The difference between assets and liabilities is the owners' interest (equity)* in the business, including personal investment (*contributed capital*) plus any profits earned by the business and not paid out to the owners (*retained earnings*). A set of financial statements contains measures of assets, liabilities, and owners' equity at the end of the fiscal period (in the balance sheet), as well as changes that have occurred in assets, liabilities, and owners' equity during the period (in the income statement, statement of retained earnings, and statement of cash flows).

Periodicity. *Periodicity* is the assumption that a company's life must be divided into periods of time in order to measure profit or loss. Ultimately, profitability can be determined only by comparing the owners' interest at the time the business began to the owners' interest at the time of dissolution. However, viewing profit or loss at the end of the business's life does not provide timely information for management, investment, and credit decisions. Therefore, accountants divide a company's life into fiscal periods—for example, a year (fiscal year) or a quarter (fiscal quarter).

Going Concern. A measurement concept, the principle of *going concern* assumes that, in the absence of contrary evidence, the company will continue to operate indefinitely. From a valuation standpoint, this allows for carryover, from period to period, of previous values placed on assets, liabilities, and owners' equity. It also requires that measurement techniques be consistent from one fiscal period to another.

Historical Cost and Unit of Measure. Assets and liabilities are recorded in the accounting records at their original or *historical cost.* For example, if we purchase land for $1 million with a $1 million mortgage, the asset land is entered at $1 million and the liability mortgage note payable is also entered at $1 million. These values continue in the accounting records until another business event indicates the need for changing them. Examples of such events are the sale of assets or the payment of liabilities.

The *unit of measure* employed in financial statements of U.S.-based entities is the *nominal dollar,* or the dollar arising from the exchange transaction unadjusted for inflation or deflation. As a result, one company may have land acquired in 1930 recorded on its books at $100,000 while another company has a similar piece of property, acquired in 1988, recorded on its books at $1 million.

Accrual Accounting. The *accrual principle* is used to translate into dollars of profit or loss the actual activities of the fiscal period. It combines two ideas—revenue recognition and matching.

The *revenue-recognition* principle requires that revenue (sales price) be recorded when the necessary activities to sell a good or provide a service have been completed. Revenue is recorded at the point of sale regardless of whether cash is collected or a receivable from the customer is created at that time.

The *matching* principle tells the accountant when to record an expense. It associates efforts (expenses) with achievements (revenues). It has three parts: cause and effect, systematic and rational allocation, and immediate recognition.

Cause and effect means that the costs directly associated with producing a certain revenue are expensed in the same period that the revenue is recorded. Sales commissions are an example of cause and effect; there is a direct association between the sale and the effort of the salesperson that can be measured by the salesperson's salary and commission.

Systematic and rational allocation is used for other costs—those for plant and equipment, for example—that are long-lived and that help produce revenue for several accounting periods. While there is not a direct causal link between plant occupancy and the sale of a unit of product, occupancy benefits the company for more than one fiscal period. The accountant expenses the cost of these types of assets over their expected lives. If a piece of equipment is expected to be used for ten years (the activity measure), its historical cost should be expensed as a cost of revenue production over that same period (i.e., depreciation).

Other costs that are not long-lived and do not have a causal relationship to revenue are *recognized immediately*—that is, when they arise. Management salaries are an example of this type of cost. It cannot be said that the company president's salary directly produces sales or that the cost of his or her services is long-lived; a president who is not paid stops working. Therefore, the cost is an expense in the period in which it arises.

Under the matching principle, an expense can be recorded before, after, or at the time a cost is actually paid. From the accountant's point of view, it is the earnings activity that gives rise to the conversion of cost to expense. It does not matter whether that cost has been paid or a liability created.

Substance Versus Form. The accountant attempts to report the economic *substance* of the transaction without regard to its *form*. Although a business pledge to a charity is not a binding obligation upon a company, an accountant still records it as a liability. The company has made a promise; it cannot avoid honoring that promise without damaging its reputation. Therefore, the company is likely to pay the pledge.

Another example of substance versus form is the capital lease, a long-term lease that transfers the basic rights of ownership and that is treated as an alternative way to purchase an asset. The business that leases the asset records an asset and a liability, just as it would have if it had financed the purchase of the asset by borrowing on a long-term note from a bank.

Conservatism. *Conservatism* does not mean preferring undervaluation to overvaluation, or understatement of income to overstatement of income. Conservatism means that when in doubt, accountants should choose the option that will least likely result in an overstatement of income or assets. The accounting practice of conservatism favors valuing assets at their historical cost even though the asset, such as land, may have increased in value each year since its acquisition. Conservatism favors recording losses even before they actually occur if they are considered likely to occur; however, the recording of a gain is postponed until the gain actually occurs even when the gain is considered likely to occur.

Materiality. *Materiality* refers to relative importance of accounting information to the user of the financial statements. A transaction must be accounted for within the measurement and reporting principles known as Generally Accepted Accounting Principles (GAAP) when the amounts involved are judged to be material.

Materiality of a transaction must be determined by its effect on the financial statement. When pooled in the financial statement, similar transactions, each involving immaterial amounts, may together have a material effect. For instance, a single purchase of a computer costing $1,500 may not be material; readers of the financial statement may not care if it is expensed or recorded as an asset. But what about 500 computers, purchased at different times during the year? It would be misleading to treat this $750,000 purchase of office equipment as an expense in the year of purchase, because the computers have a useful life of more than one year and will benefit the company over their useful life. The combined amount of the purchases is material.

CHAPTER PERSPECTIVE

In this chapter, we have discussed the forms accounting reports can take—routine and nonroutine, and the various audiences for which they are prepared—among them stockholders, managers, and government agencies. There is a purpose for each report; understanding that purpose is essential to beginning to understand the report.

Accountants use a double-entry system to record events in the accounting system according to the nine basic principles underlying all accounting reports: the accounting entity, measurement of resources and obligations, periodicity, going concern, historical cost and unit of measurement, accrual accounting, substance versus form, conservatism, and materiality.

The next section of this book focuses on annual reports; the sections that follow discuss other types of reports.

Management's Presentation, Statement Notes, and the Audit Opinion

INTRODUCTION AND MAIN POINTS

A company's annual report is produced only in part by accountants; only the financial statements included as part of the annual report are produced by the accountants. Much of an annual report is produced by the company's nonaccounting managers and discusses a variety of topics, some based on accounting figures, some not. (A second group of accountants, the company's independent external auditors, evaluates the financial information provided in the annual report and provides an expert opinion on its accuracy and completeness; this opinion is an important part of the report.)

This chapter focuses on the contents of the annual report; later chapters cover the accounting requirements of the financial statements.

After studying the material in this chapter:

- You will understand the purpose of an annual report.
- You will know the sources of the accounting principles governing financial reporting.
- You will know which components of the annual report are produced by management and which are produced by accountants.
- You will realize the importance of the notes to the financial statements.
- You will understand the importance of the auditor's opinion and the types of opinions auditors can render.
- You will be familiar with the structure of consolidated financial statements, the form of financial statements used by most companies.

THE ANNUAL REPORT

An annual report is designed to satisfy the information requirements of many different people with many different needs. Stockholders, creditors, economists, financial analysts, suppliers, and customers all look to annual reports to satisfy their information needs. Because they must satisfy such a diverse audience, annual reports are rigidly structured by both convention and legal requirements.

REPORT HIGHLIGHTS, LETTER TO SHAREHOLDERS, AND REVIEW OF OPERATIONS

Management's part of the annual report usually consists of three sections: the annual report highlights, the letter to shareholders, and the review of operations.

1. *Annual Report Highlights.* The highlights section focuses on the bright spots in the company's operations, financial statements, stock performance, or whatever management wishes to present. Frequently, graphs or tables that display the favorable trends management wishes to emphasize are included. This section also contains the company's sales, profits, and earnings per share for several years.

2. *Letter to Shareholders.* The letter to shareholders commonly begins with a statement such as "I am pleased to report . . ." and is signed by the president alone or with the chairman of the board. The key to understanding the letter to shareholders is to ask "What do I expect them to say?" and "What did they really say?" The answer to the first question is usually obvious: The letter will contain a predictably self-congratulatory, optimistic message. But the second question is harder to answer. Vague wording, colorful adjectives, and meaningless euphemisms are commonplace, and messages may be obscure.

3. *Review of Operations.* The review of operations, a public relations presentation, usually consumes the largest part of the annual report and is designed to impress the reader. The company may dwell on its products or its many locations in beautiful settings—whatever management and the public relations department decide is effective. Most of the photographs and artwork are in this section. You may enjoy it—but interpret it with caution!

FINANCIAL STATEMENTS

The heart of an annual report is the financial statement, which must conform to accounting and reporting standards established by the Financial Accounting Standards Board (FASB), the Securities and Exchange Commission (SEC), and various committees of the American Institute of Certified Public Accountants (AICPA). The requirements of these different groups are a mixed blessing. Because financial statements are very structured, they are not tailored to meet the needs of any one group precisely, and each group of users may find something lacking. But because of the high degree of structure and the involvement of the CPA, users of financial statements can be sure that the information they receive adheres to the principle of fair presentation; they can review the financial statement of a company in New York or California and decide to buy stock, lend money, or in some other way become involved with the company, solely on the basis of its audited financial statements.

Financial statements provide the substance of the annual report. At a minimum, they consist of a balance sheet, income statement, statement of cash flows, and the accompanying notes and auditor's opinion.

THE NOTES TO THE STATEMENTS

The notes to the financial statements are as important, if not more important, than the statements themselves. Many times, numbers by themselves do not adequately express material information (that which would make a difference to a financial statement user; see Chapter 1); notes to the financial statements are largely descriptive and include information on such things as accounting methods, commitments, lease obligations, contingencies, stock-based compensation, long-term debt, income taxes, and significant events affecting the company between the end of the fiscal year and the issuance of the annual report. Note disclosures relating to the following areas are discussed in this chapter:

1. Accounting methods
2. Commitments
3. Leases
4. Contingencies
5. Pensions and post-retirement benefits
6. Financial instruments

1. *Accounting Methods.* Accountants use many methods to summarize business transactions in financial statements. In many instances, several acceptable methods of reporting a transaction have evolved and are in current use. Because different methods exist for recording the same transaction, accountants have had a hard time standardizing financial reporting.

Accounting principles require that if a company has a choice of valuation methods, it must disclose the method used; traditionally, this is done in Note One. For example, different accounting methods exist for valuing inventories and computing depreciation. Acceptable inventory methods include specific identification, FIFO, LIFO, average cost, and lower of cost or market. Acceptable depreciation methods include straight-line, units of production, sum of the years' digits, and double declining balance. Note One specifies which inventory and depreciation methods have been used by a particular company.

Note One is important because the choice of accounting methods directly affects balance-sheet valuation and the computation of net income. For example, some methods of depreciation allow higher expense deductions than do other methods. Depending on the method of depreciation that is selected, net income will vary, as will the value carried in the balance sheet for the related item (asset).

Financial statements of a company are not directly comparable from year to year unless the company consistently uses the same valuation methods. Companies are required to disclose a change in accounting methods (Chapter 6 discusses disclosures relating to a company's change in accounting principle). Similarly, direct comparison of financial statements of two different companies is not possible unless they are based on the same accounting methods. Note One is very important because it tells us the methods used by the company to prepare its financial statements and therefore whether two reports are or are not comparable.

Figure 2-1 is an example of the disclosure of accounting methods in a typical Note One.

2. *Note Disclosure of Commitments.* A commitment is a contractual agreement to do something. Some of the more common types of commitments disclosed in financial statements involve long-term purchase arrangements, the terms of outstanding loans, agreements to refinance existing debt, lines of credit, lease arrangements, and employee pension plans (discussed later in this chapter). You should pay close attention to these arrangements. Many commitments affect the company in the future by adding to its debt structure and increasing the amount of cash necessary to meet current obligations.

Different types of commitments are entered into by a company. Some commitments directly affect the balance sheet at the time they occur. For example, borrowing $1 million increases assets by $1 million and liabilities by $1 million. Commitments that are unexecuted affect the company's future operations and may not be recorded on the balance sheet. An example is a commitment to purchase 5 million parts from a supplier over the next five years. Regardless of whether accounting principles require the commitment to be recorded on the balance sheet, the principle of materiality requires that the details of significant commitments be disclosed in the notes to the financial statements.

Notes to Consolidated Financial Statements

Note 1—Summary of Significant Accounting Policies:

Principles of Consolidation: The consolidated financial statements include the accounts of all significant wholly owned and majority-owned subsidiaries. Intercompany transactions and balances have been eliminated. Investments in partially-owned equity companies are accounted for under the equity method.

Inventories: Inventories are generally stated at cost that is not in excess of market. Domestic manufactured inventories of standard products are valued on the last-in, first-out (LIFO) method and all other inventories are valued using the first-in, first-out (FIFO) method.

Property and Depreciation: The company principally uses accelerated depreciation methods for both tax and financial reporting.

FIG. 2-1 *A Note One fragment showing the disclosure of accounting principles.*

3. *Notes Relating to Leases.* Leases are a type of commitment. Some noncancellable long-term leasing arrangements, known as capital leases, are viewed as alternative purchase and mortgage arrangements and transfer the risks of ownership to the lessee (the party leasing the asset). Capital leases are essentially purchases of capital assets. A typical note disclosure of lease commitments is shown in Figure 2-2.

The lessee of a capital lease records an asset "Property Subject to Capital Leases" and a liability "Obligations Under Capital Leases." The amount recorded as the "historical cost" of the leased asset is treated as if it were the purchase price of the asset. Since this is a long-term arrangement, the lease payments must allow the lessor to recover not only the original investment in the leased property but also a reasonable return—"interest."

The lessee expenses the leased asset's historical cost over the term of the lease (or the asset's economic life if the lessee will obtain ownership of the asset at the end of the lease term). Lease payments are divided between principal payments on the recorded lease obligation and interest expense, just as loan payments are divided between payments of principal and interest expense.

Note 7—Lease Commitments

The present value of net minimum lease payments, net of the current portion of the payments and any unamortized discount, totaled $64 million and $71 million at December 31, 2001 and 2000, respectively.

At December 31, 2001, future net minimum lease payments for capital and operating leases (excluding oil and gas, coal and other mineral leases) were the following (in millions):

	Capital	Operating
2002	$ 14	$ 149
2003	11	133
2004	10	115
2005	9	103
2006	9	97
Thereafter	116	690
Total minimum lease payments	$ 169	$1,287
Less—executory costs	(7)	
imputed interest	(92)	
current portion	(6)	
Present value of net minimum lease payments, net of current portion and unamortized discount	$ 64	

Rental expense for operating lease, net of immaterial sublease rentals, was $206 million in 2001, $172 million in 2000, and $142 million in 1999.

Included in the 2001 and 2000 property, plant, and equipment accounts were $243 million of property leased under capital leases and $124 million and $108 million, respectively, of related accumulated amortization.

FIG. 2-2 *Note showing the disclosure of lease commitments.*

Short-term leases and leases that do not transfer the risks of ownership are called operating leases. In such an arrangement, the lessee does not record the leased asset or obligation on the balance sheet; all lease payments are recorded as rent expense.

Care should be taken when comparing financial statements of companies that lease to the financial statements of companies that do not lease. All leases give the lessee the benefit of using an asset in exchange for payments at specified intervals. Regardless of whether accounting principles require the lease to be recorded on the balance sheet, the company has a resource to use and an obligation that must be met by cash payments. The financial statement note on leases provides you with the significant details of the lease arrangement and the lease payment schedule.

4. *Note Disclosure of Contingencies.* A contingency exists when, because of a past transaction or event, a company stands to gain or lose. The amount of gain or loss is "contingent"—that is, dependent—on another transaction or event. For example, suppose a customer who falls and is injured at your place of business then files a lawsuit. You are now in a contingency situation: The event giving rise to possible loss is the injury of the customer. The amount of loss, if any, will be determined in the future by settlement or court verdict. Typical loss contingencies relate to tax assessments, litigation, governmental investigation, and environmental issues.

All contingencies may be classified by likelihood of outcome: remote, possible, or likely. Contingencies that managers, their lawyers, and their accountants believe have only a remote chance of gain or loss are usually not disclosed. In situations in which a gain or loss is possible, the contingency must be disclosed, along with management's estimate of the range of possible gain or loss.

If a contingency is viewed as likely to result in a loss, it must be accrued (a loss recorded along with an estimated liability). The amount that must be accrued is the most reasonable estimate of loss. If a single estimate of loss cannot be determined, the smallest amount in management's estimated loss range will be accrued. The nature of the contingency and the estimated range of loss are described in footnote disclosures.

Contingencies that are likely to result in gain are not accrued, only disclosed. This is the principle of conservatism (see Chapter 1) at work. Conservatism favors recording losses before they are realized if they are considered likely to occur, but postpones recording a gain until it occurs. The nature of the gain contingency is described in the notes to the financial statements. Gain contingencies include possible receipts of cash from gifts or donations, refunds from tax disputes, and awards from a court case where a favorable action is expected.

Notes on contingencies should be evaluated with care. Contingency losses may be time bombs waiting to wreck a profitable company. Ask yourself these questions: What will be the cash-flow impact on the company if the possible or likely contingency loss comes to pass? Is the company's debt and liquidity structure capable of handling the loss?

5. *Notes Relating to Pensions and Post-retirement Benefits.* The key to understanding the cost of providing employee pension benefits

is to realize that the accounting records reflect management's best guess as to what the actual cost will be, rather than fixed, predictable costs. Employees earn pension rights through service to the company. Accountants attempt to measure the cost of these retirement benefits at the time the employee earns them, rather than when the employee actually receives them. Pension expense represents the amount of money that management should invest at the end of the year to cover future pension payments owed to employees for this additional year's service; the investment plus the interest it will earn must provide for these payments when they are made in the future.

Why is pension cost only a best guess? All kinds of assumptions about unknowable factors must be made to calculate the required annual investment. Some of these assumptions are the average years of company service of an employee at retirement, the salary level of the employee at retirement, the number of years an employee is expected to live after retirement, and the rate of interest the invested funds are expected to earn. As these estimated values change, revisions are made to pension cost. Rather than adjusting the current period's pension expense for the total change in estimate, these revisions are spread over the current and future accounting periods.

When employers adopt an employee pension plan, they usually grant employees credit for their years of service prior to the adoption of the plan. The cost of the investment to cover future pension payments for these years of service credit (prior service cost) is also spread over current and future accounting periods.

Management may choose to invest more or less than the current year's pension expense. If more than the current year's pension expense is funded, the excess funding is recorded in an asset account called "Prepaid Pension Cost." If less than the current year's pension expense is funded, the difference is recorded in a liability account called "Accrued Pension Cost."

Most invested pension funds are handled by a trustee. The trustee, typically a financial institution that specializes in pension investments, maintains separate accounting records for the invested funds. The investment is not reported on the balance sheet of the employer company.

Notes to the financial statements disclose the following:

1. A description of the pension plan, including the employee groups covered;
2. The type of benefit formula used to calculate the employees' retirement benefits;
3. Management's funding policy;
4. The current period's pension expense;

5. A schedule that reconciles the funded status of the plan with the amount reported on the balance sheet, i.e., prepaid pension cost or accrued pension cost. This reconciliation is necessary because the pension obligation (called the projected benefit obligation) and the assets available to pay the retirees (called the fair value of plan assets) are not recorded on the balance sheet. Figure 2-3 shows the reconciliation of the funded status of the plan to the amount recorded on the balance sheet;

FIG. 2-3 *Reconciliation of Funded Status of the Plan to the Amount Reported on the Balance Sheet.*

The following reconciles the funded status of the Plan to the amount recorded in the Consolidated Balance Sheet at December 31:

	2000	1999
	(Millions)	
Projected benefit obligation at beginning of year	$1,294	$1,176
Service cost—benefits earned during period	31	27
Interest cost on projected benefit obligation	88	86
Net loss	61	77
Benefits paid to participants	(74)	(72)
Projected benefit obligation at end of year	1,400	1,294
Fair value of Plan assets (primarily equity and debt securities) at beginning of year	1,347	1,232
Actual return on Plan assets	143	187
Benefits paid to participants	(74)	(72)
Fair value of Plan assets at end of year	1,416	1,347
Plan assets in excess of projected benefit obligation	16	53
Unrecognized net (asset) resulting from initial application	(15)	(20)
Unrecognized net loss (gain)	31	(4)
Unrecognized prior service cost	47	52
Asset recorded in the Consolidated Balance Sheet	$ 79	$ 81

Assumptions used in determining the projected benefit obligation at December 31 were as follows:

	2000	1999
Discount rate	6.5%	7.0%
Annual increase in future compensation levels	4.0	4.5
Expected long-term rate of return on Plan assets	9.0	9.0

FIG. 2-4 *Disclosures Relating to an Underfunded Pension Plan*

The following table sets forth the changes in the benefit obligation and the fair value of plan assets for 2000 and 1999:

	2000	1999
Change in benefit obligation:		
Benefit obligation at beginning of year	$ 5,039	$ 3,751
Service cost	711	570
Interest cost	354	283
Actuarial losses (gains)	381	546
Benefits paid	(107)	(111)
Benefit obligation at end of year	$ 6,378	$ 5,039
Change in plan assets:		
Fair value of plan assets at beginning of year	$ 3,043	$ 2,431
Actual return on plan assets	(203)	529
Company contributions	359	194
Benefits paid	(107)	(111)
Fair value of plan assets at end of year	$ 3,092	$ 3,043
Funded status of the plan (underfunded)	$(3,286)	$(1,996)
Unrecognized net actuarial losses (gains)	1,156	343
Unrecognized transition obligation	6	7
Unrecognized prior service cost	58	64
Accrued benefit cost	$(2,066)	$(1,582)

6. The discount rate, the rate of compensation increase used to measure the projected benefit obligation, and the expected long-term rate of return on plan assets.

Don't get carried away trying to analyze this data. Remember, it is only best-guess information. It is questionable whether companies even realize the magnitude of the obligation they create every time they agree to increase employee benefits.

Approximately one third of all workers in the United States participate in employer-sponsored post-retirement plans. These plans cover benefits such as medical care, dental and eye care, legal and tax services, day care, tuition, and housing assistance to retirees, their spouses, and dependents. Although the terminology relating to post-retirement benefits differs slightly from that used in pension accounting, the basic accounting principles and disclosures are the same; however, there are some significant differences between the two. One difference is that most post-retirement plans are currently not funded or are underfunded. Also, the future level of health-care use and costs is hard to predict.

Finally, many post-retirement health-care plans do not put limits on health-care benefits. These three differences can be cause for concern in determining a company's potential obligations for post-retirement benefits. If a company's workforce is young or a company does not yet have a large number of retirees, the future cost can be significant.

If you ever encounter a liability account called "Unfunded Projected Benefit Obligation," beware. This means that, given the current rate of earnings, the company's pension fund investments are not enough to cover the future benefits management expects to pay their employees. Similarly, a company whose policy is to fund less than its current year's pension expense may find itself in a tight spot down the road.

An example of the disclosures relating to an underfunded plan appears in Figure 2-4.

6. *Financial Instruments.* Traditional financial instruments consist of cash, receivables, investments, notes, and bonds. The fair value of these instruments, which can be assets or liabilities, is disclosed in the notes to the financial statements. (Most financial instruments that are assets are carried on the company's books at fair value while most liabilities are not carried at fair value.) In recent years, innovative instruments that modified the nature of these more traditional instruments have become quite common in business whereby companies can acquire, issue, or enter into a contract as a buyer or a seller. These instruments can be quite complex and have created accounting and reporting problems not only for users of financial statements, but for preparers as well. Many of these types of instruments being created today are called derivative financial instruments. A derivative is any kind of financial instrument whose value depends on a change in the underlying value of something else (e.g., the value of bonds, stocks, interest rates, or commodities). Examples include hedging options, swaps, futures contracts, or forward contracts. Derivatives are to be recorded as assets and liabilities on the balance sheet at their fair value on the balance sheet date. Changes in the fair value of derivatives should be recognized in the income statement in the period in which they occur.

Until recently, many of these financial instruments (either assets or liabilities) have not been recorded in the accounting records and did not appear in the financial statements. Examples of these types of items included financial guarantees, interest-rate swaps, and loan guarantees. When the possibility of an accounting loss from one of these financial instruments exists, a company is exposed to what is called "off-balance-sheet risk." This risk occurs because another party may fail to perform according to the terms of a contract or future changes in market prices, or because interest rates may make the financial instrument less valuable. Companies are required to disclose information about financial instruments that expose them to off-balance-sheet risk. Figure 2-5 is an example of the disclosure relating to financial instruments. For fiscal years beginning after June 15, 2000, all companies are required to record all derivative financial instruments in the balance sheet as either an asset or a liability measured at its fair value and that changes in the derivative's fair value be recognized currently in income.

FIG. 2-5 *Disclosure Relating to Financial Investments.*

The carrying amounts and related fair values of the Company's financial instruments are as follows (in thousands):

December 31	2000		1999	
	Carrying Amount	Fair Value	Carrying Amount	Fair Value
Marketable securities	$ 16,087	$ 16,087	$ —	$ —
Long-term debt	249,149	260,707	250,559	262,233
Off-balance-sheet derivative:				
Fuel contracts	—	(4,169)	—	(1,060)

Marketable securities are considered available-for-sale securities for financial reporting purposes and are classified with Equipment Deposits and Other Assets on the Consolidated Balance Sheets. Fair value for these investments is based on quoted market prices for the same securities. Unrealized holding gains on these securities, which are included in Other Comprehensive Income, were $1,540,000 as of December 31, 2000. Realized gains recognized in 2000 were $1,531,000.

Discussion regarding the fair value of the Company's long-term debt and fuel contracts is disclosed in the respective notes to the consolidated financial statements. Carrying amounts for cash, trade accounts receivable, and current liabilities approximate fair value.

OTHER DISCLOSURES
Supplementary Tables
A number of supplementary tables may accompany an annual report. Some of the most frequently encountered are reporting by segments, financial reporting and changing prices, five-year summary of operations, and two-year quarterly data. Figure 2-6 shows a typical supplementary table containing a five-year summary of selected financial data.

FIVE-YEAR SUMMARY OF SELECTED FINANCIAL DATA
(Dollar amounts in millions, except per-share amounts)

For the years ended December 31,	2000	1999	1998	1997	1996
RESULTS OF OPERATIONS:					
Net sales and operating revenues	$ 20,068	$ 19,417	$ 17,096	$ 15,344	$ 14,534
Income before extraordinary gain (loss)	256	313	184	172	455
Net income	285	302	240	181	696
Preferred dividend requirements	7	7	27	74	224
Earnings per common share before extraordinary gain (loss)	.92	1.26	.78	.66	2.21
FINANCIAL POSITION:					
Total assets	20,741	20,747	16,739	17,467	11,586
Senior funded debt, net	6,872	6,179	4,739	5,613	1,955
Subordinated debt, net	1,281	1,438	1,600	1,832	1,796
Redeemable preferred stocks	13	13	13	13	337
Stockholders' equity	5,899	6,224	5,164	4,308	3,281
Common dividends declared per share	2.50	2.50	2.50	2.50	2.50
Average shares outstanding (thousands)	269,486	243,120	200,986	149,730	103,843

See Management's Discussion and Analysis and the Notes to the Consolidated Financial Statements for information regarding business acquisitions, asset dispositions, the issuance of stock of subsidiaries and other items affecting comparability.

FIG. 2-6 *A supplementary schedule showing selected financial data.*

Management's Discussion and Analysis

Management's discussion and analysis, an objective presentation required by the Securities and Exchange Commission, covers all developments affecting three areas of the company's business: results of operations, capital resources, and liquidity.

The management discussion and analysis section, unlike the report highlights, letter to shareholders, and review of operations, is not produced by the public relations department. It is supposed to contain a discussion of all past and future conditions and uncertainties that may materially affect the business. You may find this section quite informative.

THE AUDITOR'S OPINION

The independent auditor's opinion, a short report addressed to the shareholders of the company, gives an opinion on the financial statements prepared by management. An unqualified opinion is good; any other opinion is less than good. Qualified opinions, containing the phrase "except for," should put you on guard.

The standard report form, which was adopted in 1988, is designed to increase public awareness of the nature and the limitations of the audit. As stated in the first paragraph of the report, management—not the auditors—is primarily responsible for the financial statements; the statements are prepared under management's direction.

The second paragraph of the audit report describes just what an audit is. The auditor tests the accounting records and supporting documents to form an opinion on the reasonableness of the financial statements. Standards developed by the American Institute of Certified Public Accountants offer guidance and define the auditor's responsibilities in various situations. For instance, the standards require that an auditor confirm receivables and payables; however, because auditors draw test samples, only a sample of receivables and payables is confirmed. Testing all accounting records would be too time-consuming and expensive; remember, it took a year to accumulate the data. Based on the outcome of the test samples, the auditor forms an opinion on the reasonableness of financial statement presentation.

The third paragraph of the audit report contains the auditor's opinion. An auditor may express a "clean" (unqualified), "qualified," or "adverse" opinion or "disclaim" and express no opinion at all.

The auditor also states that the financial statements are "in conformity with generally accepted accounting principles" (GAAP). GAAP, the accounting profession's collection of rules governing financial statement presentation and measurement, includes the basic accounting principles discussed in Chapter 1. The accounting profession and auditors view financial statements that follow GAAP as fair presentation.

Qualified Opinion

A qualified opinion points out to the financial-statement user the particular area the auditor believes is not fair presentation. The auditor believes that the remainder of the statements are fairly presented.

Adverse Opinion

An adverse opinion states that the auditor does not believe the financial statements are fairly presented and lists the factors that led the auditor to that opinion.

Auditors base their opinions of financial statements on evidence gathered from the test samples. Because they do not test the complete accounting records, material misstatement may exist without the auditor's being aware of it. As pointed out above, a qualified or adverse opinion raises questions of fair presentation. When a qualified or adverse opinion is given, the financial statement user should read carefully and seek to understand the auditor's objections to the presentation. Exhibit 1 shows the standard audit report.

EXHIBIT 1
Standard Audit Report Form
(Unqualified Opinion)

We have audited the accompanying balance sheet of Wiggins Battery Company as of December 31, 2000, and the related statements of income, retained earnings, and cash flows for the year then ended. These financial statements are the responsibility of the Company's management. Our responsibility is to express an opinion on these financial statements based on our audit.

We conducted our audit in accordance with generally accepted auditing standards. Those standards require that we plan and perform the audit to obtain reasonable assurance about whether the financial statements are free of material misstatement. An audit includes examining, on a test basis, evidence supporting the amounts and disclosures in the financial statements. An audit also includes assessing the accounting principles used and significant estimates made by management, as well as evaluating the overall financial statement presentation. We believe that our audit provides a reasonable basis for our opinion.

In our opinion, the financial statements referred to above present fairly, in all material respects, the financial position of Wiggins Battery Company at December 31, 2000, and the results of its operations and its cash flows for the year then ended in conformity with generally accepted accounting principles.

Simmons, Clark & Early, CPAs

January 31, 2001
Nashville, Tennessee

CHAPTER PERSPECTIVE

In this chapter, we have discussed the components of the annual report produced by a company's management and accountants. We discussed the purpose of the annual report, the source of the accounting principles that govern financial reporting, and the notes to the financial statements, emphasizing the importance and meaning of notes on accounting principles, commitments, leases, contingencies, pensions and post retirement plans, and financial instruments. Finally, we explained the involvement of the independent auditor and discussed the standard audit report and the types of opinions an auditor might render.

The Balance Sheet: Classification and Current Assets

INTRODUCTION AND MAIN POINTS

Annual reports must contain three financial statements: the balance sheet, the income statement, and the statement of cash flows. The income statement and the statement of cash flows both show business activity (earning and spending) over a period of time—usually a quarter of a year. The balance sheet, in contrast, is a report of resources owned and debts owed at a particular point in time. In this chapter, the first of three on the balance sheet, we talk about the structure of the balance sheet and the formal classification of accounts within it. We then begin our discussion of the classified accounts by examining current assets, comprising primarily cash, receivables, and inventories.

After studying the material in this chapter:

▬ You will know what a balance sheet is and how it differs from the other statements in the annual report.

▬ You will understand how accountants classify accounts within the balance sheet to assist readers of financial statements.

▬ You will know what current assets are and how accountants decide which assets belong in this group.

▬ You will know which items are included as cash on the balance sheet.

▬ You will know which items are included as receivables on the balance sheet.

▬ You will understand how the statements are affected by the allowance for uncollectible accounts.

▬ You will know what components may comprise total inventory and why they are carried at the lower of cost or market.

THE STRUCTURE OF THE BALANCE SHEET

As we explained in Chapter 1, accountants use a system of record-keeping, called double-entry bookkeeping, which is based on the relationship between business resources and the source of those resources. Business resources, or assets, are created by using funds obtained either by borrowing (creating a liability) or from the investment of the owners (creating owner's equity or property rights in the business). The relationship between assets, liabilities, and owners' equity is expressed as:

$$\text{Assets} = \text{Liabilities} + \text{Owners' Equity}$$

A balance sheet, or statement of financial position, is a report that displays the business's assets, liabilities, and owners' equity at a specific date. The recorded value of the assets always equals the recorded value of the liabilities plus owners' equity. In Chapter 1, we gave a simple definition of assets, liabilities, and owner's equity. In this chapter, we will expand those definitions.

ASSETS

Assets are those items of value that a business possesses and can use as it attempts to produce a profit. In order for a company to record an asset on its balance sheet, the resource must possess three characteristics: (1) the potential to generate positive cash flow, (2) the ability to be controlled, and (3) the right of use or control, granted in a past transaction or event.

The first characteristic, positive potential cash flow, means that management believes the resource is capable of bringing cash into the business. Controllability indicates that the resource provides an advantage that can be used as the company sees fit. The third characteristic, the right of use, results from the historical, backward-looking nature of accounting. Financial statements report only the results of past transactions or events.

To be listed as an asset on a balance sheet, a resource must also be capable of being valued. Because valuing assets can be difficult or impossible, significant resources often go unrecorded. Employees, probably the most important resource a business has, are an example. You would not hire someone unless you believed the person could contribute positively to your operations. The right to control or assign the employee job tasks belongs to management and arises out of the employment contract. But how do you measure and objectively value an employee? Obviously, you can't. Even though an employee can be considered an asset, valuation problems prevent employees from being listed as assets on a balance sheet.

Legal ownership is not a required characteristic of an asset. Equipment leased long-term that transfers the basic rights and risks of ownership is recorded as an asset on the books of the lessee.

LIABILITIES

Liabilities—the debts of the business—are the amounts owed to nonowners. Liabilities possess three characteristics: (1) they represent the possibility of a future payment of cash to settle the obligation, (2) they are obligations that management has little chance of avoiding, and (3) they are the result of a past transaction or event.

Obligations do not have to be legally binding before they are recorded as a liability on the balance sheet. A business pledge to a charity is not legally binding on management, but it is recorded as a liability, because the obligation can be valued and all three characteristics of a liability are present: an obligation exists as a result of management's signing a pledge card at some time in the past; there exists the possibility of a future payment of cash to settle the pledge; and management cannot honorably avoid payment of the pledge.

OWNERS' EQUITY

Owners' (or shareholders') equity is the difference between the recorded value of a business' assets and its liabilities. It includes amounts directly invested by the owners (contributed capital) plus any profits earned by the business that have not been paid out to the owners or shareholders (retained earnings).

When the corporation sells shares of stock, it creates ownership. The cash received increases assets and equity (contributed capital) equally. For a company to realize net income, the inflow of assets from earnings (as measured by revenues) must exceed the outflow of assets to produce those earnings (as measured by expenses). Assets

increase, and liabilities are not affected; therefore, ownership (retained earnings) must be increased. A simple example will illustrate:

John invests $100,000 to begin a business. Immediately after his investment, John draws up the following balance sheet.

Assets		Liabilities	
Cash	$100,000		$ 0
		Owners' Equity	
		Contributed Capital	100,000
	$100,000		$100,000

John pays $10,000 to buy inventory (an asset until it is resold). His balance sheet now appears as follows:

Assets		Liabilities		
Cash	$ 90,000*		$	0
Inventory	10,000	**Owners' Equity**		
		Contributed Capital		100,000
	$100,000			$100,000

*100,000 − $10,000

John eventually sells merchandise that originally cost him $4,500 (expense) for $6,500 (revenue) for a net income of $2,000. His balance sheet then appears as follows:

Assets		Liabilities		
Cash	$ 96,500*		$	0
Inventory	5,500**	**Owners' Equity**		
		Contributed Capital		100,000
		Retained Earnings		2,000***
	$102,000			$102,000

* $90,000 + $6,500
** $10,000 − $4,500
*** $6,500 − $4,500

CLASSIFIED BALANCE SHEET

To assist readers of financial statements, the accounts on a balance sheet are usually grouped according to length of life, liquidity (ease of conversion to cash), or another characteristic, such as type or expected function. A balance sheet with accounts grouped this way is called a classified balance sheet. Most classified balance sheets contain the following asset, liability, and owners' equity categories:

Assets	Liabilities
Current Assets	Current Liabilities
Long-term Investments	Long-term Liabilities
Property, Plant, and Equipment	
Intangibles	**Shareholders' Equity**
Other Assets	Capital Stock
	Additional Paid-in Capital
	Retained Earnings

Each of these categories contains many individual accounts; for example, "Current Assets" may include cash, short-term investments, and inventories. "Capital Stock" and "Additional Paid-in Capital" together are called contributed capital. These categories and the individual accounts that are included in them are discussed in this chapter and Chapters 4 and 5.

A classified balance sheet from a published annual report is shown in Figure 3-1.

A caution is in order: The balance sheet is a still picture. It presents resources, obligations, and equity at only one point in time, typically the fiscal year-end. As you can see from the simple example above, each transaction affects the balance sheet, causing it to change immediately; in addition, some assets and liabilities go unrecorded because of measurement problems. To detect such cases, you should pay close attention to the notes to the financial statements. Material information that cannot be quantified is reported in a note to the financial statements, as discussed in Chapter 2.

CURRENT ASSETS

Current assets, the first category listed in the balance sheet, are for the most part short-term assets. Current assets include cash, items that provide cash, and certain items that delay the outflow of cash in the short term. The key to understanding the current assets category of the balance sheet is to examine the accountant's definition of current assets phrase by phrase.

Accountants define *short term* as one year or one company operating cycle, whichever is greater. The meaning of short term may be different for individual companies, depending on operating cycle, or the length of time required to go from cash to cash in operations. For example, suppose cash is first invested in inventory, either by manufacturing or purchasing inventory for resale. Next, inventory is sold, creating an account receivable. Finally, the receivable is collected when cash is received; the cycle is now complete. (The length of time a company's cash is tied up in accounts receivable and inventory can be estimated using a technique explained for activity ratios in Chapter 11.)

Usually, cash is tied up for 30 to 60 days both in accounts receivable and in inventories; a company's operating cycle is usually 60 to 180 days. As a result, the time span for defining current assets is usually one year, since it is greater than the operating cycle. But some companies leave cash in inventories for very long times. For instance, a whiskey distiller who ages inventory for 12 years during the manufacturing process may have an operating cycle that is the total of the 12 years cash is invested in inventory plus the 30 days cash is invested in receivables. In this case, the time span for current assets is 12 years, 30 days. Current assets are listed on the balance sheet in order of liquidity, or the ease with which the asset can be converted to cash. Cash is always listed first since it is already cash, then accounts receivable (one step—collection—from cash), then inventories (two steps—sale and collection—from cash), and so on. There are three general types of current assets, listed here in the same order they appear on the balance sheet:

CONSOLIDATED BALANCE SHEET

ASSETS

Current assets:

Cash, including short-term cash investments of $18,038,000 and $6,157,000	$20,017,000
Accounts receivable, less allowance for doubtful accounts of $546,000 and $268,000.	24,606,000
Other notes and accounts receivable	815,000
Inventories	14,412,000
Prepaid expenses	382,000
Total current assets	60,232,000
Property and equipment, net	9,312,000
Goodwill and other intangible assets, less amortization of $1,186,000 and $1,006,000.	258,000
Other assets	211,000
Total.	$70,013,000

LIABILITIES AND STOCKHOLDERS' EQUITY

Current liabilities:

Capital lease obligations due within one year	$ 135,000
Notes payable	1,555,000
Accounts payable	5,072,000
Accrued payroll and other employee compensation	3,816,000
Income taxes payable	1,897,000
Accrued taxes, other than payroll and income taxes	782,000
Deferred income taxes	82,000
Other accrued liabilities	1,041,000
Total current liabilities	14,380,000
Capital lease obligations	344,000
Deferred income taxes	616,000
Stockholders' equity, as restated to give effect to the stock split discussed in Note 8:	
Preferred Stock, $1.00 par value per share; 500,000 shares authorized, none outstanding	—
Common Stock, $.01 par value per share; 20,000,000 shares authorized, 12,683,385 and 10,675,926 shares outstanding	127,000
Additional paid-in capital	37,247,000
Retained earnings	17,445,000
Equity adjustment for foreign currency translation	(146,000)
Total stockholders' equity	54,673,000
Total	$70,013,000

See accompanying notes to consolidated financial statements.

FIG. 3-1 *Example of a classified balance sheet from a published annual report.*

1. Cash and short-term investments.

2. Items that provide cash in one year or one operating cycle, whichever is greater—primarily accounts and short-term notes receivable, inventories of raw materials, supplies, and finished goods.

3. Items that prevent the outflow of cash in one year or one operating cycle, whichever is greater—primarily prepaid items such as prepaid insurance, prepaid rent, and salary advances to employees.

An example of the current assets section of a balance sheet is shown in Figure 3-2.

Sometimes the term "working capital" is used to refer to current assets. But you must be alert: Working capital is also used to refer to *net* current assets, or current assets net of (less) current liabilities. Long ago, the term *net working capital* was used to refer to current assets minus current liabilities and *working capital* referred to current assets, but this distinction is now seldom made.

Cash and Short-term Investments

Cash is the most active asset in a company's balance sheet. There are few business transactions that do not affect cash in some way, by either providing cash or requiring it.

Assets

Cash and marketable securities	$ 186,992	$ 163,854
Receivables	192,485	176,219
Inventories	187,643	197,330
Prepaid expenses	21,636	14,200
Current assets	$ 588,756	$ 551,603

FIG. 3-2 *Current assets section of a balance sheet.*

Cash is an unproductive asset (earning at best a nominal interest rate on time deposits), but it is vitally important to have adequate cash on hand if the business is to operate: payrolls must be met, suppliers must be paid, overhead must be covered. Cash is also the most universally desirable asset that a company possesses: It is easily transported, hard to recognize once off the company premises, and easily convertible into other goods. Cash is subject to more accounting and management controls than any other asset.

Cash is the most liquid current asset. To be reported as "cash," an item must be readily available and not restricted for use in payment of current obligations. Items classified as cash include coin and currency on hand, petty cash funds, demand deposits (basically checking accounts, which are unrestricted funds available on deposit in a bank), change funds, and negotiable instruments (such as personal checks, travelers' checks, cashiers' checks, bank drafts, and money orders).

Cash balances to be used for some special purpose are not reported as cash but are listed instead as restricted funds. An example of such a fund is an employee travel fund. This fund is not readily available to meet current obligations. Special-purpose cash balances are reported in the balance sheet as "restricted funds." Similarly, certificates of deposit, money market funds, treasury bills, and commercial paper are not readily available to meet current obligations and are generally classified as temporary investments.

Because idle cash is not productive, companies may place their cash in short-term investments such as treasury bills, certificates of deposit, bonds, stock, and debt instruments. Management invests in short-term investments all cash not needed for daily operations and to increase its return on investment. Short-term investments are classified as current assets on the balance sheet if they are readily marketable and if management intends to convert them into cash in a short period of time.

Short-term investments in stock can result in dividend revenue to a company. Similarly, short-term investments in bonds or notes earn interest for the company. The market price of many short-term investments is subject to constant fluctuation, reflecting changes in market conditions. Generally accepted accounting principles do not call for the recognition of changes in the market value of short-term investments such as certificates of deposit or treasury bills; however, they do call for the recognition of changes on certain stock and debt securities (bonds).

Equity securities are of two types—trading securities and available-for-sale securities (AFS). Securities are classified as trading if they are purchased and held principally to be sold in a short period of time. By buying and selling frequently, the company hopes to generate profits from short-term price differences. These securities are always current assets and are reported at fair value with unrealized holding gains and losses reported as a component of net income. An unrealized holding gain or loss is the change in fair value of a security from one period to another. For example, assume a company purchases 1,000 shares of Company A for $2 per share in December of the current year. In preparing its financial statements for the year ending December 31, the company determines that the fair value of Company A's stock is $3 per share. The company has a holding gain of $1,000 [($3 – $2) × 1,000 shares]. The short-term investment in Company A's stock will be shown in the current assets section of the balance sheet at $3,000, and the $1,000 holding gain will appear in the income statement.

Equity securities not classified as trading are, by default, AFS securities. Although AFS securities are marketable, their classification as current or noncurrent depends on management's intent. AFS equity securities are also reported at fair value on each balance sheet date; however, any unrealized holding gains or losses appear as a separate component of stockholders' equity rather than as a component of stockholders' equity.

Debt securities are classified as held-to-maturity (HTM) securities, trading securities, or available-for-sale securities. HTM securities are purchased by a company with the intent and ability to hold those securities until they mature. There is no HTM classification for equity securities because they do not have a maturity date. HTM securities are generally classified as noncurrent assets, are not adjusted to fair value, and are accounted for at cost. AFS and trading debt securities are reported and accounted for in the same manner as AFS and trading equity securities.

Receivables

Receivables represent all claims expected to be settled in cash. The chief source of receivables is the company's trade or business. All receivables can be classified as either trade receivables (usually either accounts or notes receivable) or nontrade receivables (accounts or notes receivable arising from claims for losses or damages, claims for tax refunds, dividends or interest receivable, advances to employees, sales of property other than inventory, or deposits held by creditors or utilities).

Trade receivables are the most common type of receivable reported in the balance sheet and usually represent the largest dollar amount. All trade receivables are current assets by definition. On the other hand, nontrade receivables can be either current or noncurrent.

Receivables may appear in the current assets section of the balance sheet as illustrated below.

	Year 2	Year 1
Receivables:		
Trade	$80,000	$74,000
Other	20,000	25,000

Certain credit transactions may require the borrower to pledge or assign receivables as security for a loan. Assignment may be general or specific, depending on whether all accounts receivable or specific accounts receivable are pledged as collateral.

Notes receivable may be "discounted" to a bank. When notes receivable are discounted, the company receives immediate cash and the bank receives repayment, with interest, when the note is collected. When notes receivable are discounted with recourse, the company will disclose in the notes to the financial statements any obligations on the discounted notes.

Uncollectible Accounts. Accounts receivable are always shown on the balance sheet net of (that is, minus) any uncollectible accounts, also known as doubtful accounts or bad debts. Details related to allowances for uncollectible accounts, when not shown on the face of the balance sheet, are found in Note One, Significant Accounting Policies.

When a company accounts for uncollectibles, both the income statement and the balance sheet are affected: The estimated bad-debt expense is shown in the income statement, and the estimate of uncollectible accounts is shown as a subtraction from total accounts receivable in the current assets section of the balance sheet. A financial statement note showing the allowance for doubtful accounts is shown in Figure 3-3.

NOTE 4: RECEIVABLES
Receivables at December 31 are summarized as follows:

(Dollars in thousands)	2000	1999
Trade	$156,456	$150,991
Other	9,926	15,043
Allowance for doubtful amounts	(1,616)	(1,782)
	$164,766	$164,252

FIG. 3-3 *Financial statement note showing allowance for bad debts (doubtful accounts).*

To understand the accounting treatment of bad debts, it is important to remember that the amounts involved are estimates of amounts that may become uncollectible. There are two goals for such accounting. One is to match the cost of bad debts to the sales revenue produced in the period. This means that, of necessity, some estimation must take place. At the end of the year, some credit sales will have been collected and others will have already proven to be uncollectible. The collectibility of the remaining receivables will not be known. Therefore, it becomes necessary to estimate the uncollectible amount that will result from these as yet uncollected accounts and to include that estimate in this year's bad-debt expense in order for the company to charge this year's profits with the bad-debt expense that resulted from this year's sales. If the company were to wait until each account proved to be uncollectible (or collectible), the costs of bad debts in one year would have to be charged against the next year. But accounting principles require that bad-debt expense be matched to the year benefited by the original sale. (The accounting concept of matching is explained in Chapter 1.)

The second goal in accounting for bad debts is to value correctly the amount of accounts receivable shown in the current assets section of the balance sheet. These accounts are all uncollected, but the company has not yet decided which accounts are definitely bad debts. (If the company judges an account to be uncollectible, it must re removed from the balance of accounts receivable.) As a result, the allowance for bad debts shown as a deduction from accounts receivable in the balance sheet is wholly an estimate.

There is some conflict between the two goals in accounting for bad debts—maximizing the accuracy of the income statement versus maximizing the accuracy of the balance sheet. Bad debt estimates are occasionally high or low, particularly on interim (monthly or quarterly) statements; bad debt estimates for annual statements are, by and large, not materially misstated. To prevent misstatement, a company that does not relate the amount of bad debts expensed to sales activity will be required to examine periodically the outstanding accounts receivable in detail and justify the amounts of the estimates that appear in the financial statements.

Inventories

Depending on the kind of business, a company may have one or more types of inventory. A retailer may have an inventory of purchased finished goods available for sale, while a manufacturer may have inventories of raw materials, inventories of partially completed work in process, and inventories of supplies used in operations, in addition to an inventory of manufactured finished goods available for sale.

Inventories are current assets, carried in the balance sheet at the lower of original, historical cost or market value. The cost of purchased goods in a retailer's inventory includes the cost of transportation or freight-in but is reduced by any purchase discounts taken by the buyer or any returns made or allowances received. A schedule of ending inventories for a retailer is illustrated below.

Schedule of Ending Inventories

Beginning inventory		$ 75,000
Purchases	250,000	
Plus: Freight-in	10,000	
Less: Purchase discounts	(5,000)	
Returns and allowances	(15,000)	
Net delivered cost of purchases		240,000
Total goods available for sale		315,000
Less: Cost of goods sold		255,000
Ending inventory		$ 60,000

The components of a manufacturer's inventories are shown either in the body of the financial statements or in the statement notes. A schedule of inventory components for a manufacturer is illustrated below.

Schedule of Manufacturer's Inventory

	12/31 Year 2	12/31 Year 1
Raw materials	$ 53,000	$ 60,000
Operating supplies	18,000	27,000
Work-in-process	95,000	87,000
Finished goods	107,000	123,000
Ending inventory	$273,000	$297,000

Inventories are usually shown on the balance sheet at that which is lower: historical cost or current market value. This prevents a company from carrying inventories at an inflated asset amount and forces a company to expense any loss in value in the period the loss occurred. Without the lower-of-cost-or-market rule, inventories could be carried as current assets with an inflated value and any loss in value would not be charged against earnings until the goods were sold, possibly in the year following the actual decline in inventory replacement prices; therefore, managers would have an incentive to delay expensing the lost inventory value in the hope that market prices would rise again in the next year.

CHAPTER PERSPECTIVE

The balance sheet is a report of assets, liabilities, and owners' equity at a particular point in time. In this chapter, we introduced the structure of the balance sheet and explained the formal classification of accounts within the balance sheet, beginning our discussion of the classified accounts by examining current assets. The current assets classification is composed primarily of cash and short-term investments, receivables (reduced by the allowance for doubtful accounts), and inventories. In the next two chapters we will discuss noncurrent assets, liabilities, and owners' equity to complete our coverage of the balance sheet.

The Balance Sheet: Noncurrent Assets

INTRODUCTION AND MAIN POINTS

Noncurrent assets consist of (1) investments, (2) property, plant, and equipment, (3) natural resources, (4) intangibles, and (5) other assets. To understand the valuation of these long-lived assets, you must understand the accounting methods used to expense them. Long-lived, tangible, productive assets are depreciated; intangible assets are amortized; and natural resources are depleted. In this chapter, we discuss each kind of noncurrent asset, the way it is valued for inclusion on the balance sheet, and the way it is expensed.

After studying the material in this chapter:

■ You will know what a noncurrent asset is.
■ You will know how the different noncurrent assets are valued at acquisition.
■ You will understand the need for different methods of depreciation for different assets.
■ You will understand the weaknesses of historical-cost depreciation and amortization.
■ You will understand the difficulties of accounting for different kinds of investments and why different accounting treatments exist.
■ You will understand each type of noncurrent asset as it is presented in the balance sheet.

INVESTMENTS

A company may invest its idle funds in many ways; for example, it can choose to leave them in a savings account, put them in certificates of deposit, or invest them in stock or bonds of other companies. This portion of the chapter discusses how a company reports its noncurrent investments in stocks and bonds in the balance sheet.

Short-term investments, those expected to be held for less than one year, are current assets and are discussed in Chapter 3. Long-term investments are generally reported in their own section of the balance sheet between Current Assets and Property, Plant, and Equipment.

Three different methods exist for reporting the value of an investment in the balance sheet: cost, fair value, and the equity method. Figure 4-1 shows the methods used to value each type of investment.

Investment	*Valuation Method*
Short-term investments	
Common Stock	Fair value
Preferred Stock	Fair value
Bonds	Fair value
(Classified as trading or available-for-sale)	
Long-term investments	
Common Stock	(If company owns < 20% of
(Classified as	outstanding shares)
available-for-sale)	Fair value
	(If company owns ≥ 20% but ≤ 50% of outstanding shares) Equity method
	(If company owns > 50% of outstanding shares, has entered into a parent-subsidiary relationship, and will prepare consolidated financial statements)
Preferred Stock	Fair value
(Classified as available-for-sale)	
Bonds	Cost or fair value
(Classified as held-to-maturity or available-for-sale)	

FIG. 4-1 *Type of investment and balance sheet valuation method.*

PROPERTY, PLANT, AND EQUIPMENT

The company's long-lived productive assets (such as land, buildings, machinery, furniture, and fixtures) make up the asset category "Property, Plant, and Equipment." These assets are carried at their historical cost less any depreciation—that is, any amount already charged off as an operating expense. The historical cost of a productive asset is the total cost of acquiring the asset and readying it for use; for example, the historical cost of a piece of machinery includes its invoice price, delivery charges, installation costs, and the cost of trial production runs to adjust the machine to the desired product quality.

In other words, all costs incurred until the time production begins are considered part of the machine's historical cost.

Historical cost may also include interest cost. Many companies borrow funds to finance the construction of plant and equipment. These companies record this additional interest cost as part of the historical cost of their plant and equipment. Accountants call this type of interest avoidable interest, payments the company makes only because it is building.

"Property, Plant, and Equipment" also includes the assets "Leasehold Improvements" and "Property Subject to Capital Leases." Leasehold improvements are the cost of improvements made to leased property that will revert to its owner at the end of the lease term; property subject to capital leases is property that has been acquired through a long-term leasing arrangement that is essentially an alternative purchase and mortgage arrangement.

Valuing an asset at historical cost causes problems for the reader of financial statements, because, while historical cost is an objective measure, it may not be relevant. For instance, a piece of land valued at its 1940 historical cost of $1 million on a balance sheet tells us little about its current sales value or loan value. Comparisons between entities are also hampered by the use of historical cost: comparing the cost of property purchased in 1940 to the cost of similar property in 2000 is misleading. Although the property purchased in 2000 has a higher historical cost, it may not be more productive than the property purchased in 1940.

DEPRECIATION

In ordinary usage, depreciation means a decline in value; to an accountant, however, depreciation is the assignment of historical cost of a long-lived productive asset to production periods—the matching of costs of production (expenses) with the results of production (revenues). Rather than recording the decline in value as depreciation, the accountant records the using-up of original cost of the asset over its productive life.

The exception to the concept of depreciation is land. Land is a renewable resource, and therefore is not used up. It is not depreciated and is valued on the balance sheet at its historical cost.

Depreciation expense reduces earnings in the income statement. In the balance sheet, the asset being depreciated is shown at its original historical purchase price less the total of all depreciation expensed to the balance sheet date. The total of depreciation expensed is maintained in an account called "Accumulated Depreciation." If a company has a $100,000 machine and has depreciated it $10,000 a year for four years, it appears in the balance sheet as:

| Machine | $100,000 | |
| Less Accumulated Depreciation | 40,000 | $60,000 |

or simply as:

| Machine (net of depreciation) | $60,000 |

Figure 4-2 shows how one company disclosed the depreciation taken on fixed assets.

Methods of Depreciation

Most companies use one (or several) of four primary depreciation methods in preparing their annual reports. These methods are straight-line, units of production, sum of the years' digits, and double declining balance.

Straight-line. Straight-line depreciation assumes that equal benefit is derived from using the productive asset each year of its useful life. The formula for straight-line depreciation is:

[(cost − salvage value) ÷ years of useful life] = 1 year's depreciation

For example, if a company purchases a machine for $10,000 and at the time of purchase estimates its productive life to be three years, after which time it will have a salvage value of $1,000, depreciation expense is $3,000 a year [($10,000 − $1,000) ÷ 3].

Units of Production. Units of production depreciation assumes that revenue produced parallels units of product produced. In other words, in years in which more product is produced, the company has greater revenue-producing ability and, hence, should incur more depreciation expense. The formula for units of production depreciation is:

[(cost − salvage value) ÷ estimated units of product that will be produced over the life of the asset] = per unit depreciation.

In the Balance Sheet:
Property, Plant, and Equipment (Note 6) $494,290 $533,427

In the Statement Notes:
NOTE 6: PROPERTY, PLANT, AND EQUIPMENT
Plant assets represent the original cost of land, buildings and equipment less depreciation computed under the straight-line method over the estimated useful life of the asset. Equipment lives range from 5 to 15 years, buildings from 10 to 30 years.

Timber resources are stated at cost. Depletion is charged to operations based on the number of units of timber cut during the year.

Depreciation and depletion expense amounted to $62,979,000 in 2000; $66,542,000 in 1999; and $54,897,000 in 1998. Details of property, plant, and equipment at December 31 are as follows:

(Dollars in thousands)	2000	1999
Land	$ 15,178	$ 18,646
Timber resources	13,955	14,637
Buildings	154,026	143,230
Machinery & equipment	634,712	628,181
Construction in progress	38,781	72,882
	856,652	877,576
Accumulated depreciation and depletion	(362,362)	(344,149)
	$494,290	$533,427

FIG. 4-2 *Balance sheet and note disclosure of fixed assets showing depreciation.*

To find a year's depreciation expense, multiply the number of units produced during the year by the per-unit depreciation rate. For example, assuming a cost of $10,000, a salvage value of $1,000, a useful life of three years, and an estimated production of 4,000,000 units of product over the three-year period, the depreciation rate per unit of product produced is:

$$(\$10,000 - 1,000) \div 4,000,000 = \$ .00225 \text{ per unit.}$$

If a million units are produced during the year, depreciation expense of $2,250 is recorded for the year (1,000,000 × .00225).

Declining Balance Methods. Two declining balance methods of depreciation are the sum of the years' digits and the double declining balance method. Both of these methods take more depreciation in the earlier years of an asset's life than in the later years, on the assumption that an asset is most productive (and therefore has the most revenue-producing ability) in the early years of the asset's life before wear and tear begin to take their toll.

1. *Sum of the years' digits.* The formula for this declining balance method of depreciation is:

$$\text{(cost} - \text{salvage value)} \times$$
$$\text{[years in reverse order} \div \text{sum of the years' digits].}$$

For a machine that has a $10,000 cost, $1,000 salvage value, and a three-year life expectancy, the first year's depreciation expense is calculated as follows:

$$[\$10,000 - \$1,000] \times [3 \div (1 + 2 + 3)] =$$
$$\$9,000 \times \tfrac{3}{6} = \$4,500.$$

The second year's depreciation expense is $\left(\$9,000 \times \tfrac{2}{6}\right) = \$3,000$; the final year's depreciation is $\left(\$9,000 \times \tfrac{1}{6}\right) = \$1,500$. Notice that the rate of depreciation declines every year $\left(\tfrac{1}{2}\text{—}\tfrac{1}{3}\text{—}\tfrac{1}{6}\right)$—the depreciation base ($9,000) remains constant.

2. *Double declining balance.* The formula for double declining balance depreciation is:

net book value of the depreciable asset $\times$
$(2 \div$ number of years estimated life$)$.

Net book value of the depreciable asset is its original cost minus all depreciation taken to date (accumulated depreciation). Using our example of an asset that cost $10,000, with $1,000 salvage value and a three-year estimated life, the first year's depreciation expense is calculated as:

$$\left[(\$10,000 - \$0) \times \tfrac{2}{3}\right] = \$6,667.$$

The second year's depreciation expense is $\left[(\$10,000 - \$6,667) \times \tfrac{2}{3}\right] = \$2,222$. While calculating depreciation expense by this formula gives us $\left[(\$10,000 - \$8,889) \times \tfrac{2}{3}\right] = \$741$ of depreciation in the third and final year of the asset's life, the company actually records only $111 of depreciation. This is the difference between net book value at the beginning of the third year and the estimated salvage value at the end of the third year [($10,000 − $8,889) − $1,000]. Double declining balance is the only one of the four primary depreciation methods that ignores estimated salvage value in its formula for annual depreciation expense. Therefore, in the final year of the asset's life, the asset must be depreciated only to a net book value equal to its expected salvage value.

Determining Depreciation Methods

As we stated, depreciation is an estimate because it is impossible to know with a high degree of certainty an asset's actual life and the pattern of its benefit. The usefulness and market value of an asset decreases because of such factors as physical wear and tear, obsolescence, and inadequacy, and these factors influence accounting estimates of the asset's useful life and salvage value. Inadequacy refers to the asset becoming incapable of meeting the increasing demands for its product or service because of a company's unexpected rapid growth. Obsolescence occurs when technological advances create new assets that make older models outdated and relatively less efficient before they physically wear out. When this happens, an asset is reduced in value. For example, because of the improvement in computers over time, older models have become inadequate, if not obsolete.

The Weaknesses of Historical-Cost Depreciation

The basis for long-lived asset valuation is historical cost. Because depreciation does not measure actual decline in value, the net book value of a long-lived asset (historical cost − accumulated depreciation) is not a good measure of the cost of replacing the asset; neither is it a good measure of what the asset would bring if sold. Long-lived assets with net book value equal to their estimated salvage value or zero (if there is no salvage value) may continue to be used by the company to earn revenue while they are minimally valued on the balance sheet.

Depreciation computations are based largely on estimates of useful life and salvage value. Should either of these estimated figures change during the life of the depreciable asset, the company recomputes depreciation from that point forward. This computation uses the net book value as the historical cost and the new estimates of salvage and remaining years of useful life. For example, suppose management decides at the beginning of the third year that an asset—which cost $10,000 and has a $1,000 salvage value and a three-year estimated useful life—has in fact a remaining useful life of three years with a new estimated salvage value of $1,500. Straight-line depreciation expense for that third year is computed as follows: [$10,000 − $6,000] = $3,000, the net book value after two years straight-line depreciation; depreciation for succeeding years is calculated at [($3,000 − $1,500) ÷ 3 years remaining life] = $500 depreciation expense per year.

Comparability is hindered by using different depreciation methods. In our examples, the first year's depreciation expense varied according to the method used: straight-line—$3,000, units of production—$2,250, sum of the years' digits—$4,500, and double-declining balance—$6,667. If four identical companies each use a different method to compute depreciation for an identical asset, their net book values of the asset and their net incomes will be different. In other words, choice of depreciation methods can create artificial differences between companies in terms of asset valuation and net income.

NATURAL RESOURCES

Many companies own assets such as stands of timber, oil fields, and mineral deposits such as coal or copper. These assets are called natural resources or wasting assets, terms that indicate that they are physically exhausted during the production process and can only be replaced by a process of nature. The basis for recording these assets is the same as that of other long-lived assets, that is, cost. Cost is defined as the outlays for the acquisition of the property that normally comprises expenditures for exploration, development, and production. These capitalized costs constitute the total amount that will be expensed over the period of removal and production of the natural resource. The process of allocating these costs to the periods of benefit is called depletion (discussed below).

INTANGIBLE ASSETS

Intangible assets are long-lived productive assets that do not have a physical existence. For the most part, they are legal rights given to the company that give it a competitive edge and aid the company in producing revenue. Examples of intangible assets are: patents, copyrights, trademarks and trade names, franchises, organization costs, and purchased goodwill.

Initially, intangible assets are recorded at historical cost. As an intangible's historical cost is expensed against production periods, the recorded value of the intangible declines. Unlike a depreciable asset whose historical cost is maintained in the asset account and reduced to net book value for the depreciation taken to date (recorded in a separate accumulated depreciation account), amortization taken to date on an intangible may be deducted directly from the asset account. If the balance sheet does not show an accumulated amortization account used to reduce the historical cost of the intangibles to their net book value, the amortization has been written off directly against the assets, and the values as shown for the intangibles are their net book values.

A company may become involved in defending its intangible in an infringement suit. If the company loses the suit, the intangible is worthless and its remaining net book value (along with legal fees) is written off (expensed). If the company wins the suit, its legal fees are added to the intangible's historical cost and expensed over the remainder of the original amortization period.

DEPLETION AND AMORTIZATION

Depletion (for natural resources) and amortization (for intangible assets), like depreciation, specify the assignment of the historical cost of a long-lived asset to operating periods; that is, they match costs of operation (expenses) with operation's results (revenues).

The method of depletion most often used is a units-of-production formula:

costs of the natural resource ÷ estimated recoverable (removable) units of the resource = per unit depletion rate

If a stand of timber costs $2 million and will produce 4 million cords, the depletion rate is $.50 per cord ($2,000,000 ÷ 4,000,000). If 500,000 cords are removed in one year, the depletion expense for that year is (500,000 × $.50) = $250,000.

For intangibles, amortization is recorded on a straight-line basis (cost ÷ number of amortization periods). The amortization period is the lesser of the intangible's economic life, legal life, or 40 years. Suppose we develop a patented process to use in the production of our product. The research-and-development costs were $15 million and were expensed throughout the research-and-development phase. However, attorneys' fees and patent application fees totaled $500,000 (the amount recorded as the historical cost of the patent). We estimate that the patented process will have an economic life of 12 years; therefore, we will expense this patent over the 12-year period rather than over its legal life of 17 years. At the end of 12 years, we do not expect the process to aid us in the production of revenues. Amortization expense will be ($500,000 ÷ 12) = $41,667 per year.

Amortization is also taken on "Leasehold Improvements" and "Property Subject to Capital Leases." If leased property will be returned to the lessor at the end of the lease term, the recorded cost of improvements and the leased property is expensed over the term of the lease. If the company will keep the property after the expiration of the lease, it should expense the improvements and property over their economic lives. In this case, the method of computing amortization should be the method we would use to depreciate similar assets that we own.

As with depreciation, the net book values of natural resources and intangibles are not good measures of either the cost of replacing these assets or the amount that could be realized if they were sold. Depletion and amortization computations are based on estimates that are subject to change. When an estimate changes, the net book value of the asset at that time becomes the basis for depletion or amortization over the remaining units of natural resource or amortization period. Management's ability to choose an arbitrary amortization period for certain intangibles such as purchased goodwill (as long as they do not exceed 40 years) may create artificial differences between companies and lessen comparability.

TYPES OF INTANGIBLES
Patents

A patent—an exclusive right to use, manufacture, or sell a product or process—is granted for 17 years. The patent's historical cost is expensed against the revenues that the patent helps produce over the lesser of its legal life (17 years) or its estimated economic life. In fields in which technology is rapidly changing, such as computer hardware and software, the economic life of a patent (the estimated period during which the patent will produce revenue) may be less than the patent's legal life.

Copyrights

A copyright gives exclusive control to the creator of a literary, musical, or artistic work, and may be assigned or sold. Currently, copyrights are granted for the life of the creator plus 50 years; however, a copyright's historical cost is expensed over the lesser of its estimated economic life or 40 years (accounting principles require that intangibles be expensed over a period that may not exceed 40 years). The historical cost of literary and musical copyrights is frequently expensed over the estimated life of the first printing (estimated economic life at the time of printing), since no one can reliably predict a best seller or other highly successful work that will enjoy a long economic life.

Trademarks and Trade Names

Trademarks and trade names are symbols or words that identify a product or company. They are granted for 20 years and are subject to indefinite renewals. Their historical cost is expensed over the lesser of their estimated economic life or 40 years.

Franchises

A franchise is the right to sell a product or service under a trade name. The cost of the franchise is expensed over the life of the franchise (40 years in the event that the franchise's life exceeds 40 years).

Organizational Costs

Organizational costs are the initial costs of creating a business entity and include attorneys' fees and state fees for incorporation. Organizational costs enable a business to produce revenue over its whole life. These costs are expensed over a period of not more than 40 years.

Purchased Goodwill

To an accountant, goodwill is the "excess of cost over the market value" of net assets purchased by a company. In other words, "net assets" are the difference between the value of a company's total assets and its total liabilities. When one business purchases another, it may be willing to pay more for that business than the market value of the individual assets minus any liabilities. This is referred to in accounting as *goodwill.*

Why might a company be willing to pay more than market value for the net assets of another company? Because the purchaser is also acquiring intangibles—the reputation of the products or service of the purchased company, the quality of its personnel, brand-name recognition, and so on. Conceptually, goodwill represents an amount paid for the above-average earnings of a company caused by these factors.

Accounting principles allow only purchased goodwill to be recorded in the accounts; internal development of a business reputation is not assigned a value and recorded. Goodwill may have an indefinite economic life, but it must be amortized over a period not to exceed 40 years. Currently, goodwill can be deducted for tax purposes over a period not to exceed 15 years.

Research-and-Development Costs

Research-and-development costs are the costs of discovering new technology and applying it to products, processes, and services. Occasionally in the past, research-and-development costs were recorded as assets and amortized over the lesser of their economic life or 40 years. However, now accounting principles require that the majority of research-and-development costs be expensed as they arise because of the uncertainty of future benefits. The majority of research-and-development projects do not result in a marketable product, process, or service.

The total amount of research-and-development cost for the fiscal period must be disclosed. While the majority of projects may not succeed, the research they require helps keep a company competitive. The proportion of dollars spent on research and development to a company's sales is one measure of that company's investment in the future and its vitality.

Methods of Valuation

Cost. When an accountant uses the cost method of valuation, the investment is recorded on the balance sheet value at its historical cost. Income from the investment is recorded when dividends are declared or interest is due. The cost method is appropriate when market prices (fair values) are not available and should be used in periods subsequent to acquisition. The cost method (normally called amortized cost) is used for debt securities classified as held-to-maturity. Held-to-maturity securities are discussed in Chapter 3.

Fair Value. When an accountant uses the fair value method, the investment is recorded on the balance sheet at its current market value and subsequently adjusted each period to its current market value. Income from the investment is recorded when dividends are declared or interest earned along with any unrealized holding gains or losses. Recall from our discussion in Chapter 3 that unrealized holding gains and losses on available-for-sale debt and equity securities do not appear on the income statement but as a separate component of stockholders' equity.

For example, suppose you own two stocks both classified as available-for-sale—UVW, Inc. and XYZ, Ltd. The cost of UVW was $100 per share; the cost of XYZ was $200 per share. At the end of the fiscal year, UVW is selling for $110 per share, and XYZ is selling for $160 per share. You should group these stocks together into a portfolio. You then compare the cost of these portfolios to their current market values. The cost of your portfolio is $300 ($100 + $200), while the stock's current market value is $270 ($110 + $160).

Because the current market value of the portfolio is $30 less than its historical cost ($300 ($270), write it down in value $30 and report it on the balance sheet at $270. The write-down is called an unrealized loss—unrealized because the stock has not yet been sold. If it were sold today, you would incur a loss of $30.

Because the investments are long term, the unrealized loss is no longer likely to occur. You then reduce the investment portfolio to its current market value and from owners' equity the "Net Unrealized Loss on Noncurrent Marketable Equity Securities."

When you prepare your next balance sheet, if the investments' current market value exceeds their recorded amount, they will be written back up to fair value. The increase will be reflected by increasing the investment account and reducing or eliminating the negative owners' equity account "Net Unrealized Loss on Noncurrent Marketable Equity Securities."

Equity Method. If the investor exercises significant influence over the affairs of the investee, the method of choice for accounting for the investment is the equity method. The investor gains such influence by buying common stock (the company's voting stock) and holding it as a long-term investment. An investor who owns 20 percent of the outstanding shares of common stock can elect one-fifth of the board of directors. Accountants assume that significant influence exists once an investor has acquired 20 percent or more of a company's common stock.

An accountant using the equity method initially records the investment at historical cost. As the investee earns income from the company, the investor records his or her share as income from investment. Income increases the value of the investee company and the value of the investment. As dividends are paid, the investor reduces the value of the investment. Dividends, paid in cash, are assumed to be a withdrawal of investment. Dividends are cash; income is only an increase in value. Recording income and dividends in this manner causes the investment account to mirror the changes that are occurring in the investee's stockholder's equity.

For example, suppose that we buy 10,000 of the outstanding shares of CDE Corp. for $2 million. This investment represents one-third of the outstanding shares. CDE's owners' equity has a recorded value of $6 million. Our investment account reflects a third of CDE's owners' equity, or:

Investor's Accounts	*Investee's Accounts*
Investment $2,000,000	CDE's Owners' Equity $6,000,000

If CDE has net income of $900,000 for the year, our investment will increase by $300,000, or:

Beginning Investment	$2,000,000	CDE's Beginning Owners' Equity	$6,000,000
+ Income	300,000	+ Income	900,000
	$2,300,000		$6,900,000

Next, suppose CDE pays $450,000 in dividends. We will receive $150,000 in dividends. The dividends are a withdrawal of investment and reduce our investment account:

Beginning Investment	$2,000,000	CDE's Beginning Owners' Equity	$6,000,000
+ Income	300,000	+ Income	900,000
Dividends	(150,000)	− Dividends	(450,000)
	$2,150,000		$6,450,000

Notice that each time CDE's equity increases or decreases, our investment increases or decreases proportionately. CDE's owners' equity is $6,450,000. Because we own one-third of CDE, our investment is recorded at one-third of the value of CDE's owners' equity.

If we had paid more than $2 million for our investment in CDE, the excess amount paid would have been considered goodwill (see page 49 of this chapter). Accounting rules require that goodwill be expensed over a period of 40 years or less. As the goodwill is expensed, the value of our investment decreases. After all the goodwill has been expensed, our investment account reflects our portion of the investee's recorded owner's equity.

Long-term investments in bonds are recorded at their present value and classified as held-to-maturity or available-for-sale. The present value of a bond is its cash value at a point in time.

Suppose we are willing to pay $1,100 for a 10-year, $1,000 bond that pays 10 percent interest annually. If we hold this bond to maturity, we will receive only $900 more than we originally invested. (We receive $1,000 in interest over the 10-year period plus the principal of $1,000 at maturity, but we invested $1,100—a $100 premium.) In this case, writing off $10 of the premium each year causes the investment to decrease $10 a year and $90 ($100 less the $10 write-off) to be recorded as interest income. In periods subsequent to recording a long-term bond (classified as held-to-maturity), we carry the bond at amortized cost. Amortized cost reflects the amortization of any premium or discount on the purchase of the bond. In our example, we paid $1,100 for a bond with a face value of $1,000, resulting in a premium of $100, to be amortized over the life of the bond. Since the bond has a ten-year life, the premium is reduced by $10 per year. Therefore, the carrying amount of the bond after the first year's amortization would be $1,090 ($1,100 recorded amount less the amortization of the premium of $10). At maturity, the bond will be valued at $1,000, its cash value.

Some industries have their own valuation methods for investments. For instance, insurance companies and brokerage firms value their short-term investments at current market value even if that value is greater than historical cost.

OTHER ASSETS

"Other Assets" is a catch-all category that includes business resources that cannot be classified as current assets, investments, property, plant, and equipment, natural resources, or intangibles—for example, long-lived assets that are awaiting sale and that are no longer being used in production. (Classifying them as property, plant, and equipment would imply that they are currently in use.) Long-term prepayments of expenses (such as a three-year insurance policy) may also be classified as "other."

CHAPTER PERSPECTIVE

Continuing our discussion of the balance sheet, this chapter discussed noncurrent assets. Noncurrent assets consist of (1) investments, (2) property, plant, and equipment, (3) natural resources, (4) intangibles, and (5) other assets. We discussed each kind of noncurrent asset and the way it is valued for inclusion on the balance sheet. Long-lived, tangible, productive assets are depreciated; intangible assets are amortized; and natural resources are depleted. The chapter discussed the weaknesses of historical-cost accounting, including the weaknesses of depreciation accounting and of valuing certain kinds of investments.

The Balance Sheet: Liabilities and Stockholders' Equity

INTRODUCTION AND MAIN POINTS

As we stated in Chapter 1, all assets are acquired with funds generated from borrowing or from stockholders' investment or, in the case of retained earnings, reinvestment. Hence, assets equal liabilities plus owners' equity. But there are many different kinds of liabilities and owners' equity accounts. Therefore, balance sheets display liabilities and owners' equity amounts separated into categories and subcategories that provide information to readers of financial statements and make analysis easier.

In this chapter, we discuss the types of liabilities and owners' equity accounts that you might find on the balance sheet omitting coverage of readily understood terms such as mortgage payable and concentrating on less widely understood concepts.

After studying the material in this chapter:

▬ You will understand how total equities are separated into useful categories and subcategories.
▬ You will know the meanings of the different equity classifications.
▬ You will know the accounts generally included in the balance-sheet equity categories.
▬ You will understand the way accountants treat several nonroutine debt transactions, such as retirement before maturity and troubled-debt restructuring.
▬ You will understand how accountants account for bonds.
▬ You will understand the different sources of invested capital and be able to identify the features of the different classes of stock.
▬ You will know what retained earnings are and will understand the significance of retained-earnings appropriations.

EQUITIES

Equities are property rights. The equity of creditors is called liability and is a liability, or debt, of the company. The equity of owners is called stockholders' equity or owners' equity. Equities are shown on the balance sheet in the general order of preference upon liquidation. For example, the liabilities or equities of creditors are shown before the equities of owners because creditors would be paid before owners if the company were liquidated. Within owners' equity, common stock and retained earnings are listed after preferred stock because common stockholders would be the last persons paid at liquidation. This is not a hard-and-fast rule, but it does represent the general order in which accountants arrange groups of equities and individual equities within each group.

The equities side of the balance sheet usually appears in the following general order:

LIABILITIES
Current Liabilities
    Trade Payables
    Notes Payable
    Unearned Revenues
    Short-term Contingencies
Noncurrent Liabilities
    Mortgages Payable
    Notes and Bonds Payable
    Other Long-term Payables
SHAREHOLDERS' OR OWNERS' EQUITY
    Preferred Stock
    Common Stock
    Retained Earnings

Figures 5-1 and 5-2 show the equities side of a balance sheet and portions of two financial statement notes that supplement the balance sheet and provide full disclosure of debt and capital structure.

CURRENT LIABILITIES

Current liabilities are obligations of the company that are expected to be paid from current assets within one year of the date on the balance sheet. The types of current liabilities shown on the balance sheet include

▬ Trade Accounts Payable: Amounts owed to suppliers for merchandise or services, such as an unpaid invoice for merchandise purchases or the utility bill.

▬ Short-term Notes Payable: Short-term interest-bearing debt. Notes are formal documents showing the amount borrowed (principal) and stating as an annual rate the percentage interest that must be paid. Only the principal is recorded on the balance sheet under the title "notes payable." Any interest the company owes is called interest payable.

Liabilities and Shareholders' Equity

Current Liabilities

Payable to suppliers and others	$151,726	$154,013
Notes payable and current portion of long-term debt....................	29,046	22,465
Taxes on income	2,347	13,284
	183,119	189,762
Long-term Debt (Note 12)	226,240	275,535
Deferred Income Taxes.................	74,199	57,676

Shareholders' Equity

Serial preferred stock, no par value
Authorized 30,000,000 shares
None issued (Note 7)

Common shares, no par value
Authorized 150,000,000 shares

Issued 45,920,440 shares (Note 7)	7,175	7,175
Capital in excess of stated value	48,319	45,982
Translation of foreign currencies	(8,238)	(3,516)
Retained earnings	485,093	417,115
Treasury shares at cost (2000–2,193,910; 1999–2,059,607).....................	(20,775)	(12,270)
	511,574	454,486
	$995,132	$977,459

FIG. 5-1 *Liabilities and Shareholders' Equity Section of Balance Sheet*

■ Current Portion of Long-term Debt: The portion of principal on long-term debt that will be paid within the year. Long-term debt is usually payable in installments (for example, mortgage payments). Any unpaid interest on long-term debt is recorded as interest payable.

■ Interest Payable: The unpaid interest on short-term and long-term debt. This is the interest charge for the days from the last payments to the balance sheet date.

■ Unearned Revenues: Payments made in advance by customers for product or services. Revenue is not recorded until the product is delivered to the customer or the service is completed.

■ Tax and Other Withholdings: Income taxes and social security taxes (FICA taxes) withheld from employees' paychecks.

NOTE 7: CHANGES IN AUTHORIZED CAPITAL

In April 2000, the shareholders approved an increase in the total number of authorized no par common shares from 75,000,000 to 150,000,000. In addition, the shareholders approved the authorization of 30,000,000 shares of preferred stock, no par value, which may consist of one or more series that the board of directors may, from time to time, establish and designate.

NOTE 12: DEBT

Debt at December 31 was as follows:

(Dollars in thousands)	2000	1999
Commercial paper, average rate of 8.8%–2000 and 9.4%–1999	$132,310	$169,590
Private placement notes payable, interest at 9.3%, due 2003 through 2009	50,000	50,000
Notes payable through 2003 with variable interest rates (average rate of 9.8% at December 31, 1999)		31,000
Foreign denominated debt average rate of 13.8% at December 31, 2000, and 15.3% at December 13, 1999	50,959	26,686
Industrial revenue bonds payable through 2018, average rate of 8.3% at December 31, 2000 and 1999.	10,151	11,147
Other notes.	11,866	9,577
Total debt.	255,286	298,000
Less current portion	29,046	22,465
Long-term debt.	$226,240	$275,535

The Company maintains fully committed bank lines of credit to support its $200 million commercial paper program. One-half of these lines expires in 2004 with the remaining one-half expiring in 2005. Accordingly, commercial paper borrowings are classified as long-term debt on the balance sheet.

The Company has two interest-rate-swap agreements with banks: $25 million due 2003 at 9.8%, and $50 million due 2005 at 10.5%. The purpose of these agreements is to reduce the Company's exposure to floating interest rates on a portion of its commercial paper borrowings.

Certain of the Company's debt agreements impose restrictions with respect to the maintenance of financial ratios and the disposition of assets. The most restrictive covenant requires that long-term debt shall not exceed 90% of net tangible assets.

FIG. 5-2 *Supporting notes for Figure 5-1*

These withholdings plus additional FICA taxes and unemployment taxes must be paid quarterly by the employer to federal and state governments.

■ Income Taxes Payable: The portion of income taxes the business has not yet paid. These are taxes due on the company's earnings (not withholdings as above).

■ Contingencies: A number of "likely to occur" contingencies are recorded as liabilities (see Chapter 7). Examples are "Vacation Wages Payable" and "Estimated Liabilities Under Warranties." "Vacation Wages Payable" is the company's estimate of vacation pay that has been earned by employees but that has not been paid because the employees have not yet taken their vacations. "Estimated Liabilities Under Warranties" is the estimated repair cost of items manufactured and sold under warranty. Only the portion of the contingencies expected to be paid in the coming year are classified as current liabilities. Be sure to read the notes to the financial statements to get a feel for possible contingencies.

NONCURRENT LIABILITIES

Noncurrent (or long-term) liabilities are obligations that are not expected to be paid for at least one year from the date on the balance sheet or are not expected to be paid from current assets. Noncurrent liabilities are carried at their present values, the amount of money the company would have to pay to settle the debt at the balance-sheet date and excluding any future interest that is not yet due. Most noncurrent liabilities call for periodic payments of principal and interest. The portion of principal that will be due within the year is classified as a current liability (see page 56).

Examples of noncurrent liabilities include long-term notes and mortgages payable, bonds payable, obligations under capital leases, accrued pension cost, and deferred tax liabilities.

Unless you carefully read the notes to the financial statements, you will not understand noncurrent liabilities. Many long-term debt covenants place restrictions on the borrower. For instance, a debt covenant may require a company to maintain a 2:1 current ratio of current assets to current liabilities. What if the current ratio is only 1.9:1? Then the company is technically in default on its long-term obligation and the debt can be called due at any time. Unless management believes it can correct the current ratio deficiency within the specified grace period, it must reclassify the debt from long-term to current.

Settling Debt Before Maturity

Sometimes a company pays off debt before it is due. Any settlement of debt before its due date causes the company to report a gain or loss—a gain if the cost of settling the debt is less than the debt's recorded value on the balance sheet (including any interest) or a loss if the cost of settling the debt is greater than the debt's recorded value on the balance sheet (including any interest due). These gains and losses must be reported on the income statement as extraordinary items (see Chapter 7). Why might a company take a loss to settle a debt before it is due? The loss may be less than the future interest payments, or the company may now be able to borrow money at lower interest rates.

Restructuring of Troubled Debt

Sometimes a company experiences problems repaying its debts. A troubled-debt restructuring is an agreement by which the creditor grants the debtor concessions to help the debtor avoid defaulting. The concessions may take the form of transferring assets to the creditor, transferring the debtor's own stock to the creditor, or modifying the terms of debt.

The creditor may agree to settle the debt for noncash assets whose market value is less than the recorded value of the debt (including any interest due). The debtor reports a gain on the restructuring equal to the amount by which the debt exceeds the market value of the assets being given to the creditor. The gain is usually reported on the income statement as an extraordinary item.

Alternatively, the creditor may agree to settle the debt for shares of the debtor's stock. In other words, the creditor becomes an owner. The debtor reports a gain on the restructuring equal to the amount by which the debt exceeds the market value of the stock being given to the creditor. The gain is usually reported on the income statement as an extraordinary item.

When the creditor agrees to modify the terms of debt (principal, interest rate, or length of time), the debtor may have to pay more or less than the recorded value of the debt plus any interest due. If all of the new payments called for by the modified terms of debt are less than the recorded value of the debt (including any interest due), the debtor records a gain, usually as an extraordinary item on the income statement. Payments made by the debtor after restructuring are considered to be payments of principal. The debtor, who could not pay even the debt owed, let alone additional interest, does not recognize interest expense.

On the other hand, what if modifying the terms of debt results in total payments that exceed the recorded value of the debt (including any interest due)? In this case, the debtor recognizes the recorded value of the debt as the principal of the restructured debt. The amount by which the new payments exceed this principal is the debtor's interest expense over the remaining term of the debt.

BONDS

Bonds are a form of long-term debt, usually repaid in ten to twenty years. When a company needs to borrow a large amount of money—say, $20 million—it has two basic choices. The company can seek to find one lender who will supply the entire $20 million, or it can find several smaller lenders, each of whom contributes part of the total amount needed. When a company issues bonds, it is taking the second option. Each bond is a debt agreement for $1,000; a $20 million debt is divided into 20,000 bonds, each carrying a debt of $1,000.

When bonds are issued, the company can obtain its $20 million from any number of lenders (up to 20,000). When an investor (lender) "buys" $50,000 in bonds, the investor has, in essence, agreed to lend the company $50,000. The debt is supported by 50 bonds of $1,000 each. Each bond is a debt agreement, with the interest rate, interest payment schedule (usually semiannually), and bond maturity date (when the principal amount is returned) all contained in the bond.

The bond debt may be secured or unsecured; unsecured bonds are called debentures. All the bonds may be retired (repaid) at the same time, or they may be structured to mature (come due) in increments. Bonds that mature in increments are called serial bonds.

Amortization of Bonds

Amortization is the accounting method that causes the bond interest expense recorded by a company to be different from the cash paid as interest on the money borrowed. For example, a typical bond might be for a debt of $1,000 for ten years, with interest at 10 percent per year, paid semiannually. The company is, in essence, making two promises: to pay the lender $1,000 in ten years, and to pay interest of $100 ($1,000 \times .10$) each year. As long as the market rate of interest is 10 percent for bonds of that particular type (secured or unsecured), for the same term and for companies in the same risk class, the company can issue the bond without a problem, receiving $1,000 and paying the principal and interest as agreed.

But suppose that the interest rate rises before the bond is issued. A lender will no longer purchase a $1,000 bond (and agree to lend $1,000) for 10 percent interest; the lender will either demand a higher return or insist on investing less than $1,000 in order to receive the payments (principal and interest) described in the bond agreement. Perhaps, at the higher market rate of interest, the lender might agree to lend only $900 in exchange for the payments described in the bond. The following would then be true. The company would pay:

1. At the end of ten years	$1,000
2. In equal semiannual payments each year ($100 × 10)	$1,000
Total amount paid	$2,000
Less amount received from lender	900
Excess paid over amount received	$1,100

The excess paid over the amount received is the true interest cost of the funds. The company pays $100 cash in interest per year, but the true average annual cost of the money borrowed is $110 (1,100 ÷ 10) per year. The company records the $100 cash outflow each year and the $110 average annual expense. The extra $10 interest expense ($110 – 100) in excess of the actual cash paid is the amortization of the excess paid over the amount received.

When bonds are presented in an annual report, details of the security agreement (if any), maturity dates, and interest rates can be found in the notes to the financial statements. The bonds are shown in the long-term liabilities section of the financial statements. When a bond is issued at face (for $1,000), the bond is presented in the balance sheet as follows:

Bond payable	$1,000

If the market interest rate is more or less than the interest in the bond agreement, the bonds are sold at a discount or premium from face, and their presentation in the balance sheet is different. If a bond is issued for $900 (as described above) it appears in the financial statement as follows:

Bond payable	$1,000	
Less discount on bonds payable	100	900

Bonds sold for more than the face amount are accounted for in a similar fashion. A bond issued for $1,100 appears in the financial statements with a premium rather than a discount:

Bonds payable	$1,000	
Plus premium on bonds payable	100	1,100

STOCKHOLDERS' EQUITY

The amount of owners' equity can be calculated by subtracting the equity of creditors (liabilities) from the total assets of the company: $A - L = OE$. Expressed in this form, owners' equity is sometimes called "net assets," meaning "assets net of (less) liabilities." When creditors have transactions with a company, the transactions are at arm's length; when owners have transactions with their own company, it is as related parties, not at arm's length. Since owners can legally remove capital as dividends only under certain conditions and only from certain sources, the focus in accounting for owners' equity is on the *detailed sources of capital.*

A complex owners' equity presentation may have capital that comes from many sources, such as donations, treasury stock transactions, preferred stock, subscribed stock, common stock, appropriated retained earnings, and unappropriated retained earnings. Each element or source of capital is fully described in a company's annual report. Some information about owners' equity is included in the body of the financial statements, and additional information is disclosed in the notes to the financial statements.

CLASSES OF STOCK

All stock issued by a company is either preferred stock or common stock, regardless of what name the issue of stock may be given. There is generally only one class of common stock; all other classes of stock, regardless of name, are preferred in some way over the one class of common stock.

If a company is liquidated, creditors are paid proceeds of the liquidation before the claims of stockholders are considered. In addition, the different classes of stock are ranked in the order in which their holders will receive the proceeds of the liquidation. The stock with the least claim to assets on liquidation is common stock. All other classes of stock are classes of preferred stock, since those stockholders have preference over common stockholders in liquidation, and perhaps in other ways as explained later.

Common Stock

Because of their bottom ranking as claimants on corporate assets at liquidation, holders of common stock are said to be residual equity holders; they receive the residual left after all creditors and all holders of other classes of stock have been paid. Holders of common stock may receive nothing or they may receive a great deal when a company is liquidated. While all creditors and preferred shareholders have a contractually stated amount that they will receive if the company is liquidated and funds are available, holders of common stock have no such contractually stated amount; they are last in line and, as such, receive whatever is left, large or small. They take the greatest risk but may also receive the greatest reward.

Holders of common stock have four rights that result from their stock ownership:

1. The right to share in assets upon liquidation (as residual equity holders);
2. The right to receive distributions of earnings as dividends;
3. The right to maintain a proportionate share of ownership when new common shares are issued (called the preemptive right);
4. To vote their opinion on company management.

Par Value. Par value (or stated value) is an arbitrary amount assigned to shares of stock, both common and preferred by the board of directors of the company. Par or stated value had real meaning decades ago when securities regulations were different, but these terms have little significance now. Originally, par or stated value referred to the legal minimum capital to be furnished by the stockholder and not removed from the corporation except by a liquidating dividend. The regulators' concern was that owners and stockholders who believed the company to be in financial trouble would remove their investment and leave creditors without recourse. Securities regulations now prevent this action, but the terms still exist and stock is shown in the balance sheet with the stockholder's investment divided into par (or stated) value and premium, "Paid in Capital in Excess of Par (or Stated) Value," or simply "Additional Paid in Capital."

Suppose stockholders paid $110,000 for shares of common stock with a total par value of $90,000. The owners' equity section of the balance sheet would disclose the following:

Common Stock (at par)	$90,000
Additional Paid in Capital	20,000

Shares Authorized and Issued. For common stock and each class of preferred stock, the number of shares authorized by the charter and the board of directors, and the number of shares issued and outstanding are disclosed in the balance sheet. Occasionally, when there is treasury stock (explained later in this chapter), the number of shares outstanding will be less than the number issued because some shares are held in the treasury.

Preferred Stock

Holders of common stock may vote to create a class of stock—preferred stock—that has first claim on assets at liquidation. In addition, the class of stock is given preference in the distribution of dividends; preferred stock dividends usually must be paid before common stock dividends are paid. If the company does not create enough earnings to declare dividends for both common and preferred shareholders, holders of common stock may receive no dividends at all.

Why would holders of common stock permit (much less vote for) the creation of a stock that receives preference with regard to dividends each year and assets on liquidation? The answer is simple: while holders of preferred stock are given precedence with regard to assets and dividends, they do not have the right to vote on company policy. Preferred shareholders have no voice in company management. They are, in fact, more like long-term bondholders (creditors) than owners: Both receive a fixed payment each year as dividend or interest, both have preference over common stockholders as to assets on liquidation, but neither has a vote in company management. Long-term bondholders will eventually be repaid their investment—the debt principal—while preferred stockholders will not.

To explain fully preferred stock, we must address three other points: dividend calculation, obligation for missed dividend payments, and conversion privileges.

1. *Dividend calculation:* The dividend rate for preferred stock is a set amount each year and is usually stated as a dollar amount per share (i.e., a $5 preferred stock pays $5 dividends) or as a percentage of par value (i.e., an 8 percent, $100 par value preferred share pays $8 dividends).

2. *Obligation for missed dividend payments:* If the dividend agreement on preferred stock is cumulative, a company must catch up any missed dividend payments to preferred shareholders before dividends can be paid to common shareholders. This is important because a company has no legal obligation to pay dividends until they are declared by the board of directors; thus, even though holders of preferred stock are entitled to dividends at a set rate, there is no guarantee that they will be paid until the dividends are declared by the board. For example, assume dividends to preferred shareholders would total $100,000 per year, but the company does not declare and does not pay dividends for years one and two. In year three, the board declares total dividends of $350,000. If the dividend agreement for preferred shareholders specifies that dividend payments are cumulative, the preferred shareholders must receive the dividend payments they missed before common shareholders can receive payments. A cumulative distribution schedule for the above example is shown below:

For Preferred Stock:	
Current year dividend (Year 3)	$100,000
Prior year dividends (Years 1 and 2)	200,000
Total dividends for preferred stockholders	$300,000
Residual amount available for dividends to common stockholders	50,000
Total dividends paid	$350,000

In contrast, if a preferred stock does not have a cumulative dividend payment agreement, the company does not have to pay dividends missed before paying dividends to common shareholders. A noncumulative distribution of the same $350,000 under the conditions described is shown below:

For Preferred Stock:	
Current-year dividend (Year 3)	$100,000
Prior-year dividend (Years 1 and 2)	-0-
Total dividends for preferred stockholders	$100,000
Residual amount available for dividends to common stockholders	250,000
Total dividends paid	$350,000

3. *Conversion privilege:* Some preferred stock agreements contain an option allowing the preferred stock to be exchanged for common shares. Since common shares do not have a fixed dividend rate, they carry more risk; however, they offer more opportunity for market price increases. To make preferred shares more attractive to investors, the stock may be convertible to common shares in some ratio (ten shares of common for one share of preferred, for example).

Preferred stock, like common stock, is shown in the balance sheet stockholders' equity section and is separated into "Par Value" and "Capital Paid in Excess of Par":

Preferred Stock (at Par)	$500,000
Paid in Capital in Excess of Par	100,000

Again, the number of shares issued and authorized is disclosed.

Treasury Stock

Stock issued by a company may later be reacquired by the company, which may then retire or cancel it. Reacquired stock that is not retired or canceled is referred to as "treasury stock."

Treasury stock is not an asset; a company cannot create an asset by holding stock in itself. Treasury stock represents a decrease in outstanding stock, just as if the shares had been retired, but the reduction in shares outstanding is not made directly to the common stock account. Instead, the treasury stock is shown as a reduction in stockholders' equity in one of two ways. (Under either method, total stockholders' equity is decreased by the purchase of treasury shares.)

1. The treasury stock may be shown at par value as reduction in common stock.

Stockholders' Equity

Contributed capital:		
Common stock at par	$500,000	
Less treasury stock at par	100,000	
	400,000	
Paid in capital in excess of par	80,000	480,000
Retained earnings		200,000
Total stockholders' equity		$680,000

2. The treasury stock may be shown at reacquisition cost as a reduction of total stockholders' equity.

Stockholders' Equity

Common stock at par	$40,000	
Paid in capital in excess of par	50,000	90,000
Retained earnings		100,000
Total		190,000
Less treasury stock at cost		10,000
Total stockholders' equity		$180,000

Just as treasury stock is not an asset, an income statement loss or gain cannot result from treasury stock transactions. Events transpire that you and I would call a "loss" (reacquiring treasury stock for $20 per share and later reissuing it for $12) or a "gain" (reacquiring treasury shares at $30 and reissuing the shares at $40). But it is illegal for a company to produce a gain or loss, in accounting terms, on transactions involving its own stock. When total stockholders' equity is decreased by treasury stock transactions, the decrease is usually taken directly from retained earnings, and no loss is recorded on the income statement. When total stockholders' equity is increased by treasury stock transactions, the increase is recorded as a separate source of capital called "paid-in capital from treasury stock transactions."

Subscribed Stock

Companies may issue stock outright—selling the stock and receiving cash, property, or services in exchange—or on a subscription basis. A stock subscription is a legally binding contract between the issuing company and the subscriber or purchaser of the stock. Stock subscription agreements allow payment for the stock to be deferred and accomplish two goals:

1. They give the company a legal claim for the contract price of the stock.
2. They give the purchaser the legal status of a stockholder (unless specific rights are withheld by state law or contract).

The company's legal claim to the stock contract price is recorded in the balance sheet (usually as a current asset) as "Stock Subscriptions Receivable." (The SEC requires the account to be treated as a contra stockholders' equity account.) Stock subscriptions are like other company receivables: The purchaser/stockholder pays against the outstanding balance according to the contract agreement. The stock certificates are ordinarily not issued until the contract price is paid in full.

When the subscription agreement is signed, the source of the new asset "Subscription Receivable" is shown in the owners' equity section of the balance sheet as an increase in two accounts:

1. The par value of the stock is recorded in an account called "Common Stock Subscribed."
2. Any excess over par value is recorded in the account "Premium on Common Stock" or "Paid-in Capital in Excess of Par."

When the subscribed stock is fully paid, there will no longer be a "Subscription Receivable" category carried in current assets, and "Common Stock Subscribed" will be transferred to "Common Stock."

Although a stock subscription agreement is a legal contract and the subscription receivable is a legitimate receivable, corporate policy and state law vary as to how a defaulted subscription is treated. When a subscriber defaults, the company may take any of the following actions:

1. It can refund the amount received.
2. It can refund the amount received less the cost of reselling the stock.
3. It can declare as forfeited the amount received from the subscriber.
4. It can issue shares equal to the amount already received.

Donated Capital
When property or services are donated to a company, the value of the asset is recorded and the source of the asset is shown as a corre-

sponding increase in owners' equity, called "Paid-in Capital from Donations." If the donation is very large, the nature of the donation may be identified, as in "Paid-in Capital from Donated Plant Site."

RETAINED EARNINGS

Retained earnings is the dollar amount of assets furnished by company earnings that were not distributed as dividends. The primary key to understanding retained earnings is to realize that retained earnings do not represent cash—they represent only a source of assets and not any particular asset.

If a company earns $500,000 and does not declare dividends, retained earnings are increased by the $500,000 retained in the business. But what does a company do with $500,000 received as profits? They may use it to expand the business (to buy new equipment or increase inventories, for instance) or to repay an outstanding loan. They would certainly *not* keep the $500,000 as cash in the bank. The $500,000 increase in retained earnings documents a source of net assets (assets minus liabilities) but does not indicate which assets were provided by the income.

In addition to being a source of assets, retained earnings are also the maximum amount that can be distributed to stockholders as dividends. The company probably does not have cash available to pay dividends in the amount of retained earnings (nor would the company wish to, if earnings could be reinvested in the business). A company frequently distributes a portion of each year's earnings as dividends in some general pattern, perhaps some amount per share or some percentage of earnings; the remainder is retained and invested in the business.

Appropriations of Retained Earnings

When a company embarks on a special project, it may limit dividend payments until the project is completed, either because it is required to do so by a major creditor or because it wishes to preserve cash for expansion. When management limits dividend payments, there are two methods of notifying stockholders:

1. Through the notes to the financial statements.
2. By appropriating a portion of retained earnings.

That portion of retained earnings listed as appropriated in the owners' equity section of the balance sheet is not available for dividend payments. Since, as we have stressed, retained earnings constitute only the source of the assets, not an asset, no cash or any other resource need be set aside to fund the project undertaken.

When the project is completed, appropriated retained earnings are unappropriated and become available for dividend payments. Cash may have been spent on the project (building a plant, retiring bonds) and the composition of assets changed, but retained earnings are unaffected except for changing the designation of the appropriated component back to unappropriated.

Companies may use an appropriation of retained earnings simply to reduce the size of unappropriated retained earnings "available" for dividends. Uninformed investors may believe they should receive more of the earnings retained in the business, or labor unions may believe that wages should be higher—neither group realizing that the earnings retained are reinvested to buy new equipment, build new plants, and create more profit for owners and higher wages for workers.

CHAPTER PERSPECTIVE

This chapter has discussed the accounts and balance sheet captions you are most likely to encounter in the liability and owners' equity sections of the balance sheet. Liabilities are usually divided into current and noncurrent categories; owners' equity may divide capital into contributed and earned capital. Each category may include many different account titles. To understand the broad array of items that you may encounter in this part of the balance sheet, you must understand how accountants treat the different events affecting these items and you must read the balance sheet and other financial statements, including the notes to the financial statements, carefully.

The Income Statement: Operating Income

INTRODUCTION AND MAIN POINTS

Accountants and financial-statement readers usually consider information in the income statement to be more important than information in the balance sheet. If, for example, a company has a high level of debt, an investor may still believe the company will be successful—*if* the company has a strong earnings record. But if a company has a more moderate level of debt, an investor may doubt the company's ability to survive—*if* the company's earnings record is poor. This chapter is the first of two chapters covering the components of the income statement.

This chapter describes each component in a classified income statement and discusses in detail the components of operating income. Different inventory flow methods are introduced and the difference between inventories held by manufacturers and inventories held by retailers is discussed. Chapter 7 covers the remainder of the classified income statement, nonoperating revenues, and expenses.

After studying the material in this chapter:

▬ You will know the components of a classified income statement.
▬ You will understand the difference that different inventory accounting flow methods can produce.
▬ You will know the difference between the kinds of inventories that may be held by a manufacturer and by a retailer.
▬ You will know how accountants determine operating income and the significance of this portion of the income statement.

INCOME STATEMENT COMPONENTS

The income statement reports the results of business activities for a period of time, typically a fiscal year. These results are classified as revenues and expenses. Revenues measure the inflow of new assets to the business from the earnings process; expenses measure the outflow of assets or the using up of assets in that same process. Net income represents an increase in assets and owners' equity, while a net loss represents a decrease in assets and owners' equity.

Annual business income or loss is computed by subtracting the expenses that occurred during the year from the revenues earned during the year. If revenues exceed expenses, the business has earned income; if expenses exceed revenues, a loss has occurred. Revenues and expenses are recorded at the time they are earned or occur, regardless of when cash is received or paid, according to the accrual concept used by accountants to measure business activity and income.

THE INCOME STATEMENT

Each income statement contains information unique to the company preparing it. Depending on the activities of the company, an income statement may contain the following sections:

Sales or Operating Revenues:	Net sales revenues (sales less returns) or service revenues are reported in this section.
Cost of Goods Sold:	This is the amount the company paid for the inventory it sold. A service organization does not have this expense.
Gross Profit:	This is the difference between net sales revenues and the cost of goods sold. From this profit margin, the company must cover all other costs if it expects to have net income. A service organization does not report a gross profit; a company may or may not show gross profit in its income statement.
Operating Expenses:	These include selling, general, and administrative expenses.
Other Revenues:	These increases in asset value occur from transactions that are not directly related to operations; for instance, interest earned on investments arises from a decision related to managing idle cash, not trying to earn a profit through sales or by providing services.
Other Expenses:	These decreases in asset value occur from transactions not directly related to operations. For instance, interest

expense arises from the decision to finance operations by increasing debt. That decision is not related to trying to earn a profit through sales or by providing services.

Pretax Income Continuing Operations:
This figure is the sum of all the revenues from and expenses related to the portion of the business that is continuing.

Income Tax Expense:
This figure is a function of pretax income from continuing operations and the appropriate tax rates.

Income from Continuing Operations:
This is the after-tax income of the portion of the business that is continuing.

Discontinued Operations:
This may either be an after-tax gain or loss on a segment of the business that management intends to sell or has sold.

Income Before Extraordinary Items: This is a subtotal.

Extraordinary Items:
These are after-tax gains or losses on transactions that are unusual and that are not expected to reoccur.

Cumulative Effect of a Change in Accounting Principle:
A change in accounting principle occurs when management changes from one acceptable accounting principle to another. This is a catch-up adjustment. For example, suppose we change depreciation methods to a method that would have recorded more depreciation expense than was recorded under the old method. To make the records look as if we have always used the new method, we must take the additional depreciation—the cumulative effect of the change in accounting principle.

When a company reports a change in accounting principle, it also shows pro forma income figures in a schedule attached to the income statement. These pro forma income figures show what past net incomes would have been if the new principle had been used in those reporting years.

Net Income (Loss):	This is the total of all reported revenues (gains) and expenses (losses).
Earnings per Common Share:	Publicly traded companies that are required to present several ratios summarize the assumed income earned by each holder of a share of common share. Earnings-per-share ratios are an income figure divided by an average number of common shares assumed to be outstanding.

Not all income statements include the sections presented above. For instance, in a year in which a company does not have discontinued operations or a change in accounting principle, those sections drop out of the income statement. Care should be taken when comparing income statements over time; for example, income from continuing operations is comparable only to a later year's net income taken from an income statement that does not have discontinued operations, extraordinary items, or a change in accounting principle. Figure 6-1a contains an example of a simple income statement taken from actual financial statements; Figure 6-1b contains a more complex example.

REVENUE FROM SALES AND SERVICES

Revenues (the price charged by the company for its merchandise or services) are generally recorded at the time of sale or completion of the service. However, two conditions must be met before revenue can be recorded: The earnings process must be substantially complete, and the company must be reasonably certain the revenue can be collected.

The earnings process is not substantially complete if:

■ The seller and buyer have not agreed on the price of the merchandise or service.

■ The buyer does not have to pay the seller until the merchandise is resold.

■ The buyer does not have to pay the seller if the merchandise is stolen or physically destroyed.

■ The buyer and seller are related parties (for example, parent company and subsidiary).

STATEMENT OF INCOME
(Years ended December 31)

(Dollars in thousands except per share)	2000	1999
Sales	$ 1,655,830	$ 1,599,751
Cost and expenses		
Cost of products sold	1,306,758	1,263,978
Selling, general and administrative		
expenses	161,546	148,417
Interest expense	29,440	25,175
Acquisition consolidation charges		
Income from operations before income taxes .	158,086	162,181
Taxes on income (Note 16)	60,906	67,029
Income from operations before equity in		
earnings of affiliates.................	97,180	95,152
Equity in earnings of affiliates (Note 10) ...	6,381	1,125
Net income.........................	$ 103,561	$ 96,277
Average shares outstanding	43,897,002	43,816,224
Net income.........................	$2.36	$2.20
Dividends per share	$.81	$.64

FIG. 6-1a *A simple income statement.*

■■■ The seller must still provide significant services to the buyer or aid in reselling the product.

If substantial performance has occurred and the collectibility of the revenue is reasonably certain, the sale of product or service can be recorded. If a company cannot estimate the collectibility of a sale, it records revenue as the customer makes payments. This has the effect of recording the sale on a cash basis rather than when it is earned.

Accountants use one of two methods to record revenue as the customer makes payments: the installment method or the cost-recovery method. The *installment method* records part of each payment as revenue. Suppose, for example, we sold merchandise that cost us $40 for $100. The gross profit on the sale is $60 ($100 − $40) or 60 percent of the sales price ($60/$100). As the customer makes payments, $.60 of each $1 collected is reported as revenue. (The remaining $.40 is cost of goods sold expense.)

Statement of Income

In the thousands except per share amounts For the years ended December 31	2000	1999	1998
Net sales	$3,021,352	$2,647,900	$2,799,481
Cost of goods sold	2,264,736	1,947,335	2,105,587
Administrative, selling and service engineering expenses	471,120	431,986	455,457
Restructure of operations	—	—	23,000
Operating income	285,496	268,579	215,437
Interest expense	32,672	38,641	60,900
Other income (expense), net	(24,603)	(26,233)	(16,592)
Dresser-Rand income (loss)	2,567	(42,569)	—
Nonrecurring gains	—	—	33,694
Nonrecurring charges	—	—	17,305
Earnings before income taxes, extraordinary item and cumulative effect of accounting change	230,788	161,136	154,334
Provision for income taxes	69,200	53,200	53,700
Earnings before extraordinary item and cumulative effect of accounting change	161,588	107,936	100,634
Extraordinary item—(net of income tax benefit of $5,673)	—	(6,660)	—
Cumulative effect of accounting change—(net of income tax provision of $9,004)	—	9,755	—
Net earnings	$161,588	$ 117,691	$ 93,974
Earnings per share of common stock:			
Net earnings before extraordinary item and cumulative effect of accounting change	$3.00	$1.98	$1.92
Extraordinary item	—	—	(.13)
Cumulative effect of accounting change	—	.19	—
Net earnings per share	$3.00	$2.17	$1.79

Pro forma amounts, assuming the new method of accounting had been applied retroactively for 1999 and 1998, are $107.9 million ($1.98 per share) and $100.1 million ($1.91 per share), respectively, for earnings before extraordinary item and $107.9 million ($1.98 per share) and $93.4 million ($1.78 per share), respectively, for net earnings.
See accompanying notes to consolidated financial statements.

FIG. 6-1b *A detailed income statement.*

The revenue that has not yet been collected is recorded as "Deferred Gross Profit" in the liability section of the balance sheet.

In contrast, the *cost-recovery method* does not record revenue until the customer has paid the seller an amount equal to the cost of the merchandise sold. Using the example given above, we have to recover the $40 cost from the customer before any revenue is recorded. After we recover the $40 cost of the merchandise, each dollar received is recorded as revenue.

Long-Term Contract

If a company provides services on a long-term contract, revenue may be recorded over the life of the contract. For example, the construction industry records revenue on major long-term contracts as the work is performed rather than at the point of sale. If dependable estimates of selling price, construction costs, and the stage of construction exist, the construction company records revenue as the work is performed. Accountants refer to this as the percentage-of-completion method.

For instance, suppose we are involved in a three-year construction project. At the end of the first year, we estimate the project is one-third completed; after the second year, it is two-thirds complete. We finish the project in the third year. We record one-third of the estimated gross profit (sales price less the total estimated construction cost) as revenue in the first year, and another third of the estimated gross profit in the second year ($\frac{2}{3} - \frac{1}{3}$ reported the first year). The final one-third is recorded as revenue in the third year.

While the percentage-of-completion method departs from the concept of recording revenue at the point of sale, it is consistent with the accrual concept of measuring activities in the period in which they occur. If a company does not have dependable estimates of the sales price, construction costs, and stage of construction, it does not recognize revenue until the project is complete (year three in our example).

COST OF GOODS SOLD AND INVENTORIES

Inventories were discussed in Chapter 3 as a component of the current assets section of the balance sheet. This discussion explains the relationship between cost-of-goods-sold category in the income statement and the balance-in-inventory-on-hand category in the balance sheet.

The total inventory available for sale each year is the total of the beginning inventory (that available at the beginning of the year) and the inventory purchased during the year. At year end, the total inventory available for sale each year is either still on hand or sold. The total available for sale is split between ending inventory in the balance sheet and cost of goods sold in the income statement.

At first glance, this may seem to be no problem—and if all units were purchased at the same price all year, there would in fact be no problem. A problem develops, however, because companies purchase units at many different prices, and, depending on the method used to flow costs through inventory, ending inventory and cost of goods sold can be any one of several different figures—all of which are acceptable for financial reporting.

For example, suppose that a company has no beginning inventory and purchases three identical units during the first quarter of the year: one in January, one in February, and one in March. The units were purchased for $4, $6, and $8, respectively. Now assume that one unit is sold for $10. What would the gross profit be?

If the company charges the $4 cost of the first unit purchased to cost of goods sold, gross profit is $6 and ending inventory is $14 ($6 + $8) for the two units still on hand. If the company charges the $6 cost of the second unit purchased to cost of goods sold, gross profit is $4 and ending inventory is $12 ($4 + $8). Finally, if the last unit purchased is expensed first, gross profit and ending inventory will be $2 and $10, respectively. These three possibilities are shown below.

	Possibility 1	Possibility 2	Possibility 3
In the income statement:			
Selling price	$10	$10	$10
Cost of goods sold	4	6	8
Gross profit	$ 6	$ 4	$ 2
In the balance sheet:			
Ending inventory	$14	$12	$10
	($6 + $8)	($4 + $8)	($4 + $6)

There are three inventory accounting methods in common use; depending upon which is used, any one of these results described above is possible. The three methods are First-In-First-Out (FIFO), Last-In-First-Out (LIFO), and Weighted Average.

FIFO Inventory

Accountants using FIFO inventory flow record costs the way merchants typically flow goods: The oldest units are sold first, and the most recently purchased units wind up in ending inventory. In the above example, using a FIFO inventory flow produces the first possibility.

The key to understanding inventory and cost of goods sold is to realize that when units are identical, accountants are free to flow costs through the accounting records in ways that do not mimic the way the actual goods are handled.

LIFO Inventory

The third possibility in the example given above results from the use of the LIFO method of inventory flow, by which the cost of the most recent purchases are charged to cost of goods sold and the old costs remain in inventory, regardless of how the company flows the physical units.

To understand the accounting logic behind LIFO inventory, think about the result of the sale. How much better off is the company after selling one unit for $10? Is it $6 better off? Or $4? Or $2? To answer this question, you must consider replacement costs. If the company is to remain in business, management must replace any units sold. How much will the next unit purchased cost? The last unit purchased cost $8. Prices have been rising from $4 to $6 to $8 per unit. The next unit probably will cost $8 per unit or more. If the company, having sold one unit for $10, must replace the unit sold, it is only $2 better off ($10 − $8 = $2). The logic that supports LIFO increases the accuracy of the income statement, flowing costs in a LIFO pattern regardless of the flow pattern of physical units.

Figure 6-2 contains one company's note disclosure of inventory methods and the difference between values obtained using LIFO and FIFO.

Weighted-Average Inventory

Weighted-average inventory, the third method, is a compromise between flowing costs as merchants flow inventory and maximizing the accuracy of the income statement. This method charges both ending inventory and cost of goods sold with the weighted average cost of all units available for sale. The weighted-average cost per unit for our example is $4 + $6 + $8 or $18, divided by three units, or $6 per unit. This result is shown in Possibility 2 on the previous page.

Inventories are stated at the lower of cost or market. The last-in, first-out (LIFO) method was used to determine costs of approximately 45% of the total inventories in 2000 and 49% in 1999. The remaining inventories are determined on the first-in, first-out (FIFO) method.

(Dollars in thousands)	2000	1999
Finished and in process	$ 65,989	$ 60,367
Materials and supplies	85,660	103,339
	$151,649	$163,706

If the FIFO method of accounting had been used for all inventories, the totals would have been higher by $11,536,000 in 2000 and $8,057,000 in 1999.

FIG. 6-2 *Note disclosure of inventory methods and the difference between results based on LIFO and FIFO.*

MANUFACTURERS' INVENTORIES

A manufacturer may have several different kinds of inventory: raw materials, work in process, and finished goods held for sale (in contrast to a retail company which has only an inventory of units held for sale). In addition, manufacturing costs differ from nonmanufacturing costs in the timing of their charge against earnings. Nonmanufacturing costs, such as selling or administrative costs, are called *period costs* because they generally become expenses as a result of the passing of time. When a sales salary is paid, it is immediately charged to sales salaries expense, because the benefit of the salary (the salesperson's work) was consumed in the period during which the salesperson made sales calls. In contrast, when a year's insurance is paid on the corporate office building, the insurance cost is expensed month by month and the insurance (with its benefit as an asset) expires over a period of time.

Manufacturing costs, in contrast, are assets (the cost of inventory of manufactured units) until the units are sold. When an assembly-line worker or factory foreman is paid, the wages are charged, not to a wage expense account, but directly, or through overhead, to an inventory of unfinished work in process (an asset). When prepaid insurance on the factory expires month by month, it is charged, not to insurance expense, but through overhead to an inventory of unfinished work in process (an asset).

All manufacturing costs—labor, materials, and overhead—are charged to the asset work-in-process inventory. When financial statements are prepared, work-in-process inventory is shown in the current assets section of the balance sheet or disclosed in the notes to the financial statements.

When units are completed, the costs charged to work-in-process inventory are transferred to finished-goods inventory, another asset account. Only when the finished goods are finally sold are the manufacturing costs transferred to an expense account, cost of goods sold. Because manufacturing costs are not expensed until the product is sold, manufacturing costs are called *product costs.*

Inventory might appear in a note to the financial statements, supporting both the balance sheet amount and the calculation of cost of goods sold as shown below.

Inventories	
Raw materials	$ 1,050,000
Work in process	2,790,000
Finished goods	10,500,500
Total inventories	$14,340,500

The flow of manufacturing costs is illustrated below:

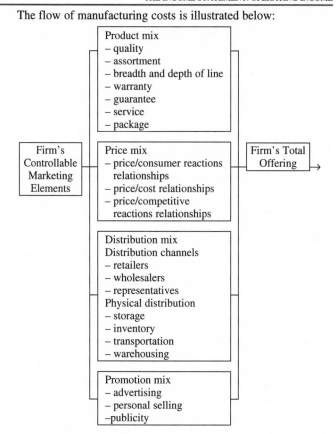

Factory Overhead

Factory overhead is the total of all the indirect costs of production (all manufacturing costs except raw materials and labor used directly in the product). Factory overhead includes the costs of supervisory labor, maintenance, factory and equipment depreciation, manufacturing supplies used, energy, insurance, and any other manufacturing cost associated only indirectly with individual units produced.

Distorted Profit

The accounting method that charges all manufacturing costs to units produced is called *full* or *absorption costing*. Because absorption costing charges fixed capacity costs (such as supervision and factory depreciation) to individual units produced, net income is biased optimistically (high) when inventories are increasing and pessimistically (low) when inventories are decreasing. The full explanation of why this happens is very complex, but the net effect is that in times of growth, when inventories are increasing, profits may not be quite as great as reported, and in times of recession, when inventories are shrinking, profits may not be as dismal as financial statements indicate.

OTHER OPERATING EXPENSES

In a business that sells merchandise, the major operating expense is the cost of goods sold. Other operating expenses are reported on the income statement after gross profit on sales and are generally divided into selling and administrative expenses.

Selling Expenses

Selling expenses are the costs associated with producing sales. They include sales personnel salaries and commissions, sales manager and office staff salaries, payroll taxes expense (related to the sales staff), pension expense (related to the sales staff), travel and entertainment, advertising expense, delivery expense and shipping supplies expense, sales office supplies expense, telephone expense (related to sales staff), and sales equipment depreciation expense.

Administrative Expenses

Administrative expenses are the costs associated with managing the company. They include officers' salaries, office staff salaries, payroll tax expense (related to the administrative staff), pension expense (related to administrative staff), legal and professional services, research-and-development expense, utilities expense, telephone expense (related to administrative staff), insurance expense, building depreciation expense, office equipment depreciation expense, office supplies expense, and miscellaneous office expenses.

The foregoing are only representative of the types of costs that are classified as selling or administrative expenses. Actual costs and breakdowns vary, depending on the nature of the company's business. For instance, a service-oriented business such as a dentist's office may not break out its expenses into the selling and administrative categories.

CHAPTER PERSPECTIVE

This chapter, the first of two on the components of the income statement, introduced the classified income statement. The components of operating income were discussed in detail: sales, cost of goods sold, selling expenses, and administrative expenses. The different inventory flow methods—LIFO, FIFO, and weighted average—were introduced and their logic explained. The difference between inventories held by a manufacturer and a retailer was discussed and the flow of costs in a manufacturing company was introduced.

The Income Statement: Nonoperating Items, Deferred Taxes, and Earnings per Share

INTRODUCTION AND MAIN POINTS

Accountants make the income statement easier to understand by separating the income (or loss) generated by ongoing, normal operations from income that is derived from activities or events that are not expected to be ongoing or are neither normal nor ongoing. This chapter discusses the two most frequently occurring items in these categories: discontinued operations and extraordinary items.

Accountants also seek to make the income statement more informative by calculating and displaying earnings per common share, but this effort results in a much-used statistic that is poorly understood by accountants and financial-statement readers alike. The second half of the chapter discusses earnings per share and deferred income taxes, another controversial area that affects both the income statement and the balance sheet.

After studying this material:

▬ You will understand the financial statement impact of a decision to discontinue a business operation and will see how accountants present that impact in the financial statements.

▬ You will be able to distinguish gains and losses that are classified as extraordinary and will see how accountants present these items in the income statement.

▬ You will understand why tax expense on the income statement is not always the same as the taxes paid during the year and will understand how accountants resolve this difference.

▬ You will understand the basic calculation of earnings per share and the multitude of factors that complicate this otherwise simple statistic.

DISCONTINUED OPERATIONS

The decision by a company to discontinue one of its business operations creates a contingency. In Chapter 2, we defined a contingency as a situation in which the company stands to gain or lose as the result of a past transaction or event. Only the amount of gain or loss that is dependent on another transaction or event is "contingent." At the point management decides to sell a segment of the business (the event giving rise to future gain or loss) a contingency exists, because management may not know whether the sale will result in a gain or loss. Management may intend to sell and not yet have a buyer lined up, or, even if management has a buyer, the exact gain or loss may not be known until the disposal date.

While the precise amount of gain or loss may be unknown at the point management decides to sell, the contingency is classified as "likely to occur" because the decision to sell makes the incurrence of either a gain or loss certain. Therefore, disclosure of discontinued operations follows the guidelines for disclosure of "likely" contingencies as discussed in Chapter 2. If management expects a loss on disposal, the loss is reported on the income statement in the period in which management makes the decision to sell. If management expects a gain on the disposal, the gain is postponed until the fiscal year in which the actual disposal occurs. (Remember, conservatism, which governs the reporting of contingencies, favors recording losses that are likely to occur before they occur but recording gains when they actually occur.)

Separate Disclosure

Gains or losses on discontinued operations are reported on the income statement in a special section that follows income from continuing operations and precedes extraordinary items. Discontinued operations are reported net of their tax effects. (Gains on disposal of such an operation generally give rise to additional taxes, while losses generally result in tax savings.) It is necessary to report discontinued operations net of their tax consequences because of the structure of the income statement. Income tax expense has been computed on income from continuing operations. Gains or losses reported on the income statement below the continuing operations section either increase tax expense or save taxes.

In the year in which management decides to sell the segment, two categories of discontinued operations may appear on the income statement: a gain or loss from operating the discontinued segment, and a gain or loss on disposal of the segment. The gain or loss from operating the discontinued segment is the segment's net income or loss from the beginning of the fiscal year to the date when management adopts the plan of disposal. The second component, gain or loss on disposal of the segment, is the contingency—the anticipated gain or loss generated by the segment from the adoption of the disposal plan to the actual date of disposal. This includes winding-down operations as well as the actual disposal of the segment's assets.

Discontinued Operations—An Illustration

Most dispositions are reported on more than one annual income statement because the winding down of operations and the disposal of the segment normally transcends two accounting periods. Because disposal of a large business segment is a lengthy process, it is seldom accomplished within one fiscal period. Let's look at a simple example of a disposal.

Whatsit, Inc., decides to sell the Widget division to Sangsung, Ltd. The decision to sell is made at the October 1, 1999 board meeting. From January 1 to October 1, 1999 Widget experienced an after-tax operating loss of $1 million. Whatsit estimates that operations from October 1, 1999, through September 1, 2000 (the date Sangsung will take over operations), and the actual sale will generate a $5 million after-tax loss. Whatsit's income statement for the year ended December 31, 1999, will show discontinued operations of:

1999
Discontinued Operations:
Loss from Operating Widget Division	$1,000,000	
Estimated Loss on Disposal of Widget	5,000,000	
		$6,000,000

Remember that the estimated loss on disposal is a contingency. Because Whatsit is estimating a loss, it will record the loss in the fiscal year in which the disposal decision was made. If, instead of estimating a loss on disposal, Whatsit had estimated a gain, only the "Loss from Operating Widget Division" would have been reported on the 1999 income statement. The gain would be recorded in 2000 when operations are actually turned over to Sangsung.

Because Whatsit must use estimates to recognize the "Loss on Disposal of Widget Division," any difference between the estimated loss and the actual loss will be reported in 2000. Suppose Whatsit experiences an actual after-tax "Loss on Disposal" of $5,750,000. The discontinued operations section of Whatsit's 2000 income statement will appear as follows:

2000
Discontinued Operations:
Loss on Disposal of Widget Division	$750,000

Together, the 1999 and 2000 income statements report the full loss on disposal ($5,750,000).

Notice that Whatsit did not report any gain or loss from operating the Widget division during 2000. There cannot be an additional "gain or loss from operating" the discontinued segment in 2000; gains or losses from operations experienced after the decision to sell has been made are part of the gain or loss on disposal of the segment.

Now suppose that instead of the estimated $5 million loss on disposal, Whatsit's actual loss is $4,800,000. The discontinued operations section of Whatsit's 2000 income statement would then appear as follows:

2000
Discontinued Operations
  Gain on Disposal of Widget Division $200,000

Together, the 1999 and 2000 income statements report the full loss on disposal of $4,800,000 ($5 million estimated loss in 1999 minus the $200,000 gain reported in 2000).

Disposals That Are Not Discontinued Operations

Segregating gains or losses on discontinued operations on the income statement is important. Segregation alerts the reader of the financial statements to the fact that a major portion of the business will no longer be contributing to the company's earnings. In this situation, income from continuing operations (rather than net income) becomes the important figure when trying to forecast the future earnings of the company. However, not all sales of business assets, segments, or divisions are reported as discontinued operations.

Only those operations that represent a completely separate line of product (service) or class of customer (client) are considered segments when reporting discontinued operations. Gains or losses on disposal of business assets, segments, or divisions that are not sales of a completely separate product line or class of customer are reported as part of income from continuing operations.

EXTRAORDINARY ITEMS

Before a company can classify a gain or loss as an extraordinary item, two criteria must be met:

1. The gain or loss must come from a transaction or event that is unusual. An unusual transaction or event is one that is unrelated to the typical activities of the business.

2. That transaction or event must be nonrecurring—that is, one that management does not expect to occur again.

The classification as extraordinary is company-specific. A natural disaster such as an earthquake, for example, meets the definition of unusual (unrelated to the typical activities of the business). But, if our business is located in southern California on the San Andreas fault, the quake would not be considered nonrecurring and therefore could not be considered extraordinary. On the other hand, an earthquake in New York City would give rise to an extraordinary loss. In general, the criteria of "unusual" and "nonrecurring" must be looked at from the perspective of the reporting company: Is the transaction or event unusual given the nature of that company's business and its geographical location?

Presentation of Extraordinary Items

Extraordinary gains or losses are reported in their own section on the income statement, between discontinued operations and the cumulative effect of a change in accounting principle. A net extraordinary gain (gain less additional income taxes) increases income, while a net extraordinary loss (loss reduced by income tax savings) decreases income. Accountants report extraordinary items net of their tax consequences because of the structure of the income statement: Income tax expense has been computed on income from continuing operations. Gains or losses reported on the income statement below the continuing operations section either increase tax expense or save taxes.

Segregating extraordinary gains or losses on the income statement is important. By classifying a gain or loss as extraordinary, management is saying, "This is an unusual gain or loss and we do not expect it to reoccur." Segregating extraordinary items also allows comparability between years. Because extraordinary items are not expected to reoccur, "Income Before Extraordinary Items" can be compared to "Net Income" in years when there are no extraordinary gains or losses. Companies required to report earnings per share must report "Per Share Income Before Extraordinary Items" so that figure may also be compared to "Per Share Net Income" for years in which there were no extraordinary gains or losses.

Exceptions to the Rules

There are exceptions to the criteria for evaluating gains and losses. Accounting principles require that certain types of gains and losses not be treated as extraordinary items, while other gains and losses must be given extraordinary item treatment.

Gains or losses that may not be treated as extraordinary items include:

1. Losses from the write-down or write-off of receivables, inventories, equipment, or intangible assets (a write-down or write-off of an asset occurs when an asset's value has been impaired, and the asset is reduced or written down)
2. Gains or losses related to exchanging foreign currencies
3. Gains or losses from the sale of a business segment
4. Gains or losses from the sale or abandonment of property, plant, or equipment that has been used in the business
5. Losses resulting from strikes by employees

The company's type of business and geographical location are not important, because these gains or losses cannot receive extraordinary-item treatment.

Gains or losses on settlement of debt before its due date (the difference between the recorded value of the debt and the amount paid to settle the debt) are reported as extraordinary items. Again, the company's type of business and geographical location are not important because these gains or losses must receive extraordinary-item treatment. Figure 7-1 presents the income statement and footnote disclosure for our extraordinary item from the 2000 annual report of Center City Enterprises. Note also that Center City had a change in accounting principle in 1998.

TAXES AND TAX DEFERRALS

Income tax regulations do not always require that a company use the same accounting method on the tax return that it has used on the income statement. Tax expense as shown on the income statement is derived from the revenues and expenses listed on the income statement. In other words, taxes are recorded on the income statement in the same year as the revenues and expenses giving rise to the taxes. This is done in adherence to the matching concept. However, the taxes actually due the government are derived from the figures on the tax return. The difference between these two tax amounts is called "deferred taxes."

Different Depreciation Methods

Suppose we decide to use a different method of depreciation on the income statement than we use on the tax return (which both the accounting profession and the government allow us to do). In order to stimulate capital investment through faster write-offs and to bring more uniformity to write-off periods, Congress enacted the Modified

	For the Years Ended January 31,		
	2000	1999	1998
	(in thousands, except per share data)		
Revenues			
Sales and operating revenues	$324,249	$293,150	$276,381
Interest and other income	17,046	17,566	14,948
Equity in earnings of affiliates	1,128	1,702	2,251
Total revenues	342,423	312,418	293,580
Operating costs excluding depreciation and amortization			
Interest incurred	120,086	96,983	78,609
Less interest capitalized for projects under development. .	30,600	17,077	11,641
	89,486	79,906	66,968
Operating costs of rental properties	134,051	117,957	109,266
Other operating expenses	82,239	84,795	90,603
	305,776	282,658	266,837
Operating earnings before depreciation and amortization and gain on disposition of properties and other provisions.	35,647	29,760	26,743
Depreciation and amortization.	31,341	25,450	20,844
Operating earnings before gain on disposition of properties and other provisions. . . .	5,306	4,310	5,899
Gain on disposition of properties and other provisions	5,760	10,753	597
Earnings from continuing operations before income taxes	11,066	15,063	6,496

FIG. 7-1 *Consolidated Statements of Earnings for Center City Enterprises, Inc., and Subsidiaries*

Income taxes			
Current.	(287)	571	(950)
Deferred.	5,562	6,659	3,749
	5,275	7,230	2,799
Net earnings from continuing operations	5,791	7,833	3,697
Net loss from discontinued operations	(1,565)	—	(511)
Net earnings before extraordinary gain and cumulative effect of an accounting change	4,226	7,833	3,186
Extraordinary gain, net of tax.	1,690	—	—
Cumulative effect on prior years of a change in accounting principle relating to income taxes	—	—	9,187
Net earnings	$ 5,916	$ 7,833	$ 12,373
Earnings (loss) per share			
Continuing operations	$ .70	$ .99	$ .47
Net discontinued operations	(.19)	—	(.06)
Extraordinary gain, net of tax.	.21	—	—
Cumulative effect of a change in accounting principle . . .	—	—	1.15
Net earnings.	$ .72	$ .99	$ 1.56

FIG. 7-1 *Consolidated Statements of Earnings for Center City Enterprises, Inc., and Subsidiaries*

Extraordinary Gain

The Company signed an agreement on November 15, 2000 with a savings and loan association, settling a dispute that arose over the Company's right to extend the maturity dates of various loans on certain of its land parcels. The Company had commenced a civil action against the lender but the civil action was settled by a compromise agreement whereby the Company agreed to retire the outstanding debt at a reduced cost, resulting in a gain before income taxes of $4,611,000.

In connection with the early extinguishment of certain letters of credit, the Company has expensed the unamortized procurement costs and early cancellation penalties and fees totaling $1,634,000. These letters of credit, which are required under the related debt agreements, guarantee repayment by the Company of principal and interest on certain tax-exempt Industrial Revenue Bonds issued by various community redevelopment agencies.

The net effect of these transactions resulted in an extraordinary gain of $1,690,000, net of tax.

Cost Recovery System (MACRS) in the Tax Reform Act of 1986. MACRS applies to depreciable assets placed in service in 1987 and later years. Tables are provided that indicate the amount of depreciation to be taken based on the specific class of asset. The table computation of tax depreciation under MACRS differs from the computation under GAAP because 1) the tax life is generally shorter than the economic life of the asset; 2) the salvage value is zero; and 3) the cost of recovery of the asset is on an accelerated basis. Depreciation expense on the income statement and tax return will be different at various times in the equipment's useful life. Consider this example:

Annual Depreciation

	Year 1	Year 2	Year 3	Year 4	Total
Income Statement	$10,000	$10,000	$10,000	$10,000	$40,000
Tax Return	$13,332	$17,780	$5,924	$2,964	$40,000
Difference *	($3,332)	($7,780)	$4,076	$7,036	$-0-
× Tax Rate of 30 percent	($1,000)	($2,334)	$1,223	$2,111	$-0-

* A negative (or parenthetical) difference in this example means that more depreciation will be recorded on the tax return, decreasing the amount of taxes currently due.

In years 1 and 2, this company records more depreciation on the tax return than on the income statement ($3,332 and $7,780, respectively). This causes it to pay less in tax than it is showing as tax expense on its income statement ($1,000 and $2,334, respectively). By claiming more depreciation on the tax return, the company postpones taxes in years 1 and 2.

In years 3 and 4 the company shows more depreciation on the income statement than on the tax return ($5,924 and $2,964, respectively). This causes it to pay more taxes than are showing in tax expense for years 3 and 4 ($1,223 and $2,111, respectively). This is the payment of the postponed taxes from years 1 and 2.

Notice that there is no difference between the total depreciation taken on the income statement and tax return over the four-year period. Over the four-year period, tax expense also equals the amount of taxes due. The difference is simply in the timing of the reporting.

In this example, a liability for future taxes is created in years 1 and 2. This liability is paid in years 3 and 4. The balance sheet prepared at the end of year 1 and year 2 shows the "deferred tax liability" as noncurrent because the deferred tax liability relates to a noncurrent asset—a depreciable asset. The balance sheet prepared at the end of year 1 shows $1,000 as the deferred tax liability and $3,334 ($1,000 + $2,334) as a noncurrent liability at the end of year 2.

Temporary Differences

Recording revenues and expenses on the income statement and tax return in different periods can also produce a "deferred tax asset." Suppose that our fiscal year ends on December 31 and that in December 2000 we collect January 2001 rents. Income tax regulations require that we pay tax on the rents in 2000, the year in which they are collected. Under the accrual accounting concept (see Chapter 1), the rents are not earned until January 2001 and are not reported as revenue on the 2000 income statement. They are unearned at year end 2000 and are reported as a current liability on the December 31, 2000 balance sheet (we must furnish the premises or return the rent money). The 2000 tax payment (which includes tax on the rent received) is more than the expense showing on the income statement; we have paid taxes on revenue we have not yet earned. This prepayment is treated as an asset—"deferred tax asset"—which is essentially a "prepaid" tax.

Changing Tax Rates

If the company experiences a change in tax rates, it must revise the recorded amount of the "deferred tax liability" or "deferred tax asset."

This adjustment is made through tax expense. Suppose the income statement shows $10,000 more in revenue than does the tax return. At a 30 percent rate, this creates a $3,000 "deferred tax liability." If the tax rate increases to 40 percent, the "deferred tax liability" must be increased by $1,000 [($10,000 × 40 percent) − $3,000]. This adjustment is made by increasing income tax expense by $1,000 when the tax rate changes, either by legislation or because the company moves into a higher (or lower) tax bracket through changes in earnings.

A company should use temporary differences to its advantage. If income tax regulations allow, it can use methods on the tax return that minimize the amount of taxes currently due, creating a "deferred tax liability." This postpones the payment of tax to a later period. Postponing the payment of tax as long as legally possible allows the company to use those funds to earn additional profits.

EARNINGS PER SHARE

Earnings per share (EPS) is a simple, almost intuitive accounting measure carried (of necessity) to its most complicated, confusing extreme. Generally accepted accounting principles require a publicly held company to calculate its earnings per share and display that figure on its income statement. The official pronouncement on EPS is long and is very complicated. Still, earnings per share is often cited as the single most used financial ratio; it can be understood if you ignore the complications and concentrate on the purpose of this ratio.

Basic EPS

Earnings per share is simply the earnings of the company divided by the number of shares of stock outstanding. When a financial-statement reader examines a company's earnings per share over a period of several years, a pattern of growth or contraction may become apparent. Reducing the company's total earnings to a measure of earnings per ownership share helps an investor determine how successful the company is in creating earnings for individual shareholders. If a company sells additional shares of stock, for instance, you would expect total earnings to increase as a result of the additional investment received from owners; the additional shareholder investment might be used to build a new plant or to expand operations in some other way.

An increase in total earnings achieved in this way can be misleading. Suppose a company with 100,000 shares of stock outstanding issues an additional 20,000 shares of stock and expands production facilities with the cash received. Assume that, as a result, the company's earnings increase from $200,000 to $220,000 per year.

If an investor looks only at total earnings, an increase of 10 percent may appear good. But if we look at the earnings per share for the two years, we see that the earnings per share of ownership actually fell:

Before investment:
EPS = $200,000/100,000 shares = $2.00/share
After investment:
EPS = $220,000/120,000 shares = $1.83/share

As companies increase and decrease the number of shares outstanding, by issuing or retiring shares of stock, by combining with other companies, or by fulfilling obligations to convert bonds or meet employee stock options, the earnings per share figure relates the company's reported earnings to the number of shares of stock outstanding. The basic equation for earnings per share is:

$$\text{Basic EPS} = \text{Earnings / number of shares outstanding}$$

EPS Complications

But now for the complications. Suppose there are preferred stockholders as well as common stockholders. In that case, some of the company's earnings must be paid as dividends to preferred stockholders just as interest must be paid on debt. Dividend payments to preferred stockholders, like interest, are a cost of capital and must be subtracted from earnings to determine the earnings available to common stockholders. (Interest is already deducted as an operating expense in calculating earnings.) So, if we are interested in the earnings per share for common stockholders, we must modify the EPS equation to read:

$$\text{EPS} = \text{Earnings available to common stockholders / number of shares outstanding}$$

Suppose further that the company issues or retires common stock during the year. A correct calculation now requires that a weighted-average number of shares be used as the denominator.

$$\text{EPS} = \text{Earnings available to common stockholders / weighted-average number of shares outstanding}$$

This is the formula for what is called "Basic EPS" that appears in published annual reports.

When a company has issued bonds or preferred stock that is convertible to shares of common stock or has stock warrants or options outstanding, the calculation of EPS becomes even more complex. The

"Basic EPS" computation fails to recognize the impact of these potentially dilutive securities on EPS when these types of dilutive securities are present in a company's capital structure. So most companies published a second EPS figure called "Diluted EPS."

Stock warrants entitle the holder to acquire shares of stock at a fixed price within a specified period. The holder may sell the warrants or exercise them by paying the fixed price and converting the warrants into shares of common stock. Stock warrants are purchased in the open market from individual investors or from an issuing corporation. The warrants are issued either separately or as part of other securities, such as bonds or preferred stock. When issued with other securities, the warrants are used as a *sweetener* to make the securities more attractive to potential investors. Investors can detach the warrants and sell them or, if they choose, exercise them.

Corporate employees and officers are issued stock rights under *stock option* plans, which are similar to warrants. These selected individuals are given the option of purchasing common stock at a specified price over a stipulated period of time. Corporations adopt stock option plans for a variety of reasons: 1) to attract and retain high-quality personnel, 2) to raise capital for expansion, and 3) to spread ownership of common stock among employees. Figure 7-2 presents the footnote disclosure relating to Elmo Electronics Corporation's stock option plan from its 2000 annual report.

Transactions in 2000 are summarized below:

	Shares	Price per Share
Options outstanding at Jan. 1, 2000	1,572,351	$10 $\frac{3}{8}$–26 $\frac{5}{8}$
Granted	107,750	16 $\frac{1}{2}$–20
Exercised	(44,705)	10 $\frac{3}{8}$–15 $\frac{3}{8}$
Cancelled or expired	(162,430)	12 $\frac{3}{8}$–26 $\frac{5}{8}$
Options outstanding at Dec. 31, 2000	1,472,966	10 $\frac{3}{8}$–26 $\frac{5}{8}$
Options exercisable at Dec. 31, 2000	1,407,616	
Shares available for grant at Dec. 31, 2000	679,773	

The company had 92,400 and 121,900 restricted stock awards issued and outstanding as of December 31, 2000 and 1999, respectively. The market value of the restricted shares is deferred in the additional paid-in capital account and amortized over the years the restrictions lapse. Total compensation expense in 2000 and 1999, related to these awards, was not material.

FIG. 7-2 *Footnote disclosure relating to stock option plan of Elmo Electronics Corporation.*

Stock warrants and options can be thought of as essentially shares of common stock (it is assumed that they will be exercised and increase the number of shares outstanding).

To calculate a useful measure of EPS, the number of shares is increased to reflect the increase resulting from those items that are essentially shares of common stock (called potentially dilutive securities). The end result is that accountants calculate two measures of EPS and publish both of them with the income statement in the annual report. The two measures of EPS are called *basic* earnings per share (containing only a weighted average of common shares and *diluted* earnings per share (representing a worst-case scenario with all items that could reasonably be converted to common stock or shares in the denominator).

When accountants treat an item as if it were converted into common stock—increasing the number of shares outstanding—an adjustment must frequently be made to the numerator as well. For example, if an issue of convertible bonds is treated as if it were converted into common stock in an EPS calculation, the accountant must also correct earnings by adding back the interest expense that would not have been subtracted if the bonds had actually been converted. Corrections must also be made for dividends that would not accrue to preferred shareholders if convertible preferred shares are treated as converted to common stock.

An excerpt from the consolidated statements of income for the Franco Petroleum Company is presented in Figure 7-3. Basic and diluted EPS for 2000 are $.92 and $.91, respectively.

FRANCO PETROLEUM

	2000	1999	1998
Net Income (in millions)	**$ 237**	$ 959	$ 1,303
Net Income Per Share of Common Stock			
Basic	**$ .92**	3.64	4.96
Diluted	**.91**	3.61	4.91
Average Common Shares Outstanding (in thousands)			
Basic	**258,274**	263,392	262,919
Diluted	**260,152**	265,419	265,256

FIG. 7-3 *Franco Petroleum Company—Consolidated Statement of Income, Years Ended December 31, 2000, 1999, 1998.*

Note 11—Stock options and awards

The 1998 Stock Incentive Plan authorizes the granting of incentive and nonqualified stock options, restricted stock awards and stock appreciation rights to key management personnel. Stock options have been granted and are currently outstanding under this and prior plans. The purchase price of shares under option is the market price of the shares on the date of grant. Options expire 10 years from the date granted.

CHAPTER PERSPECTIVE

Accountants make the income statement easier to understand by separating the income (or loss) generated by ongoing, normal operations from income that is derived from discontinued operations and extraordinary items. We have defined the terms associated with these nonoperating items and given examples of how each is presented in an income statement. The chapter also discussed deferred income taxes, explaining why tax expense on the income statement is not always the same as the taxes paid during the year, illustrating how accountants present the difference in the financial statements, and explaining the calculation of deferred income taxes. The chapter explained the basic calculation of earnings per share and discussed the factors that complicate this otherwise simple statistic.

The Statement of Cash Flows and Consolidated Statements

INTRODUCTION AND MAIN POINTS

In this chapter we introduce the Statement of Cash Flows (SCF), the third statement (in addition to the balance sheet and the income statement) required in published financial statements such as annual reports. The primary purpose of the SCF is to furnish information regarding a company's cash receipts and cash payments for a period of time. A secondary purpose is to explain the change in cash over that same period. The SCF is a flow statement like the income statement and shows the results of activities over a period of time—a quarter of a year, for example. All cash flows are presented in the SCF as either operating, investing, or financing cash flows. Financial-statement readers can use the SCF to examine a company's liquidity and cash management.

The final portion of this chapter discusses consolidated financial statements issued by companies that own a controlling interest in other companies, called subsidiaries. Almost all large companies publish consolidated financial statements.

After studying the material in this chapter:

■ You will understand the purpose and general structure of the SCF.

■ You will know the general sources and uses of cash.

■ You will be able to distinguish among operating, investing, and financing cash flows.

■ You will understand why companies publish consolidated financial statements.

■ You will see how the statements of affiliated companies are combined to show the relationship and economic activity of the consolidated group.

CASH VERSUS ACCRUAL ACCOUNTING

Before you can understand the usefulness of the Statement of Cash Flows, you must clearly understand the difference between accrual accounting—as used to create the income statement—and cash-basis accounting. Accrual accounting attempts to translate into dollars of profit or loss the actual activities of the fiscal period. Remember from Chapter 1 that the accrual principle is a combination of two ideas: revenue recognition and matching.

Revenue Recognition

The revenue recognition principle provides that revenue (sales price) be recorded when the necessary activities to sell a good or provide a service have been completed. Revenue is recorded at the point of sale regardless of whether cash is collected or a receivable from the customer is created at that time.

Matching

The matching principle tells the accountant when to record a production cost as expense. Costs directly associated with producing a certain revenue are expensed in the same period that the revenue is recorded. The accountant expenses the cost of long-lived assets over their expected lives. Other costs that benefit only the current period are expensed as they arise.

Under the matching principle, an expense can be recorded before, after, or at the time a cost is actually paid. From the accountant's point of view, it is the earnings activity that gives rise to the conversion of cost to expense. It does not matter whether that cost has been paid or a liability created.

Cash-basis reporting, on the other hand, is concerned only with the business's checkbook. Cash inflows are treated as revenues of the period; cash outflows are treated as the period's expenses. Cash flows do not capture the earnings activities of the period. For instance, a company sells merchandise to a customer at the end of the year and the customer makes payment next period. On the cash basis, the sale is not recorded until the collection is made, even though the effort to generate the sale was made this period. Similarly, if the salesperson will not be paid for that day's work until next period, their salary is not an expense on the cash basis.

Accrual accounting provides a measure of the period's earnings activities. Comparing accrual income measures over time can give us a feel for what the company can do in the future, but it does not provide us with a measure of the company's liquidity—its ability to pay its debts as they come due.

Cash-flow accounting does not isolate the earnings activities of the period. However, it does provide us with a liquidity measure. Combining accrual income measures with cash flow measures creates a base from which to estimate future operations, measure liquidity, and determine the timing between producing sales and collecting on sales. This combination takes place when we use all the financial statements together—the balance sheet, the income statement, and the statement of cash flows.

THE STATEMENT OF CASH FLOWS

The statement of cash flows is like a bridge. The balance sheet tells us what a business's assets, liabilities, and owners' equity are at a point in time. But what about the changes that have occurred in the business between two balance-sheet dates (from the end of one fiscal year to the end of another)? The statement of cash flows provides this bridge. It describes all of the changes that have occurred in the balance sheet during the fiscal year in terms of their effect on cash. What changes in the assets, liabilities, and owners' equity provided cash? What changes in assets, liabilities, and owners' equity used cash? These are the questions a statement of cash flows answers.

A company can obtain cash from operations, of course. It can also issue stock, borrow, and sell assets other than inventory. These are the four general sources of cash.

The general uses of cash are corollaries of the sources of cash, with one addition. Operations can consume cash (instead of providing cash), the company may reacquire its stock, repay debt, and buy assets other than inventory; it may also pay dividends. The general sources and uses of cash are shown in Figure 8-1.

Sources	Uses
Operations	Operations
Issue Stock	Reacquire Stock
Borrow	Repay Debt
Sell Assets	Buy Assets
	Pay Dividends

FIG. 8-1 *General sources and uses of cash.*

A company is required to present its sources and uses of cash according to three classes of activities: operating activities, investing activities, and financing activities. Figure 8-2 shows the general format of a statement of cash flows incorporating the three classes of activities. In this example, operating activities provided $70,000 in cash, financing activities (issuing stock and borrowing, perhaps) provided $30,000, and investing activities (lending money or buying stock in other companies, perhaps) used $50,000. Cash was $40,000 at the beginning of the year and $90,000 at year end.

Cash provided by (or used in):	
Operating Activities	$70,000
Investing Activities	(50,000)
Financing Activities	30,000
Increase (or decrease) in cash or cash equivalents	$50,000
Cash and cash equivalents, beginning of year	40,000
Cash and cash equivalents, end of year	$90,000

FIG. 8-2 *Statement of cash flows for the year ended December 31, 2000.*

Operating Activities

Cash from operating activities is cash-basis net income. It includes all collections during the year from sales of merchandise or providing services. It also includes dividends and interest received from investments. It is reduced by the payment of operating costs, including interest and taxes. A schedule reconciling accrual-based net income for the year to the cash collected from operating activities must accompany the SCF if it is not included in the body of the statement. Figure 8-3 presents this information from an actual Statement of Cash Flows.

Investing Activities

Cash from or for investing activities refers to changes in the company's long-term assets. Decreases in investments, property, plant and equipment, intangibles, and other assets indicate that sales or disposals that provide the company with cash have taken place. Increases in these same assets indicate that the company has purchased additional assets—a major use of cash.

Financing Activities

Often shown as "Net cash provided (used) by financing activities," financing activities are changes in a company's long-term liabilities and/or owners' equity. Increasing long-term debt or selling stock (ownership) provides the company with cash, while decreasing liabilities (indicating payment of debt) and distributing dividends to shareholders are major uses of cash.

Consolidated Statements of Cash Flows

Fiscal Year Ended (dollars in thousands)	May 2, 2000	May 3, 1999	April 27, 1998
Operating Activities:			
Net income	$504,451	$440,230	$386,014
Adjustments to reconcile net income to cash provided by operating activities:			
Depreciation and amortization	168,523	148,104	133,348
Deferred tax provision	37,921	65,271	27,560
Other items, net	(31,572)	(45,454)	(10,595)
Changes in current assets and liabilities, excluding effects of acquisitions and divestitures:			
Receivables	(104,818)	(69,818)	(72)
Inventories	(86,549)	(134,582)	(12,251)
Prepaid expenses and other current assets	17,634	(13,650)	19,908
Accounts payable	46,751	25,290	38,145
Accrued liabilities	(35,837)	19,855	18,940
Income taxes	11,333	(18,929)	(33,837)
Cash provided by operating activities	527,837	416,317	567,160
Investing Activities:			
Capital expenditures	(355,317)	(323,325)	(238,265)
Acquisitions, net of cash acquired	(56,328)	(167,470)	(287,597)
Proceeds from divestitures	6,398	72,712	18,880
Purchases of short-term investments	(342,228)	(382,550)	(513,408)
Sales and maturities of short-term investments	368,767	412,365	666,272
Other items, net	10,434	12,627	5,005
Cash (used for) investing activities	(368,274)	(375,641)	(349,113)
Financing Activities:			
Proceeds from long-term debt	231,584	227,291	45,108
Payments on long-term debt	(28,095)	(34,683)	(165,832)
Proceeds (payments) on short-term debt	87,596	49,110	(41,305)
Dividends	(207,500)	(178,474)	(154,573)
Purchase of treasury stock	(279,899)	(97,508)	(123,519)
Exercise of stock options	56,752	30,393	23,463
Cash loaned to ESOP, net	(47,000)	—	—
Sale of treasury stock to ESOP	50,000	—	—
Other items, net	—	(1,590)	1,589
Cash (used for) financing activities	(136,562)	(5,461)	(415,069)
Effect of exchange rate changes on cash and cash equivalents	211	(8,098)	280
Net increase (decrease) in cash and cash equivalents	23,212	27,117	(196,742)
Cash and cash equivalents at beginning of year	102,605	75,488	272,230
Cash and cash equivalents at end of year	$125,817	$102,605	$ 75,488

FIG. 8-3 *Cash flows statement showing operating, investing, and financing activities.*

Other Activities

Some transactions do not have a direct effect on cash. That is, these transactions affect assets or liabilities, but not cash. For example, a purchase of land on a long-term mortgage with no cash-down payment does not affect the company's cash balance. However, for the statement of cash flows to be a complete bridge between two balance sheets (describing all the changes that have occurred in assets, liabilities, and owners' equity), this transaction must be reported. Major investing and financing activities that do not directly affect cash are summarized in a schedule that accompanies the statement of cash flows or in narrative form. These types of transactions are normally referred to as "significant noncash transactions."

Figure 8-4 contains an expanded presentation of the statement of cash flows assuming that land costing $1,000,000 was acquired by agreeing to pay a 20-year mortgage payable for $1,000,000.

Cash flows from operating activities:	
Received from customers	$2,418,500
Paid suppliers and employees	(1,255,000)
Dividends and interest received	150,000
Interest paid	(260,500)
Taxes paid	(320,000)
Net cash provided by operating activities	$ 733,000
Cash flows from investing activities:	
Received—sale of plant	3,000,000
Received—sale of equipment	550,000
Paid—new equipment purchases	(1,015,000)
Paid—new plant	(4,950,000)
Net cash used in investing activities	(2,415,000)
Cash flows from financing activities:	
Received—sale of bonds	2,000,000
Paid—dividends to shareholders	(100,000)
Net cash provided by financing activities	1,900,000
Net increase in cash	218,000
Cash at the beginning of the year	50,000
Cash at the end of the year	$ 268,000
Noncash investing and financing activities:	
Acquisition of land by incurrence of mortgage payable	$1,000,000

FIG. 8-4 *Statement of cash flows for the year ended December 31, 2000.*

CONSOLIDATED STATEMENTS

To understand consolidated financial statements, you must realize that they are more or less the sum of the parts—that is, they are the combined financial statements of a parent company and its subsidiaries. A parent/subsidiary relationship is created when a company acquires more than 50 percent of the common stock of another company. Because common stock is the voting stock of a corporation, acquiring more than 50 percent entitles the acquiring company (parent) to majority representation on the board of directors of the acquired company (subsidiary). This allows the acquiring company to control the affairs of the acquired company.

The Concept of Consolidating Statements

When management of a parent company owns stock in any company that it intends to hold for more than one year, the stock is shown both in the accounts and on the balance sheet of the parent as a noncurrent asset as "Investments." When the parent company owns a majority of the stock in a company, creating a subsidiary, the two companies are, for all practical purposes, combined; the financial statements of the two companies are consolidated and shown as if the two companies were one economic entity and the parent and its subsidiary (or subsidiaries) are referred to as affiliated companies. Accounting principles require that the assets, liabilities, revenues, and expenses of majority-owned subsidiaries be included in the financial statements of their parents.

An economic entity is an activity for which separate accounting records can be created. The parent and its subsidiary are each economic entities for which separate accounting records are kept and for which separate financial statements are issued. But because of the common control by stockholders who control the parent and, through it, the subsidiary, the combined companies can also be treated as a single economic entity. Stockholders, creditors, and others must see the financial statements of the combined entity if they are to understand the relationship between the companies and its economic implications. The requirement that affiliated companies publish consolidated financial statements reflects the concept of substance over form: The affiliated companies are, in substance, one economic entity, regardless of their separate legal form. As we stated at the outset of the chapter, virtually all large companies issue consolidated statements. The requirement to consolidate does not preclude the affiliated companies from also issuing separate individual financial statements.

The Mechanics of Consolidating Statements

Suppose Acme, Inc., buys 100 percent of the stock of Baker Company for the book value of its owners' equity (common stock plus retained earnings). The balance-sheet equation for Baker is shown below:

Assets	=	Liabilities	+	Owners' Equity
$400,000	=	$300,000	+	$100,000

The Acme purchase of Baker stock is recorded on the Acme books by creating "Investment in Baker, $100,000," and reducing cash by $100,000. But what has Acme purchased? Since the value of the Baker owners' equity is $100,000, Acme has purchased $100,000 of property rights. If Acme shows the stock in its balance sheet simply as an investment of $100,000, the true nature of its relationship with Baker is not disclosed. Now Acme owes every debt that Baker owes and owns every asset that Baker owns. If Acme is to properly disclose its ownership of Baker, its balance sheet must show every debt owed and asset owned by Baker.

The balance-sheet equation for Acme before and after the purchase of the Baker stock is shown in Figure 8-5. Total assets for Acme are the same before and after the investment in Baker (the $100,000 asset "cash" has been traded for an equal asset, "Investment in Baker").

	Assets	=	Liabilities	+	Owners' Equity
Before	$1,000,000	=	$700,000	+	$300,000
Minus cash	(100,000)				
Plus stock investment	100,000				
After	$1,000,000	=	$700,000	+	$300,000

FIG. 8-5 *Effect of Baker purchase on Acme balance sheet.*

When Acme wishes to prepare financial statements, Acme must remove the $100,000 "Investment in Baker" and replace it with the individual assets and liabilities of Baker, as shown in Figure 8-6. The process of combining the companies is called *consolidation,* and the financial statements of a parent company combined with its subsidiary are called *consolidated financial statements.* Note that the total owners' equity of Acme is not changed by the consolidation.

	Assets	=	Liabilities	+	Owners' Equity
Acme before consolidation	$1,000,000	=	$700,000	+	$300,000
Less the investment	(100,000)				
Plus the assets and liabilities of Baker	400,000		300,000		
Acme's consolidated balance sheet	$1,300,000	=	$1,000,000	+	$300,000

FIG. 8-6 *Acme and Baker Consolidated.*

Eliminating Intercompany Transactions

In preparing the consolidated financial statements, accountants eliminate any transactions between the parent and its subsidiaries. If these transactions were not eliminated, assets, liabilities, revenue, and expense of the combined company would be overstated.

Consider another example. If a parent company "Y" has lent $5 million to its subsidiary "X," it will have a $5 million "Receivable from Subsidiary X" (an asset) recorded and Subsidiary X will have a $5 million "Payable to Parent Y" (a liability) recorded. Because parent and subsidiary are treated as one company in the consolidated financial statements, it does not make sense to include the $5,000,000 "Receivable from Subsidiary X" and the $5,000,000 "Payable to Parent Y" in assets and liabilities. One company cannot borrow from or owe itself. When the consolidated balance sheet is prepared, the parent's $5 million "Receivable from Subsidiary X" cancels the subsidiary's $5 million "Payable to the Parent Y"; if this were not done, consolidated assets and liabilities would be reported as $5 million more than they actually are.

Because transactions between the parent and its subsidiaries are eliminated, consolidated financial statements reflect only the transactions that have taken place between the combined companies and outsiders. However, when consolidating the financial statements of a parent and those subsidiaries that are not wholly owned (that is, in which the parent does not own 100 percent of the voting stock), "minority interest"—the owners' equity of the other shareholders of the subsidiary—is created. If we own 60 percent of a subsidiary, there is a 40 percent minority interest. Because accounting principles allow all of the assets and liabilities of a subsidiary to be reported in the consolidated financial statements, the portion of those assets and liabilities that belong to the minority shareholders must be labeled "minority interest" and may be shown on the consolidated balance sheet as either a liability (the amount the parent "owes" the minority shareholders) or as a part of consolidated owners' equity. Another form of presentation is to show the minority interest between the liability and stockholders' equity sections of the balance sheet.

Goodwill

Another account that frequently appears on the consolidated balance sheet is "Excess of Cost over Net Assets Acquired," or purchased goodwill. Purchased goodwill is an intangible asset that is amortized (expensed) over a period of time that cannot exceed 40 years. Goodwill is discussed in Chapter 4.

Additional information on the activities of the subsidiaries is included in the notes to the financial statements dealing with "segments." A business segment is a major product line, an industry, a class of customer, domestic operations, or foreign operations.

When Affiliated Companies Need Not Consolidate

We have stated that affiliated companies always issue consolidated statements; however, there are exceptions to this statement. Each company in an affiliated group (parent or subsidiary) may issue separate financial statements for regulatory agencies or for special purposes such as obtaining financing or credit from suppliers. Additionally, consolidated statements are not required if control is only temporary or if control does not rest with the majority owners.

CHAPTER PERSPECTIVE

This chapter has described the statement of cash flows, the third statement required in published financial statements. We discussed the general sources and uses of cash common to all companies and the way companies are required to present cash flows in the statement of cash flows—separated into flows from operating, investing, and financing activities. Finally, we explained the organization of consolidated financial statements, the type of financial statement published by most companies, and showed how to combine statements to show the relationship and economic activity of an affiliated group.

Quarterly Statements, Reports on Specified Elements, Reviews, and Compilations

INTRODUCTION AND MAIN POINTS

Financial statements included in an annual report have been audited by an independent Certified Public Accountant (CPA); because the statements are audited, financial-statement readers can rely on the fairness of the financial-statement presentation. But there are other statements, such as interim, or quarterly, reports issued by publicly held companies and financial statements by nonpublic companies, that may have been reviewed by a CPA at a lower level of thoroughness than that required for a full audit. Accountants may also be called upon to issue reports on specified elements, accounts, or items in a financial statement.

This chapter discusses these other types of evaluations that are often requested of CPAs. After studying the material in this chapter:

■ You will understand the levels of assurance and the conclusions expressed by the accountant, in engagements other than audits.

■ You will understand the form of the financial statements issued by the CPA when he or she reviews unaudited interim financial statements or information (the quarterly report) of a public company.

■ You will understand the form of the financial statements issued by the CPA who reviews the financial statements of a nonpublic company.

■ You will understand the types of financial information presented by the CPA who reports on specified elements, accounts, or items in a financial statement.

■ You will understand the types of financial information presented by the CPA who performs agreed-upon procedures.

■ You will understand the type of report issued by the CPA who compiles the financial statements of a nonpublic company.

■ You will understand the reporting responsibilities assumed by the CPA for each type of engagement.

TYPES OF ENGAGEMENTS

A CPA may be called upon to prepare a variety of reports relating to financial statements. In an *audit,* the accountant performs the *attest* function; that is, the accountant gathers a sufficient amount of competent evidence to provide a high level of assurance that the information contained in the financial statements is presented fairly in accordance with generally accepted accounting principles (GAAP) or some other comprehensive basis of accounting. This high level of assurance by the CPA regarding the credibility of the financial statements is sometimes referred to as positive assurance.

CPAs provide other types of *attestation* services in which they issue written communications expressing a conclusion as to the reliability of the financial statements or other financial information being reported on.

A *review* is another example of an attestation service offered by a CPA. The procedures performed by the accountant during a review are not as extensive as those performed in the course of an audit and normally consist of client inquiries and analytical review. As you might expect, a review provides only a moderate level of assurance—normally referred to as negative assurance—compared to a full audit. When giving negative assurance, the auditor, in effect, says only "I know of nothing wrong." In contrast, positive assurance says, in effect, "Having tested, I believe the statements to be presented fairly." There is a big difference. This type of service can be categorized as:

1. Reviews of the interim financial information a) of a public company that is either presented alone or that is included in the company's audited annual financial statements, or b) that is included in a note to the annual audited financial statements of either a public or nonpublic company.

2. Reviews of the financial statements of nonpublic companies.

3. Reviews of annual and interim financial statements of public companies whose annual statements are not audited.

Reports on specified elements, accounts, or items in a financial statement normally fall into one of two categories:

1. Reports expressing an audit opinion on one or more specified elements or accounts. In these, the CPA expresses positive assurance in the audit report only for the item or items audited.

2. Reports issued by the CPA after performing *agreed-upon procedures,* procedures agreed to by the accountant, the party requesting the engagement, and the intended users of the accountant's report. The accountant's report in such a case expresses negative assurance.

A *compilation,* a check of financial statements for form, appropriateness, and arithmetic accuracy, is not an attestation service because the accountant does not express a conclusion regarding the financial statements and specifically disclaims any level of assurance regarding those statements. However, because some limited procedures have been performed by the accountant, he or she is associated with the financial statements and a report accompanies the statements.

A sample report for each type of engagement is provided in this chapter. Figure 9-1 summarizes the evidence examined and the types of conclusions reached by CPAs in different situations.

Type of Engagement	Amount of Evidence Collected	Level of Assurance	Conclusion Reached
Audit	Substantial	High	Positive
Review	Significant	Moderate	Negative
Audit of Specified Elements, Accounts, or Items	Substantial	High	Positive
Agreed Upon Procedures	Varying	As Agreed Upon	Negative
Compilation	None	Minimal	Disclaimer (none)

FIG. 9-1 *Summary of types of engagements.*

QUARTERLY STATEMENTS OF A PUBLIC COMPANY

Both the New York Stock Exchange and the Securities and Exchange Commission (SEC) require that listed or registered companies provide their shareholders with quarterly financial statements. (The content of the quarterly report (the 10-Q) filed with the SEC is discussed in Chapter 10.) Quarterly financial statements are prepared for the first three quarters of a company's fiscal year; fourth-quarter statements are unnecessary because annual financial statements are issued at that time. However, many companies do issue fourth-quarter statements to their shareholders and other interested parties.

Quarterly financial statements look much the same as annual financial statements; however, there are some major differences. For one thing, because accounting principles require that the same methods of recording revenues, expenses, assets, and liabilities be used in the quarterly statements and the annual statements, it is necessary to estimate some key figures. For instance, because taking a physical inventory count is time-consuming and costly, it is done only once a year. In order to prepare the quarterly financial statements, ending inventory for the quarter is therefore estimated. The annual tax rate must also be estimated so that quarterly taxes can be recorded at the rate the company actually expects to pay.

Accounting principles also require that seasonality in the quarterly statements be pointed out. For instance, if second quarter sales are normally greater than sales in the other quarters, this fact should be indicated in the second quarter's financial statements. This has the effect of reminding the reader that sales are not level throughout the year.

A third difference is that footnote disclosure is often minimal in quarterly statements. However, certain items must be disclosed if they are applicable. These items are significant changes in estimates or provisions for income taxes; contingent items; changes in accounting principles or estimates; significant changes in financial position; and disposal of a segment of a business and extraordinary, unusual, or infrequently occurring items. The reader may find the details of one or more of these items in a section of the quarterly report normally authored by the company president or chairman of the board.

A final difference is that quarterly financial statements are unaudited. Although public companies whose securities are listed on a stock exchange are required to have their annual financial statements audited and to release interim financial information quarterly, a review of the interim reports by an independent CPA is not required.*

Figure 9-2 shows the second quarter report for Ford Motor Company for the second quarter of 1999. Notice that in addition to the quarterly financial statements, it includes a discussion of Ford's business segments by location and by business entity. There is no review report by an independent CPA. Normally, the basic financial data presented in the quarterly report closely parallel those found in the annual report. The discussion of earnings, announcements by management, and selected news briefs are included to keep investors and analysts informed of interim changes in the company's operations and financial position.

---

*In fact, many companies do have a review performed by their independent CPA, but the review report is not published with the interim financial statements because of management's concern that the review report might be misinterpreted as an audit report.

FIG. 9-2 *Ford Motor Company's second quarter report.*

FORD NEWS
Contact: Shareholder Inquiries
FOR RELEASE AT 7:00 A.M. (EASTERN DAYLIGHT)
Ford Posts Record Second Quarter Operating Earnings of $2.5 Billion; 13th Consecutive Quarter of Operating Improvement

DEARBORN, Mich., July 14, 1999—Ford Motor Company [NYSE: F] earned $2,338 million in the second quarter of 1999, or $1.89 per diluted share of common and Class B stock. These earnings include the results of Volvo Car, which was acquired on March 31, and a one-time profit reduction of $146 million, or $0.11 per share, related to the acquisition. Under U.S. accounting rules, Ford was required to write-up the value of inventory acquired to fair value, resulting in a one-time increase in cost of sales in the second quarter of 1999.

On an operating basis, a measure that excludes the Volvo Car inventory-related profit reduction, Ford's second quarter earnings were a record $2,484 million. Earnings in the second quarter of 1998 were $2,381 million. On a per-share basis, second quarter 1999 operating earnings were $2.00 per share, up nine cents, or 5 percent, from last year's second quarter. Ford now has posted improved operating results for 13 consecutive quarters.

"Throughout its history, Ford Motor Company has been constantly evolving to improve its competitive position, deliver consistent financial results and provide better value to consumers," said President and CEO Jac Nasser. "Our strong earnings momentum over the last 13 quarters is the result of our intense drive to improve quality, lower costs and become more nimble. Progress in these areas has given us the confidence to pursue our twenty-first century vision of becoming the world's leading consumer company for automotive products and services. What this means, in practice, is that Ford wants to become the 'and' company—one that delivers the highest quality products *AND* the best customer satisfaction *AND* the best shareholder returns."

During the second quarter, Ford announced several major consumer-focused initiatives, including:

━━In Europe, Ford will introduce low emissions powertrains five years ahead of regulatory requirements. These powertrains, initially available in the Ford Ka and Ford Fiesta in early 2000, will be at least 50 percent cleaner than what next year's European Union standard requires.

━━All pickup trucks in the United States and Canada will be Low Emission Vehicles beginning with the 2000-model year Ford F-Series and 2001 Ford Ranger. This action will bring a significant number of Ford trucks into compliance with an initial U.S. Environmental Protection Agency standard proposed for the 2004 model year.

"Ford has moved ahead of the industry to bring clean air technologies to high-volume production quickly and cost effectively to make real contributions to environmental quality. It's simply the right thing to do," Nasser said.

AUTOMOTIVE OPERATIONS

Worldwide net income from automotive operations was $1,931 million in the second quarter of 1999, down $120 million from the second quarter of 1998. Excluding the one-time $146 million profit-reduction related to the Volvo Car acquisition, worldwide automotive earnings were a record $2,077 million, up $26 million.

Worldwide automotive revenues increased 15 percent from the second quarter of 1998 to a record $35.9 billion, and after-tax return on sales (ROS) was 5.4 percent, down 1.2 points. Automotive cash was a record $24 billion at the end of the second quarter, up from $22.3 billion in the same period a year ago. Net cash was $12.6 billion, down from $14.1 billion a year ago because of acquisition spending.

In the first half of 1999, earnings from automotive operations increased 9 percent to $3,582 million. The Volvo Car inventory-related profit reduction was more than offset by a $165 million first quarter gain on the sale of AutoEuropa. In the first half of 1998, automotive operations earned $3,286 million. Worldwide automotive revenues in the first half of 1999 were a record $67.9 billion, up 12 percent compared with the first half of 1998, and ROS was 5.3 percent, down two-tenths of a point.

Total automotive costs declined $300 million at constant volume and mix in the second quarter of 1999, compared with the same period a year ago. Year-to-date, costs are down

$400 million. The company's full-year milestone is to reduce total costs by $1 billion compared with 1998.

North America: Automotive earnings in North America in the second quarter of 1999 were a record $1,969 million, up $314 million from a year ago. ROS was 7.7 percent, up four-tenths of a point.

For the first half of 1999, earnings in North America were a record $3,557 million and ROS was 7.1 percent. The full-year milestone for 1999 is to achieve a ROS greater than 5 percent. In the first half of 1998, earnings in North America were $2,665 million and ROS was 6.2 percent.

Vehicle sales in the U.S. in the first half of 1999 set a new all-time industry record, with the annual selling rate reaching 17.1 million units. Ford expects full-year sales to exceed the record of 16.3 million units set in 1986.

"There are so many positive factors at work in the U.S. economy right now. We're confident vehicle sales will remain strong through the balance of 1999 and into the year 2000," Nasser said. "If slightly higher short-term interest rates help to prolong the economic expansion, that's great news for consumers and our shareholders."

Among the other drivers of Ford's North American results is exceptional productivity. In the 1999 Harbour Report, a widely recognized analysis of manufacturing productivity in the North American automotive industry, Ford plants ranked first in nine of 12 vehicle segments evaluated.

Europe: Including a $125 million share of the Volvo Car inventory-related profit reduction, automotive earnings in Europe in the second quarter of 1999 were $89 million, compared with $310 million in the same period a year ago. Excluding the one-time profit reduction related to the Volvo Car acquisition, earnings in Europe were $214 million.

These results reflect lower volumes and market share for Ford-branded vehicles, principally Ford Fiesta and Mondeo, and lower export volumes, offset partially by the success of the Ford Focus and higher volumes at Jaguar.

First half 1999 earnings totaled $254 million, including the AutoEuropa gain and the Volvo Car inventory-related profit reduction, compared with $540 million a year ago. Although Volvo Car will contribute to operating earnings in 1999, it will be a challenge for Ford to achieve its full-year 1999 milestone for Europe, which is to grow earnings compared with 1998.

"Ford Motor Company's market share is up in Europe, but restoring our profits in the region to a more robust level will take time and a continued focus on great products, quality, and lower costs," Nasser said.

South America: Ford lost $120 million in South America in the second quarter of 1999, compared with earnings of $14 million a year ago. First half losses totaled $285 million, compared with losses of $31 million a year ago. Industry sales in Brazil, Ford's largest market in the region, were down more than 20 percent in the first half of 1999, compared with a year ago, and the Brazilian economy is expected to remain weak for the balance of this year.

"Ford's problems in Brazil are not intractable, but meaningful improvement will take creativity and ingenuity on our part, a continued focus on costs, and government policies that encourage sustainable economic growth," Nasser said. "The core of our strategy includes a new, highly competitive manufacturing facility in Brazil, improved service and distribution, and new products designed to meet the needs of our South American customers."

VISTEON AUTOMOTIVE SYSTEMS

In the second quarter of 1999, Visteon earned a record $282 million, compared with $241 million a year ago, and ROS improved six-tenths of a point to 5.7 percent. Visteon's earnings are included in the company's automotive results.

In the first half of 1999, Visteon earned a record $490 million, up $60 million compared with the first half of 1998, and won future new business contracts worth $1.1 billion annually. ROS in the first half of 1999 was five percent, up three-tenths of a point from the same period a year ago. Visteon is on-track to achieve its full-year 1999 milestones, which are to grow earnings and win $2 billion in new business contrasts.

FORD CREDIT

Earnings were $335 million in the second quarter of 1999, up $35 million, or 12 percent, from a year ago. Return on Equity (ROE) in the second quarter of 1999 was 12.3 percent, up four-tenths of a point. The earnings growth reflects higher financing volumes, improved credit-loss performance and lower taxes, offset partially by lower net financing margins.

Earnings in the first half of 1999 were $635 million, up $57 million, or 10 percent, compared with a year ago. Ford Credit is on track to meet its 1999 full-year milestone to grow earnings by 10 percent compared with 1998. ROE in the first half of 1999 was 11.8 percent, up one-tenth of a point compared with the first half of 1998.

HERTZ

The Hertz Corporation [NYSE: HRZ] earned a record $88 million in the second quarter of 1999, compared with $75 million a year ago, up 17 percent. Ford's share of Hertz's second quarter 1999 earnings was $71 million.

Hertz's earnings in the first half of 1999 were a record $137 million, up $27 million, or 24 percent compared with a year ago. Ford's share of Hertz's first half 1999 earnings was $111 million. Hertz is on track to meet its 1999 full-year milestone to post record earnings.

Ford Motor Company and Subsidiaries

HIGHLIGHTS

	Second Quarter (unaudited)		First Half (unaudited)	
	1999	1998	1999	1998
Worldwide vehicle unit sales of cars and trucks (in thousands)				
- North America	1,237	1,124	2,457	2,181
- Outside North America	691	669	1,246	1,340
Total	1,928	1,793	3,703	3,521
Sales and revenues (in millions)				
- Automotive	$ 35,921	$ 31,309	$ 67,854	$ 60,385
- Financial Services	6,361	5,980	12,313	13,488
Total	$ 42,282	$ 37,289	$ 80,167	$ 73,873
Net income (in millions)				
- Automotive	$ 1,931	$ 2,051	$ 3,582	$ 3,286
- Financial Services (excl. The Associates)	407	330	735	609
Subtotal	2,338	2,381	4,317	3,895
- The Associates	-	-		177
- Gain on spin-off of The Associates	-	-		15,955
Total	$ 2,338	$ 2,381	$ 4,317	$ 20,027
Capital expenditures (in millions)				
- Automotive	$ 1,755	$ 1,659	$ 3,093	$ 3,760
- Financial Services	140	153	284	251
Total	$ 1,895	$ 1,812	$ 3,377	$ 4,011
Automotive capital expenditures as a percentage of sales	4.9%	5.3%	4.6%	6.2%
Stockholders' equity at June 30 - Total (in millions)	$ 26,242	$ 23,070	$ 26,242	$ 23,070
- After-tax return on Common and Class B stockholders' equity	36.9%	43.0%	35.0%	33.2%

Automotive net cash at June 30 (in millions)				
– Cash and marketable securities	$ 23,959	$ 22,276	$ 23,959	$ 22,276
– Debt	11,406	8,220	11,406	8,220
– Automotive net cash	$ 12,553	$ 14,056	$ 12,553	$ 14,056
After-tax return on sales				
– North American Automotive	7.7%	7.3%	7.1%	6.2%
– Total Automotive	5.4%	6.6%	5.3%	5.5%
Shares of Common and Class B Stock (in millions)				
– Average number outstanding	1,211	1,212	1,211	1,211
– Number outstanding at June 30	1,210	1,212	1,210	1,212
Common Stock price (per share) (adjusted to reflect The Associates spin-off)				
– High	$67-7/8	$59-1/8	$67-7/8	$59-1/8
– Low	52-5/8	41-11/64	52-5/8	28-15/32
AMOUNTS PER SHARE OF COMMON AND CLASS B STOCK AFTER PREFERRED STOCK DIVIDENDS				
Income assuming dilution				
– Automotive	$ 1.56	$ 1.65	$ 2.89	$ 2.65
– Financial Services (excl. The Associates)	0.33	0.26	0.59	0.49
Subtotal	1.89	1.91	3.48	3.14
– The Associates	–	–	–	0.14
– Premium on Series B Preferred Stock repurchase	–	–	–	(0.07)
– Gain on spin-off of The Associates	–	–	–	12.90
Total	$ 1.89	$ 1.91	$ 3.48	$ 16.11
Cash dividends	$ 0.46	$ 0.42	$ 0.92	$ 0.84

VEHICLE UNIT SALES

For the Periods Ended June 30, 1999 and 1998
(in thousands)

| | Second Quarter | | First Half | |
	1999	1998	1999	1998
	(unaudited)		(unaudited)	
North America				
United States				
Cars	448	367	852	758
Trucks	679	662	1,419	1,226
Total United States	1,127	1,029	2,271	1,984
Canada	80	68	137	142
Mexico	30	27	49	55
Total North America	1,237	1,124	2,457	2,181
Europe				
Britain	136	149	262	291
Germany	111	117	201	223

Italy	61	48	111	118
Spain	54	45	97	82
France	53	42	91	82
Other countries	154	103	253	211
Total Europe	569	504	1,015	1,007
Other international				
Brazil	34	52	56	94
Australia	33	34	64	64
Taiwan	15	19	32	48
Argentina	14	29	29	59
Japan	9	6	16	14
Other countries	17	25	34	54
Total other international	122	165	231	333
Total worldwide vehicle unit sales	1,928	1,793	3,703	3,521

Vehicle unit sales generally are reported worldwide on a "where sold" basis and include sales of all Ford-badged units, as well as units manufactured by Ford and sold to other manufacturers.

Prior period restated to correct reported unit sales.

CONSOLIDATED STATEMENT OF INCOME
For the Periods Ended June 30, 1999 and 1998
(in millions)

	Second Quarter		First Half	
	1999	1998	1999	1998
	(unaudited)		(unaudited)	
AUTOMOTIVE				
Sales	$35,921	$31,309	$67,854	$60,385
Costs and expenses (Note 2)				
Costs of sales	30,526	26,156	58,141	51,510
Selling, administrative and other expenses	2,497	2,231	4,428	4,147
Total costs and expenses	33,023	28,387	62,569	55,657
Operating income	2,898	2,922	5,285	4,728
Interest income	348	318	688	640
Interest expense	346	208	639	407
Net interest income	2	110	49	233
Equity in net income/(loss) of affiliated companies	0	18	50	8
Net expense from transactions with Financial Services	(17)	(39)	(45)	(87)
Income/(loss) before income taxes - Automotive	2,883	3,011	5,339	4,882
FINANCIAL SERVICES				
Revenues	6,361	5,980	12,313	13,488
Costs and expenses				
Interest expense	1,825	1,825	3,713	4,195
Depreciation	2,391	2,158	4,548	4,195

Operating and other expenses	1,101	1,086	2,098	2,669
Provision for credit and insurance losses	372	360	763	1,068
Total costs and expenses	5,689	5,429	11,122	12,127
Net revenue from transactions with Automotive	17	39	45	87
Gain on spin-off of The Associates (Note 6)	-	-	-	15,955
Income before income taxes - Financial Services	689	590	1,236	17,403
TOTAL COMPANY				
Income before income taxes	3,572	3,601	6,575	22,285
Provision for income taxes	1,198	1,192	2,203	2,164
Income before minority interests	2,374	2,409	4,372	20,121
Minority interests in net income of subsidiaries	36	28	55	94
Net income	$ 2,338	$ 2,381	$ 4,317	$20,027
Income attributable to Common and Class B Stock after preferred stock dividends	$ 2,334	$ 2,377	$ 4,310	$19,928
Average number of shares of Common and Class B Stock outstanding	1,211	1,212	1,211	1,211
AMOUNTS PER SHARE OF COMMON AND CLASS B STOCK				
Basic Income (Note 7)	$ 1.93	$ 1.96	$ 3.57	$ 16.47
Diluted Income (Note 7)	$ 1.89	$ 1.91	$ 3.48	$ 16.11
Cash dividends	$ 0.46	$ 0.42	$ 0.92	$ 0.84

The accompanying notes are part of the financial statements.

Prior period costs of sales and selling, administrative and other expenses were reclassified.

CONSOLIDATED BALANCE SHEET
(in millions)

	June 30, 1999 (unaudited)	December 31, 1998
ASSETS		
Automotive		
Cash and cash equivalents	$ 4,392	$ 3,685
Marketable securities	19,567	20,120
Total cash and marketable securities	23,959	23,805
Receivables	3,713	2,604
Inventories (Note 8)	6,347	5,656
Deferred income taxes	3,342	3,239
Other current assets	3,952	3,405
Current receivable from Financial Services	581	0
Total current assets	41,894	38,709
Equity in net assets of affiliated companies (Notes 4 & 5)	4,680	2,401
Net property	39,775	37,320
Deferred income taxes	3,355	3,175
Other assets	10,348	7,139
Total Automotive assets	100,052	88,744
Financial Services		
Cash and cash equivalents	1,227	1,151
Investments in securities	915	968
Net receivables and lease investments	141,665	132,567
Other assets	16,694	13,227
Receivable from Automotive	752	888
Total Financial Services assets	161,253	148,801
Total assets	$261,305	$237,545
LIABILITIES AND STOCKHOLDERS' EQUITY		
Automotive		
Trade payables	$ 13,286	$ 13,368
Other payables	3,979	2,755
Accrued liabilities	19,419	16,925

Income taxes payable	2,641	1,404
Debt payable within one year	1,348	1,121
Current payable to Financial Services	141	70
Total current liabilities	40,814	35,643
Long-term debt	10,058	8,713
Other liabilities	32,973	30,133
Deferred income taxes	981	751
Payable to Financial Services	611	818
Total Automotive liabilities	85,437	76,058
Financial Services		
Payables	4,158	3,555
Debt	132,226	122,324
Deferred income taxes	5,653	5,488
Other liabilities and deferred income	6,332	6,034
Payable to Automotive	581	0
Total Financial Services liabilities	148,950	137,401
Company-obligated mandatorily redeemable preferred securities of a subsidiary trust holding solely junior subordinated debentures of the Company (Note 9)	676	677
Stockholders' equity		
Capital stock		
Preferred Stock, par value $1.00 per share (aggregate liquidation preference of $177 million)	*	*
Common Stock, par value $1.00 per share (1,151 million shares issued)	1,151	1,151
Class B Stock, par value $1.00 per share (71 million shares issued)	71	71
Capital in excess of par value of stock	5,036	5,283
Accumulated other comprehensive income	(2,173)	(1,670)
ESOP loan and treasury stock	(697)	(1,085)
Earnings retained for use in business	22,854	19,659
Total stockholders' equity	26,242	23,409
Total liabilities and stockholders' equity	$261,305	$237,545

- - - -
*Less than $1 million

The accompanying notes are part of the financial statements.

CONDENSED CONSOLIDATED STATEMENT OF CASH FLOWS

For the Periods Ended June 30, 1999 and 1998

(in millions)

	First Half 1999		First Half 1998	
	Automotive	Financial Services	Automotive	Financial Services
	(unaudited)		(unaudited)	
Cash and cash equivalents at January 1	$ 3,685	$ 1,151	$ 6,316	$ 1,618
Cash flows from operating activities before securities trading	9,798	4,074	9,989	8,148
Net sales/(purchases) of trading securities	762	(86)	(2,936)	(43)
Net cash flows from operating activities	10,560	3,988	7,053	8,105
Cash flows from investing activities				
Capital expenditures	(3,093)	(284)	(3,760)	(251)
Purchase of leased assets	–	–	(110)	–
Acquisitions of receivables and lease investments	–	(39,237)	–	(45,322)
Collections of receivables and lease investments	–	25,292	–	29,787
Net acquisitions of daily rental vehicles	–	(1,901)	–	(1,855)
Purchases of securities	(878)	(533)	(341)	(1,416)
Sales and maturities of securities	669	609	410	988
Proceeds from sales of receivables and lease investments	–	5,005	–	5,448

Net investing activity with Financial Services	(100)	-	786	-
Cash paid for acquisitions (Notes 3-5)	(6,342)	-	-	-
Other	(92)	(6)	(89)	(629)
Net cash used in investing activities	(9,836)	(11,055)	(3,104)	(13,250)
Cash flows from financing activities				
Cash dividends	(1,122)	(2)	(4,274)	(3)
Issuance/(Purchases) of Common Stock	(246)	-	210	-
Preferred stock - Series B repurchase, Series A redemption	-	-	(420)	-
Changes in short-term debt	84	6,263	180	3,871
Proceeds from issuance of other debt	1,653	13,874	337	14,820
Principal payments on other debt	(160)	(13,596)	(1,182)	(11,507)
Net financing activity with Automotive	-	100	-	(786)
Spin-off of The Associates cash	-	-	-	(508)
Other	544	(26)	(658)	(169)
Net cash (used in)/provided by financing activities	753	6,613	(5,807)	5,718
Effect of exchange rate changes on cash	(53)	(187)	(26)	64
Net transactions with Automotive/Financial Services	(717)	717	458	(458)
Net increase/(decrease) in cash and cash equivalents	707	76	(1,426)	179
Cash and cash equivalents at June 30	$ 4,392	$ 1,227	$ 4,890	$ 1,797

The accompanying notes are part of the financial statements.

NOTES TO FINANCIAL STATEMENTS

(unaudited)

1. **Financial Statements** - The financial data presented herein are unaudited, but in the opinion of management reflect those adjustments necessary for a fair presentation of such information. Results for interim periods should not be considered indicative of results for a full year. Reference should be made to the financial statements contained in the registrant's Annual Report on Form 10-K (the "10-K Report") for the year ended December 31, 1998. For purposes of Notes to Financial Statements, "Ford" or the "Company" means Ford Motor Company and its majority owned subsidiaries unless the context requires otherwise. Certain amounts for prior periods were reclassified to conform with present period presentation.

2. Selected Automotive costs and expenses are summarized as follows (in millions):

| | Second Quarter | | First Half | |
	1999	1998	1999	1998
Depreciation	$802	$679	$1,548	$1,359
Amortization	590	620	1,162	1,338

Acquisition of AB Volvo's worldwide passenger car business "Volvo Car" - Second quarter 1999 financial results include a one-time profit reduction of $146 million, or $0.11 per share of diluted Common and Class B Stock, related to the acquisition of Volvo Car. Under U.S. accounting rules, we were required to write-up inventory acquired to fair value, resulting in a one-time increase to cost of sales.

Dissolution of AutoEuropa Joint Venture - Effective January 1, 1999, our joint venture for the production of minivans with Volkswagen AG in Portugal (AutoEuropa) was dissolved resulting in a $255 million pre-tax gain ($165 million after-tax) in the first quarter of 1999.

3. **Purchase of AB Volvo's Worldwide Passenger Car Business** - On March 31, 1999, we purchased Volvo Car for approximately $6.45 billion. The acquisition price consisted of a cash payment of approximately $2 billion on March 31, 1999, a deferred payment obligation to AB Volvo of approximately $1.6 billion due March 31, 2001, and existing Volvo Car automotive net indebtedness of approximately $2.9 billion. Most automotive indebtedness was repaid on April 12, 1999. The purchase price payment and automotive debt repayments were funded from our cash reserves.

The acquisition has been accounted for as a purchase. The assets purchased, liabilities assumed and the results of operations, since the date of acquisition, are included in our financial statements on a consolidated basis.

The purchase price for Volvo Car has been allocated, on a preliminary basis, to the assets acquired and liabilities assumed based on estimated fair values as of the acquisition date. The excess of the purchase price over the estimated fair value of net assets acquired is approximately $2.5 billion and is being amortized on a straight-line basis over 40 years. The purchase price allocation included a write-up of inventory to fair value; the sale of this inventory in the second quarter of 1999 resulted in a one-time increase in cost of sales of $146 million after-tax.

Assuming the acquisition had taken place on January 1, 1999 and 1998, unaudited pro forma revenue for Ford (Automotive and Financial Services) would have been approximately $83.5 billion and $80.1 billion for each of the six month periods ended June 30, respectively. Excluding the unfavorable inventory profit effect in the second quarter of 1999, pro forma effects on net income and earnings per share would not have been material.

4. Purchase of Kwik-Fit Holdings plc – As of June 30, 1999, we acquired approximately 96% of the outstanding stock of Kwik-Fit Holdings plc ("Kwik-Fit"). Kwik-Fit is Europe's largest independent vehicle maintenance and light repair chain, with over 1,600 service centers in the United Kingdom, Ireland and continental Europe. Our offer price is £5.60 (approximately the equivalent of $9.05) per share, or an aggregate of £1,013 million including acquisition-related costs (approximately the equivalent of $1.6 billion). The payments through June 30, 1999 amounted to approximately £966 million which was a combination of a cash payment of £862 million and a payable to certain shareholders of £104 million. We expect to purchase the remaining Kwik-Fit shares by the end of July 1999. The purchase has been funded from our cash reserves.

The acquisition will be accounted for as a purchase. The assets purchased, liabilities assumed and the results of operations of Kwik-Fit will be included in our financial statements on a consolidated basis beginning in the third quarter of 1999. Our investment in Kwik-Fit at June 30, 1999, is included in Equity in Net Assets of Affiliated Companies on our financial statements.

NOTES TO FINANCIAL STATEMENTS

(unaudited)

5. **Purchase of Plastic Omnium** - On June 30, 1999, we purchased (through Visteon) Plastic Omnium's automotive interior business for approximately $500 million. The automotive interior business of Plastic Omnium has 14 facilities in four countries in Europe: France, Spain, Italy and the UK. The purchase was funded from our cash reserves.

   The acquisition will be accounted for as a purchase. The assets purchased, liabilities assumed and the results of operations of Plastic Omnium will be included in our financial statements on a consolidated basis beginning in the third quarter of 1999. Our investment in Plastic Omnium at June 30, 1999 is included in Equity in Net Assets of Affiliated Companies on our financial statements.

6. **Spin-off of The Associates** - On March 2, 1998, the Board of Directors of the Company approved the spin-off of The Associates by declaring a dividend on Ford's outstanding shares of Common and Class B Stock consisting of Ford's 80.7% interest (279.5 million shares) in The Associates. The Board of Directors also declared a dividend in cash on shares of Company stock held in U.S. employee savings plans equal to the market value of The Associates stock to be distributed per share of the Company's Common and Class B Stock. Both the spin-off dividend and the cash dividend were paid on April 7, 1998 to stockholders of record on March 12, 1998.

   Holders of Ford Common and Class B Stock on the record date received 0.262085 shares of The Associates common stock for each share of Ford stock, and participants in U.S. employee savings plans on the record date received $22.12 in cash per share of Ford stock, based on the volume-weighted average price of The Associates stock of $84.3849 per share on April 7, 1998. The total value of the distribution (including the $3.2 billion cash dividend) was $26.8 billion or $22.12 per share of Ford stock.

   As a result of the spin-off of The Associates, Ford realized a gain of $15,955 million based on the fair value of The Associates as of the record date, March 12, 1998, in the first quarter of 1998. Ford received a ruling from the U.S. Internal Revenue Service that the distribution qualifies as a tax-free transaction for U.S. federal income tax purposes.

   The Company's results in the first quarter of 1998 include Ford's share of The Associates earnings through the record date, March 12 ($177 million, or $0.14 a share).

7. Income Per Share of Common and Class B Stock - Basic income per share of Common and Class B Stock is calculated by dividing the income attributable to Common and Class B Stock by the average number of shares of Common and Class B Stock outstanding during the applicable period, adjusted for shares issuable under employee savings and compensation plans.

The Company had Series A Preferred Stock convertible to Common Stock until January 9, 1998. Other obligations, such as stock options, are considered to be dilutive potential common stock. The calculation of diluted income per share of Common and Class B Stock takes into account the effect of dilutive potential common stock.

Income per share of Common and Class B Stock was as follows (in millions, except per share amounts):

	Second Quarter 1999		Second Quarter 1998	
	Income	Shares	Income	Shares
Net income	$2,338	1,211	$ 2,381	1,212
Preferred stock dividend requirements	(4)	-	(4)	-
Issuable and uncommitted ESOP shares	-	(3)	-	(2)
Basic income and shares	$2,334	1,208	$ 2,377	1,210
Basic income per share	$ 1.93		$ 1.96	
Basic income and shares	$2,334	1,208	$ 2,377	1,210
Net dilutive effect of options	-	29	-	33
Convertible preferred stock and other	-	-	-	-
Diluted income and shares	$2,334	1,237	$ 2,377	1,243
Diluted income per share	$ 1.89		$ 1.91	

NOTES TO FINANCIAL STATEMENTS

(unaudited)

| | First Half 1999 | | First Half 1998 | |
	Income	Shares	Income	Shares
Net income	$4,317	1,211	$20,027	1,211
Preferred stock dividend requirements	(7)	–	(99)	–
Issuable and uncommitted ESOP shares	–	(4)	–	(1)
Basic income and shares	$4,310	1,207	$19,928	1,210
Basic income per share	$ 3.57		$ 16.47	
Basic income and shares	$4,310	1,207	$19,928	1,210
Net dilutive effect of options	–	30	–	26
Convertible preferred stock and other	–	–	–	1
Diluted income and shares	$4,310	1,237	$19,928	1,237
Diluted income per share	$ 3.48		$ 16.11	

8. Automotive Inventories are summarized as follows (in millions):

	June 30, 1999	December 31, 1998
Raw materials, work in process and supplies	$3,705	$2,887
Finished products	2,642	2,769
Total inventories	$6,347	$5,656
U.S. inventories	$2,176	$1,832

9. Company-Obligated Mandatorily Redeemable Preferred Securities of a Subsidiary Trust – The sole asset of Ford Motor Company Capital Trust I (the "Trust"), which is the obligor on the Preferred Securities of such Trust, is $632 million principal amount of 9% Junior Subordinated Debentures due 2025 of Ford Motor Company.

10. Comprehensive Income – Other comprehensive income includes foreign currency translation adjustments, minimum pension liability adjustments, and net unrealized gains and loses on investments in equity securities. Total comprehensive income is summarized as follows (in millions):

	Second Quarter		First Half	
	1999	1998	1999	1998
Net income	$2,338	$2,381	$4,317	$20,027
Other comprehensive income	(353)	(80)	(503)	(268)
Total comprehensive income	$1,985	$2,301	$3,814	$19,759

11. Segment Information – Ford has identified four primary operating segments: Automotive, Visteon, Ford Credit and Hertz. Segment selection was based upon internal organizational structure, the way in which these operations are managed and their performance evaluated by management and our Board of Directors, the availability of separate financial results and materiality considerations. Segment detail is summarized as follows (in millions):

Second Quarter	Automotive Sector		Financial Services Sector			Elims/ Other	Total Auto Sector	Total Fin Svcs Sector
	Auto-motive	Visteon	Ford Credit	Hertz	Other Fin Svcs			
1999								
Revenues								
External customer	$35,545	$ 449	$ 4,928	$ 1,162	$ 280	$ (82)	$ 35,921	$ 6,361
Intersegment	1,517	4,614	91	8	22	(6,252)	0	0
Total Revenues	$37,062	$ 5,063	$ 5,019	$ 1,170	$ 302	$ (6,334)	$ 35,921	$ 6,361
Net income	$ 1,649	$ 282	335	88	3	(19)	$ 1,931	407
1998								
Revenues								
External customer	$31,042	$ 362	$ 4,786	$ 1,045	$ 145	$ (91)	$ 31,309	$ 5,980
Intersegment	1,256	4,363	65	7	(27)	(5,664)	0	0
Total Revenues	$32,298	$ 4,725	$ 4,851	$ 1,052	$ 118	$ (5,755)	$ 31,309	$ 5,980
Net income	$ 1,810	$ 241	300	75	(31)	(14)	$ 2,051	330

NOTES TO FINANCIAL STATEMENTS

(unaudited)

First Half	Automotive Sector		Financial Services Sector			Elims/ Other	Total Auto Sector	Total Fin Svcs Sector
	Auto- motive	Visteon	Ford Credit	Hertz	Other Fin Svcs			
1999								
Revenues								
External customer	$67,142	$ 866	$ 9,791	$ 2,189	$ 336	$ (157)	$ 67,854	$ 12,313
Intersegment	2,705	8,969	148	16	93	(11,931)	0	0
Total Revenues	$69,847	$ 9,835	$ 9,939	$ 2,205	$ 429	$(12,088)	$ 67,854	$ 12,313
Net income	$ 3,092	$ 490	$ 635	$ 137	$ (9)	$ (28)	$ 3,582	$ 735
Total assets	$94,829	$11,208	$147,996	$10,123	$10,607	$(13,458)	$100,052	$161,253
1998								
Revenues								
External customer	$59,908	$ 669	$ 9,278	$ 1,938	$ 2,262	$ (182)	$ 60,385	$ 13,488
Intersegment	2,487	8,434	132	15	104	(11,172)	0	0
Total Revenues	$62,395	$9,103	$ 9,410	$ 1,953	$ 2,366	$(11,354)	$ 60,385	$ 13,488
Net income	$ 2,856	$ 430	$ 578	$ 110	$16,116 a/	$ (63)	$ 3,286	$ 16,741
Total assets	$81,994	$9,080	$128,219	$ 8,741	$ 7,619	$ (7,382)	$ 86,921	$141,350

- - - -

a/ Includes $15,955 non-cash gain (not taxed) on spin-off of The Associates in the first quarter of 1998 (Note 6).

"Other Financial Services" data is an aggregation of miscellaneous smaller Financial Services Sector business components, including Ford Motor Land Development Corporation, Ford Leasing Development Company, Ford Leasing Corporation, and Granite Management Corporation, and certain unusual transactions (footnoted). Also included is data for The Associates, which was spun-off from Ford in 1998.

"Eliminations/Other" data includes intersegment eliminations and minority interest calculations. Interest income for the operating segments in the Financial Services Sector is reported as "Revenue". Included in the Visteon segment's external customer revenues are sales to outside fabricators for inclusion in components sold to Ford's Automotive segment.

A review of interim financial information provided by a public company is viewed in the framework of an annual audit of its annual financial statements; that is, the scope of the review and the sufficiency of evidence collected by the CPA are influenced by findings from the previous annual audit. Note that this type of review is performed only for companies whose annual financial statements are audited. The accountant's standard report on the review of interim financial information of a public company appears in Figure 9-3.

Independent Accountant's Report

We have reviewed the accompanying (describe the statements or information reviewed) of XYZ Company and consolidated subsidiaries as of September 30, 20XX, and for the three-month and nine-month periods then ended. These financial statements (information) are (is) the responsibility of the company's management.

We conducted our review in accordance with standards established by the American Institute of Certified Public Accountants. A review of interim financial information consists principally of applying analytical procedures to financial data and making inquiries of persons responsible for financial and accounting matters. It is substantially less in scope than an audit conducted in accordance with generally accepted auditing standards, the objective of which is the expression of an opinion regarding the financial statements taken as a whole. Accordingly, we do not express such an opinion.

Based on our review, we are not aware of any material modifications that should be made to the accompanying financial statements (information) for them (it) to be in conformity with generally accepted accounting principles.

(Signature)

(Date)

FIG. 9-3 *Standard review report for interim information for a public company.*

The review report states that the review was made in accordance with AICPA standards and identifies the interim information reviewed. The report also contains a brief description of the procedures for a review of interim information. The CPA essentially says nothing more than "I do not know of any material changes that must be made to make the statements conform to GAAP" (see Chapter 1 for a discussion of GAAP). But the accountant has not made tests of the underlying accounting records to see if they support the figures in the financial statements—to do so would be to conduct an audit. Note the title to the review report includes the words "independent accountant." And the reader is put on notice that a review is substantially narrower in scope than an audit.

Reviews are normally performed at the request of the board of directors so that the accountant can report to management, the board, and the stockholders on significant matters found through inquiry and analytical procedures. Reviews thereby protect the company from potential legal liability by alerting management to unusual or irregular matters found during their review.

In recent years certain states have passed legislation that allow public companies to sell securities and raise a limited amount of capital without presenting audited financial statements. Many of these states require reviewed statements for companies engaged in this type of activity. This type of review differs from the quarterly review of a public company in that the accountant is not required to obtain an understanding of the company's internal control structure.

FINANCIAL STATEMENT REVIEWS OF NONPUBLIC COMPANIES

Similar to a public company, a nonpublic company might include a review of interim financial information in a note to its audited financial statements. The requirements and report are identical to that of a public company. However, many CPAs work with nonpublic client companies that do not need audits, perhaps because the business is closely held, has little debt, or is not subject to government regulations that require an audit. Examples of such companies include small (sometimes family-owned) businesses and professional firms or partnerships such as those formed by doctors and lawyers. Many times these companies need tax services or assistance preparing unaudited financial statements in order to obtain credit; you may occasionally run across a set of financial statements for a nonpublic company that has been reviewed by an independent CPA. These reviews do not carry the same weight as a formal audit, which concludes an opinion by the CPA on the fairness of financial-statement presentation. This type of review service was originally created as a low-cost alternative to an audit, and resulted in a lower level of assurance.

Figure 9-4 is an example of a review report for a nonpublic company.

I (we) have reviewed the accompanying balance sheet of XYZ Company as of December 31, 20XX, and the related statements of income, retained earnings, and cash flows for the year ended, in accordance with Statements on Standards for Accounting and Review Services issued by the American Institute of Certified Public Accountants. All information included in these financial statements is the representation of the management (owners) of XYZ Company.

A review consists principally of inquiries of company personnel and analytical procedures applied to financial data. It is substantially less in scope than an audit in accordance with generally accepted auditing standards, the objective of which is the expression of an opinion regarding the financial statements taken as a whole. Accordingly, I (we) do not express such an opinion.

Based on my (our) review, I am (we are) not aware of any material modifications that should be made to the accompanying financial statements in order for them to be in conformity with generally accepted accounting principles.

FIG. 9-4 *Review report for a nonpublic company.*

The report for a nonpublic company is substantially the same as that prepared for a public company. The essential difference is that in the review report relating to the interim financial statements for a public company, the CPA makes reference to "obtaining an understanding of the system for the preparation of interim financial information."

Like those in a review for a public company, the procedures performed for a review for a nonpublic company are limited to inquiry of company personnel and analytical review. Notice that the CPA states in the review report that he or she is not aware of any material changes needed to make the financial statements conform to GAAP. The report also states that the financial statements were not audited, and no opinion is expressed as to their fairness of presentation.

PROCEDURES PERFORMED IN AUDITS AND REVIEWS

Whether a public or a nonpublic company, a review consists of questioning management about the preparation of the financial statements and analyzing past and present financial statements to determine if unusual relationships exist. For instance, assume that for the last several years accounts receivable have averaged $2 million, but this year they are reported at $4 million. What is the cause of the unexpected relationship? Have the sales been recorded twice? It is up to the CPA to determine if the statements are wrong. The CPA does not investigate relationships that appear normal.

There are procedural differences between conducting an audit and a review. When performing an audit, the CPA is present at the counting of year-end inventories; in a review, the CPA merely asks questions about the procedures used to count inventories. Auditing standards require the CPA to obtain written confirmations from customers of the amounts they owe the company (accounts receivable) and from suppliers confirming the amounts owed by the business (accounts payable); the CPA would not perform such procedures in a review and would merely ask management whether all sales and payments from customers and all purchases and payments to suppliers have been recorded.

REPORTS ON COMPONENTS OF A FINANCIAL STATEMENT

A CPA may be requested to report on some specific aspect of a financial statement, a financial statement item, a forecast or projection, or a schedule; typical components are trade accounts receivable, projected income statement, and the schedule of royalties under a licensing agreement. As we stated, these types of engagements generally fall into one of two categories: reports on components that express an audit opinion and reports based on applying agreed-upon procedures.

Reports Expressing an Audit Opinion on Components

Suppose a shopping mall charges its tenants rent in accordance with a lease agreement that specifies that the rent is based on a percentage of the tenant's gross sales. The mall management might require an audit report on the fair presentation of those gross sales figures in accordance with GAAP. The tenant then engages an auditor to perform an examination of the sales account. The auditor's unqualified opinion on a schedule of gross sales is shown in Figure 9-5. Similar reports might be requested to determine royalty agreements or participation in profit-sharing plans.

There are several similarities and differences between an audit report on specified elements and the auditor's standard audit report (discussed in Chapter 2).

Independent Auditor's Report

We have audited the accompanying schedule of gross sales (as defined in the lease agreement dated March 24, 2000, between Smith Company, as lessor, and Jones Stores Corporation, as lessee) of Jones Stores Corporation at its Yellowstone Street store, Pocatello, Idaho, for the year ended December 31, 2000. This schedule is the responsibility of Jones Store Corporation's management. Our responsibility is to express an opinion on this schedule based on our audit.

We conducted our audit in accordance with generally accepted auditing standards. Those standards require that we plan and perform the audit to obtain reasonable assurance about whether the schedule of gross sales is free of material misstatement. An audit includes examining, on a test basis, evidence supporting the amounts and disclosures in the schedule of gross sales. An audit also includes assessing the accounting principles used and significant estimates made by management, as well as evaluating the overall schedule presentation. We believe that our audit provides a reasonable basis for our opinion.

In our opinion, the schedule of gross sales referred to above presents fairly, in all material respects, the gross sales of Jones Stores Corporation at its Yellowstone Street store, Pocatello, Idaho, for the year ended December 31, 2000, as defined in the lease agreement referred to in the first paragraph.

This report is intended solely for the information and use of the boards of directors and managements of Jones Stores Corporation and Smith Company and should not be used for any other purpose.

FIG. 9-5 *Report relating to amount of sales for the purpose of computing rental.*

Similarities

1. The report title includes the word "independent."
2. The report states that the specified elements, accounts, or items identified in the report have been audited.
3. The report states that the specified elements, accounts, or items are the responsibility of the company's management and that the auditor is responsible for expressing an opinion on the specified elements, accounts, or items based on the audit.
4. The second paragraph regarding generally accepted auditing standards and the definition of an audit is the same as that found in the standard audit report except that the reference is to the specified element rather than to the financial statements as a whole.
5. The opinion paragraph is the same as the standard report except that reference is made to the identified element rather than to the financial statements as a whole.

Differences

1. While not included in the sample report shown in Figure 9-5, an additional paragraph might be needed above the opinion paragraph to describe the accounting basis on which the specified elements, accounts, or items are presented if different from GAAP. If necessary,

the auditor should also comment in this paragraph on the sources of significant client interpretations relating to the provisions of a relevant agreement (such as the lease agreement).

2. Our example contains a paragraph after the opinion paragraph restricting the distribution of the report to Smith Company and Jones Stores Corporation. This restriction is necessary because the basis of presentation is determined by reference to a document (the lease agreement) that is not generally available to other third parties. A similar restriction is necessary if the presentation of the element, account, or item was not in conformity with GAAP. On the other hand, if a CPA were engaged to simply audit a schedule of accounts receivable for a company, such a restriction would be unnecessary.

Reports Based on Applying Agreed-Upon Procedures

When the scope of an examination of specified elements, accounts, or items is limited, the engagement becomes one based on *agreed-upon procedures.* This means that the accountant is applying selected auditing procedures, rather than the full set of procedures that would normally be performed in an audit.

When this type of engagement is performed, the parties involved arrive at an understanding of the specific audit procedures to be performed by the CPA through discussions; this understanding is stated in a draft copy of the report or in the engagement letter distributed to the concerned parties, who are asked to respond with any comments before a report is issued.

The accountant's report contains the following information:

1. The specified elements, accounts, or items to which the agreed-upon procedures were applied.
2. The intended distribution of the report.
3. The procedures applied, along with the accountant's findings.
4. A disclaimer of opinion (negative assurance) with respect to the specified elements, accounts, or items.
5. A statement that the report relates only to the specified elements, accounts, or items and not to the client's financial statements taken as a whole.

Figure 9-6 provides an example of an agreed-upon procedures engagement in which the accountant has performed limited procedures on a statement of investment performance statistics for a company fund. The reference in the report to "Note 1" refers to footnote 1. In footnote 1, the CPA enumerates the measurement and disclosure criteria used to evaluate the fund. That is, the CPA identifies the established, stated, or agreed-upon criteria in this footnote.

Board of Directors

X Company

We have applied certain agreed-upon procedures, as discussed below, to accounting records of Y Company, Inc., as of December 31, 20XX, solely to assist you in connection with the proposed acquisition of Y Company, Inc. It is understood that this report is solely for your information and is not to be referred to or distributed for any purpose to anyone who is not a member of management of X Company. Our procedures and findings are as follows: (The following paragraph enumerates the procedures and findings.)

Because the above procedures do not constitute an audit conducted in accordance with generally accepted auditing standards, we do not express an opinion on any of the accounts or items referred to above. In connection with the procedures referred to above, no matters came to our attention that caused us to believe that the specified accounts or items should be adjusted. Had we performed additional procedures or had we conducted an audit of the financial statements in accordance with generally accepted auditing standards, matters might have come to our attention that would have been reported to you. This report relates only the accounts and items specified above and does not extend to any financial statements of Y Company, Inc., taken as a whole.

FIG. 9-6 *Report on agreed-upon procedures for the statement of investment performance statistics of XYZ Fund.*

COMPILATION REPORTS FOR NONPUBLIC COMPANIES

When doing a compilation, the CPA reads the financial statements, decides whether they are in proper form and appear to contain appropriate disclosures, and checks the mathematics of the statements (for instance, for the balance sheet, do assets equal liabilities plus owners' equity?). The CPA is not required to analyze relationships or to ask management questions about the preparation of the statements. However, the accountant should be familiar enough with the company's business transactions and the proper accounting to be used to know if the information supplied by the company has obvious flaws.

The accountant's report should state that a compilation has been performed and that a compilation is limited to presenting information that is the representation of management or the owners. The report must state that the accountant has not audited or reviewed the financial statements and is not expressing an opinion as to their fairness of presentation. Compilations can be performed on the financial statements taken as a whole or on only one financial statement. Figure 9-7 shows a sample compilation report on the financial statements of PLT Company.

We have compiled the accompanying balance sheet of PLT Company as of December 31, 2000, and the related statements of income, retained earnings, and cash flows for the year then ended, in accordance with Statements on Standards for Accounting and Review Services issued by the American Institute of Certified Public Accountants.

A compilation is limited to presenting in the form of financial statements information that is the representation of management. We have not audited or reviewed the accompanying financial statements and, accordingly, do not express an opinion or any other form of assurance on them.

FIG. 9-7 *Accountant's Compilation Report.*

An accountant who is not independent of a company can still compile the financial statements of the company and issue a report. In this instance, an additional paragraph is added noting that the accountant is not independent of the company.

CHAPTER PERSPECTIVE

In this chapter we described services other than full audits that can be provided by CPAs. These services include reviews of both public and nonpublic companies; audits of specified elements, accounts, or financial statement items; agreed-upon procedures engagements; and engagements to compile the financial statements of nonpublic companies.

Each of these engagements carries a different level of assurance. These levels of assurance are communicated through the report issued by the CPA and may be positive (as in an unqualified audit opinion), negative (as in a review of a nonpublic company), or unstated (as in a disclaimer of opinion in a compilation engagement of a nonpublic company).

We described the reports and responsibilities of the CPA when performing reviews of public and nonpublic companies, audits of specified elements, agreed-upon procedures engagements, and compilations of the financial statements of nonpublic companies. We also included in each section an illustration of a CPA's report for that particular engagement.

Reports to the Securities and Exchange Commission

INTRODUCTION AND MAIN POINTS

While annual reports containing audited financial statements are used by a number of groups, including some government agencies, the Securities and Exchange Commission (SEC) requires that companies under its jurisdiction file separate reports according to specified formats. The SEC filings discussed in this chapter include the registration, the required annual filing (Form 10-K), the required quarterly filing (Form 10-Q), and the required filing of significant changes (Form 8-K). After studying the material in this chapter:

■ You will understand the general goal of the SEC in ensuring equal access to information.

■ You will understand the accountant/auditor's involvement in the SEC registration process and the information contained in a registration statement.

■ You will know what an auditor's comfort letter is and why underwriters request them.

■ You will know the difference between Forms 10-K, 10-Q, and 8-K and the information they require.

■ You will know which forms contain audited data and which do not.

Prior to the establishment of the SEC, many states enacted legislation to curb abuses relating to the issuance of securities. The state laws dealing with the regulation of securities became known as "blue sky laws," a phrase that originated more than fifty years ago in a judicial comment denouncing speculative schemes that were an intangible as "so many feet of blue sky." "Blue sky law" is often used interchangeably with "state law" to refer to state laws that govern issuance and trading of securities.

State laws never really proved to be totally effective in regulating the securities markets, largely because companies that were engaged in interstate commerce could simply choose to issue securities in a state where there were no regulations governing their issuance. Also, in states where regulations existed, exemptions were commonplace, along with selective prosecution of those companies found to have violated the law.

Because the state laws proved to be ineffectual, a large number of state and local officials looked to the federal government for action regarding the regulation of the securities markets. The results were the Securities Acts of 1933 and the Securities Exchange Act of 1934.

THE REASON FOR SEC REPORTING REQUIREMENTS

If the markets for both debt and stock are to be orderly and if investors are to make informed investment decisions, all parties must have equal access to reliable information about the companies that borrow money or issue stock. Part of the job of the SEC is to ensure that current and potential investors and creditors have equal access to information about companies whose securities are publicly traded. In attempting to ensure that investors are provided with the information necessary to make informed investment decisions, the SEC has expanded its regulations to encompass four areas:

1. Offerings of securities, both as original issuances and as secondary distributions
2. The information a prospective investor is entitled to receive
3. The information an investor is entitled to receive periodically
4. Disclosure of significant events

The SEC accomplishes its mission by requiring publicly held companies to provide financial information at regular intervals. This information is then made available to potential investors or others with an interest in it.

By overseeing the filing of information—determining what information should be filed and how it should be presented—the SEC acts as a kind of clearinghouse. (However, requests for annual reports should be addressed to the company and requests for SEC filings should be addressed to the company or the SEC. This information can also be found on each company's website or the SEC's site (http://www.sec.gov).) This chapter discusses the registration process and SEC Forms 10-K, 10-Q, and 8-K. These reports are compared in Figure 10-1.

Form	Filing Frequency	Contains Audited Data?
Registration (including S-1)	At issue	yes
10-K	Annually	yes
10-Q	Quarterly	no
8-K	As needed (following significant changes)	no

FIG. 10-1 *Forms required by the SEC.*

REGISTRATION

Registration is the process of filing information about stock and the issuing company with the proper regulatory agency. At the federal level, registration statements are filed with the SEC. The SEC does not approve the company or its stock issue, but looks only at the adequacy of the information disclosed. State laws may also require registration.

The registration process normally begins with the selection of an investment banker or underwriter. The underwriter agrees to assist the company in the registration process by marketing and distributing the securities. The underwriter usually requests a *comfort letter* from the independent CPA auditor to indicate that the company has fulfilled all of the necessary accounting requirements in the registration process. The comfort letter says, in essence, that the CPA knows of nothing wrong with the financial information provided by the company issuing the securities.

Underwriters request comfort letters to acquire information and to show their reliance on the CPA auditor. Comfort letters are not required by the SEC or by either of the Securities Acts. They are simply one way accountants are involved with stock issues.

The registration statement is a document presented in narrative form, similar to a brochure. The SEC requires companies to file a registration statement before a public offering of stock is made in interstate commerce or through the mails, unless the offering qualifies for an exemption. Exemptions are divided into two categories: exempt securities and exempt transactions. Securities offered by banks, nonprofit organizations, common carriers, state governments, as well as intrastate offerings, are examples from the first category. Exempt transactions are private offerings to a limited number of persons or institutions who already have access to the type of information that registration would disclose and who do not intend to redistribute the securities. The SEC also has the authority to exempt other offerings when the amount of capital to be raised is small and the offering is limited to a modest group of investors. This "small issue exemption" has a $5 million limit on the amount that can be solicited. Exemption from registration does not relieve the company from legal liability. The registration statement, which is available to the public, serves only to provide investors with a source of information and does not imply approval of the investment by the SEC.

A company selects one form from more than 20 different forms. The most common are *Form S-1, Form S-2,* and *Form S-3.*

A Form S-1 consists of two principal parts: a prospectus, or selling document, that must be furnished to all purchasers of the stock, and a supplemental part containing more detailed information, such as a listing of expenses related to issuing the securities, information about officers and directors, and additional exhibits and financial statement schedules.

Form S-1 is the basic, most commonly used form for full registration of an initial stock offering. Instructions for the financial statement portions of the registration forms are found in Regulation S-X and, for the nonfinancial aspects of registration, in Regulation S-K. The company must provide whatever information is necessary to make the registration statement complete and not misleading.

As stated, a prospectus is included in Form S-1. A prospectus is any offer made in writing to sell stock; as used by the SEC, the term refers to the document the SEC requires companies to provide to prospective investors in stock registered with the SEC. It is unlawful to sell registered stock in interstate commerce without providing the investor with a prospectus.

The registration statement does not become effective immediately when it is filed, and no sales of stock can be made until it becomes effective. Nonetheless, expressions of interest can be solicited from investors by showing them a preliminary prospectus called a "red herring." This document includes on its face a legend in red ink stating that the registration statement has not become effective and that a formal offer to sell can be made only after the effective date of the registration. Ordinarily, information about offering price, commissions to dealers, and proceeds accruing to the issuer is excluded from the red herring.

Though the SEC does not pass judgment on the value of the offering as an investment, it frequently requires amendments to the registration to improve disclosure. The accountant may assist in the preparation of tables and other data contained in the registration statement in addition to the audited statements, but must make it clear he or she does not assume responsibility for any matters not within his or her expertise as an accountant.

In some states, an effective federal registration fulfills all state blue sky requirements. State securities administrators can provide this information.

THE ANNUAL FILING (FORM 10-K)

Form 10-K must be filed annually with the SEC by publicly traded companies within 90 days after the close of the company's fiscal year. Form 10-K requires much the same information that companies include in their annual reports but also asks for additional information. Some companies issue a combined annual report and 10-K, a procedure allowed under the SEC's integrated disclosure rules.

The 10-K is divided into four parts, each of which is subdivided into individual items. If information has been provided elsewhere, the company may reference those sources rather than repeating the information. The financial statements contained in the 10-K are audited; the 10-K contains a copy of the auditor's report (Item 8, below) as do the financial statements in the annual report.

The contents of the 10-K are:

Part 1

Item 1	A description of the company's business, including information on different segments of the company (for example, product lines, industries, domestic and foreign operations, and major classes of customers).
Item 2	A description of the company's property.
Item 3	A description of any legal proceedings in which the company is involved.
Item 4	A discussion of matters that have been voted on by the shareholders.

Part 2

Item 5	A description of the market for the company's common stock, including disclosures of the principal American markets on which the company's common stock is traded, quarterly high and low stock prices for the last two years, the approximate number of shareholders, the number of times and the amount of cash dividends paid in the last two

years, and any restrictions on the company's ability to pay dividends.

Item 6   A five-year summary of selected financial data, including net sales (operating revenues), income or loss from continuing operations, income or loss from continuing operations per common share, total assets, long-term debt and redeemable preferred stock, and cash dividends per common share.

Item 7   Management's discussion of the company's financial condition, changes that have occurred in financial condition, and the results of operations. This discussion includes management's analysis of the company's liquidity, resources, and operations, the impact of inflation, the cause of major changes in the financial statements that have occurred during the year, and any material contingencies.

Item 8   The financial statements, supplementary data, and auditor's report.

Item 9   Changes in accounting principles and disagreements with the company's auditors.

Part 3

Item 10   The company's directors and executive officers.

Item 11   Compensation of the executive officers.

Item 12   Company securities owned by management and major stockholders.

Item 13   Information on related-party transactions, including transactions between the company and management, its subsidiaries, and major stockholders.

Part 4

Item 14   Exhibits, financial-statement schedules, and reports on Form 8-K.

Figure 10-2 provides excerpts from the 1999 10-K report of Dell Computer Corporation.

FIG. 10-2 *Excerpts from the 1999 10-K report of Dell Computer Corporation.*

UNITED STATES
SECURITIES AND EXCHANGE COMMISSION
Washington, D.C. 20549

Form 10-K

**ANNUAL REPORT PURSUANT TO SECTION 13 OR 15(d) OF THE
SECURITIES EXCHANGE ACT OF 1934**

For the Fiscal Year Ended January 29, 1999

Commission File Number: 0-17017

Dell Computer Corporation

(Exact name of registrant as specified in its charter)

Delaware	**74-2487834**
(State or other jurisdiction of incorporation or organization)	(I.R.S. Employer Identification No.)

One Dell Way, Round Rock, Texas 78682-2244
(Address, including Zip Code, of registrant's principal executive offices)

(512) 338-4400
(Registrant's telephone number, including area code)

Securities registered pursuant to Section 12(g) of the Act:

Common Stock, par value $.01 per share
Preferred Stock Purchase Rights

Indicate by check mark whether the registrant (1) has filed all reports required to be filed by Section 13 or 15(d) of the Securities Exchange Act of 1934 during the preceding 12 months (or for such shorter period that the registrant was required to file such reports), and (2) has been subject to such filing requirements for the past 90 days. Yes ☒ No ☐

Indicate by check mark if disclosure of delinquent filers pursuant to Item 405 of Regulation S-K is not contained herein, and will not be contained, to the best of registrant's knowledge, in definitive proxy or information statements incorporated by reference in Part III of this Form 10-K or any amendment to this Form 10-K. ☐

**Aggregate market value of common stock held by non-affiliates of the registrant as of
March 31, 1999** **$88,625,556,895**
Number of shares of common stock outstanding as of March 31, 1999 . . . . **2,536,184,711**

DOCUMENTS INCORPORATED BY REFERENCE

The information required by Part III of this Report, to the extent not set forth herein, is incorporated by reference from the Registrant's definitive proxy statement relating to the annual meeting of stockholders to be held in 1999, which definitive proxy statement shall be filed with the Securities and Exchange Commission within 120 days after the end of the fiscal year to which this Report relates.

Statements in this Report that relate to future results and events are based on the Company's current expectations. Actual results in future periods may differ materially from those currently expected or desired because of a number of risks and uncertainties. For a discussion of factors affecting the Company's business and prospects, see "Item 1 — Factors Affecting the Company's Business and Prospects."

PART I

ITEM 1 — BUSINESS

General

Dell Computer Corporation (the "Company") is the world's largest direct computer systems company, with revenue of $18.2 billion for the fiscal year ended January 29, 1999. The Company was founded in 1984 by Michael Dell on a simple concept: By selling computer systems directly to customers, the Company could most efficiently understand and satisfy the computing needs of customers. The Company offers its customers a full range of computer systems, including desktop computer systems, notebook computers, workstations and network server and storage products, as well as an extended selection of peripheral hardware and computing software. The Company's "direct model" offers in-person relationships with corporate and institutional customers, as well as telephone and Internet purchasing; build-to-order computer systems; telephone and on-line technical support and next-day, on-site product service. The Company sells its products and services to large corporate, government, medical and education customers, small-to-medium businesses and individuals.

The Company is a Delaware corporation that was incorporated in October 1987, succeeding to the business of a predecessor Texas corporation that was originally incorporated in May 1984. Based in Round Rock, Texas, the Company conducts operations worldwide through wholly owned subsidiaries. See "Item 1 — Business — Geographic Areas of Operations." Unless otherwise specified, references herein to the "Company" are references to the Company and its consolidated subsidiaries. The Company operates in one principal industry segment.

The Company's common stock, par value $.01 per share, is listed on The Nasdaq National Market under the symbol "DELL." See "Item 5 — Market for Registrant's Common Equity and Related Stockholder Matters — Market Information."

Business Strategy

The Company's business strategy is based on its direct business model. The Company's business model seeks to deliver a superior customer experience through direct, comprehensive customer relationships, cooperative research and development with technology partners, computer systems custom-built to customer specifications and service and support programs tailored to customer needs. The Company believes that the direct model provides it with several distinct competitive advantages. The direct model eliminates the need to support an extensive network of wholesale and retail dealers, thereby avoiding dealer mark-ups; avoids the higher inventory costs associated with the wholesale/retail channel and the competition for retail shelf space; and reduces the high risk of obsolescence associated with products in a rapidly changing technological market. In addition, the direct model allows the Company to maintain, monitor and update a customer database that can be used to shape future product offerings and post-sale service and support programs. This direct approach, combined with the Company's efficient procurement, manufacturing and distribution processes, allows the Company to bring relevant technology to its customers faster and more competitively priced than many of its competitors.

Comprehensive Customer Relationships

The Company develops and utilizes direct customer relationships to understand end-users' needs and to deliver high quality computer products and services tailored to meet those needs. For large corporate and institutional customers, the Company works with the customer prior to the sale to plan a strategy to meet that customer's current and future technology needs. After the sale, the Company continues the direct relationship by establishing account teams, consisting of sales, customer service and technical personnel, dedicated to the Company's large corporate and institutional customers. The Company also establishes direct relationships with small-to-medium businesses and individuals, through account representatives, telephone sales representatives or Internet contact. These direct customer relationships provide the Company with a constant flow of information about its customer's plans and requirements and enable the Company to weigh its customer's needs against emerging technologies.

Cooperative Research and Development

The Company has successfully developed cooperative, working relationships with many of the world's most advanced technology companies. Working with these companies, the Company's engineers manage quality, integrate technologies and design and manage system architecture. This cooperative approach allows the Company to determine the best method and timing for delivering new technologies to the market. The Company's goal is to quickly and efficiently deliver the latest relevant technology to its customers.

Custom-Built Computers

The direct model is based on the principal that delivering custom-built computers is the best business model for providing solutions that are truly relevant to end-user needs. This concept, together with the Company's flexible, build-to-order manufacturing process, enables the Company to achieve faster inventory turnover and reduced inventory levels and allows the Company to rapidly incorporate new technologies and components into its product offerings.

Custom-Tailored Service and Support Programs

In the same way that the Company's computer products are built-to-order, service and support programs are designed to fit specific customer requirements. The Company offers a broad range of service and support programs through its own technical personnel and its direct management of specialized service suppliers. These services range from telephone and Internet support to on-site customer-dedicated systems engineers.

The Internet

The Company is committed to refining and extending the advantages of its direct model approach by moving even greater volumes of product sales, service and support to the Internet. The Internet, perhaps the purest and most efficient form of the direct model, provides greater convenience and efficiency to customers and, in turn, to the Company. As of March 31, 1999, the Company was receiving in excess of two million visits per week to www.dell.com, where it maintains 44 country-specific sites. Company sales generated through the Internet achieved $14 million per day by the end of the fourth quarter of fiscal year 1999 and approximated 25% of revenue for that quarter.

Through the Web site, customers and potential customers can access a wide range of information about the Company's product offerings, can configure and purchase systems on-line and can access volumes of support and technical information. The Company also develops custom Internet sites, called Premier Pages[SM], for various corporate and institutional customers, allowing these customers to simplify and accelerate procurement and support processes. Through these custom sites, the Company offers the customer paperless purchase orders, approved product configurations, global pricing, real-time order tracking, purchasing history and account team information. The Company currently provides more than 15,000 Premier Pages. The Company also provides an on-line "virtual account executive" for its small business customers. And, for all customers, the Company provides a spare-parts ordering system, and a "virtual help desk" featuring natural-language search capabilities and direct access to more than 50,000 pages of technical-support data.

Subsequent to fiscal year 1999, the Company expanded its Internet presence with the launch of www.gigabuys.com, an on-line source for more than 30,000 competitively-priced computer-related products, including software and peripherals.

The Company believes that it has significant opportunities for continued growth in all parts of the world, in all customer groups and in all product categories, ranging from enterprise systems, such as network servers, high-end workstations and storage, to home PCs. While the Company believes that its business strategy provides it with competitive advantages, there are many factors that may affect the Company's business and the success of its operations.

. . .

Products and Services

The Company offers a wide range of products and services, including desktop computer systems, notebook computers, workstations and network server and storage products, as well as software, peripherals and service and support programs.

. . .

Executive Officers of the Company

The following table sets forth the name, age and position of each of the persons who were serving as executive officers of the Company as of March 31, 1999.

Name	Age	Position
Michael S. Dell	34	Chairman of the Board, Chief Executive Officer and Director
Morton L. Topfer	62	Vice Chairman
Kevin B. Rollins	46	Vice Chairman
Paul D. Bell	38	Senior Vice President, Americas Home and Small Business Group
G. Carl Everett, Jr.	48	Senior Vice President, Personal Systems Group
Jan Gesmar-Larsen	38	Senior Vice President, and President — Dell Europe, Middle East and Africa
Thomas B. Green	44	Senior Vice President, Law and Administration, and Secretary
Jerome N. Gregoire	47	Senior Vice President and Chief Information Officer
Michael D. Lambert	52	Senior Vice President, Enterprise Systems Group
John J. Legere	40	Vice President, and President — Dell Asia Pacific
Joseph A. Marengi	45	Senior Vice President, Americas Relationship Group
Keith Maxwell	50	Senior Vice President, Worldwide Operations Group
Thomas J. Meredith	48	Senior Vice President and Chief Financial Officer
Rosendo G. Parra	39	Senior Vice President, Americas Public and International Group
Charles H. Saunders	55	Vice President and President — Dell Japan
James M. Schneider	46	Senior Vice President, Finance

. . .

ITEM 3 — LEGAL PROCEEDINGS

The Company is subject to various legal proceedings and claims arising in the ordinary course of business. The Company's management does not expect that the results in any of these legal proceedings will have a material adverse effect on the Company's financial condition, results of operations or cash flows.

ITEM 4 — SUBMISSION OF MATTERS TO A VOTE OF SECURITY HOLDERS

No matter was submitted to a vote of the Company's stockholders, through the solicitation of proxies or otherwise, during the fourth quarter of fiscal year 1999.

PART II

ITEM 5 — MARKET FOR REGISTRANT'S COMMON EQUITY AND RELATED STOCKHOLDER MATTERS

Market Information

The Company's common stock is traded on The Nasdaq National Market under the symbol "DELL." Information regarding the market prices of the Company's common stock may be found in Note 13 of Notes to Consolidated Financial Statements included in "Item 8 — Financial Statements and Supplementary Data."

Holders

As of March 31, 1999, there were 26,173 holders of record of the Company's common stock.

Dividends

The Company has never paid cash dividends on its common stock. The Company intends to retain its earnings for use in its business and, therefore, does not anticipate paying any cash dividends on the common stock for at least the next 12 months.

On each of March 6, 1998, September 4, 1998 and March 5, 1999, the Company effected a two-for-one common stock split by paying a 100% stock dividend to stockholders of record as of February 27, 1998, August 28, 1998 and February 26, 1999, respectively.

Sales of Unregistered Securities

The Company has an active stock repurchase program, which is more fully described in Note 6 of Notes to Consolidated Financial Statements included in "Item 8 — Financial Statements and Supplementary Data." One element of such program is the sale of put obligations. During fiscal year 1999, the Company sold 200,000 put obligations to a financial institution and received proceeds of $1.5 million in connection with such sale. The put obligations entitle each holder to sell to the Company, by physical delivery, cash delivery or net-share settlement, at the Company's option, one share of common stock at a specified price. The put obligations expire on January 7, 2000 and have an exercise price of $40 per share. The transaction was exempt from registration under Section 4(2) of the Securities Act of 1933, as amended. The transaction was privately negotiated and the purchaser of the put options was an accredited investor and qualified institutional buyer. No public offering or public solicitation was made by the Company in the placement of these securities.

ITEM 6 — SELECTED FINANCIAL DATA

The following selected financial data should be read in conjunction with the Consolidated Financial Statements, including the related notes, and ''Item 7 — Management's Discussion and Analysis of Financial Condition and Results of Operations.''

	Fiscal Year Ended				
	January 29, 1999	February 1, 1998	February 2, 1997	January 28, 1996	January 29, 1995
	(in millions, except per share data)				
Results of Operations Data:					
Net revenue	$18,243	$12,327	$7,759	$5,296	$3,475
Gross margin	4,106	2,722	1,666	1,067	738
Operating income	2,046	1,316	714	377	249
Income before extraordinary loss	1,460	944	531	272	149
Net income	1,460	944	518	272	149
Income before extraordinary loss per common share(a)(b):					
Basic	$ 0.58	$ 0.36	$ 0.19	$ 0.09	$ 0.06
Diluted	$ 0.53	$ 0.32	$ 0.17	$ 0.08	$ 0.05
Number of weighted average shares outstanding(a):					
Basic	2,531	2,631	2,838	2,863	2,473
Diluted	2,772	2,952	3,126	3,158	3,000
Balance Sheet Data:					
Working capital	$ 2,644	$ 1,215	$1,089	$1,018	$ 718
Total assets	6,877	4,268	2,993	2,148	1,594
Long-term debt	512	17	18	113	113
Total stockholders' equity	2,321	1,293	806	973	652

(a) All share and per share information has been retroactively restated to reflect the two-for-one splits of common stock. See Note 6 of Notes to Consolidated Financial Statements.

(b) Excludes extraordinary loss of $0.01 basic per common share for fiscal year 1997.

ITEM 7 — MANAGEMENT'S DISCUSSION AND ANALYSIS OF FINANCIAL CONDITION AND RESULTS OF OPERATIONS

The Company's objective is to maximize stockholder value by executing a strategy that focuses on a balance of three priorities: growth, profitability and liquidity. The following discussion highlights the Company's performance in the context of these priorities. This discussion should be read in conjunction with the Consolidated Financial Statements, including the related notes.

Results of Operations

The following table summarizes the results of the Company's operations for each of the past three fiscal years. All percentage amounts were calculated using the underlying data in thousands.

	Fiscal Year Ended				
	January 29, 1999	Percentage Increase	February 1, 1998	Percentage Increase	February 2, 1997
	(dollars in millions)				
Net revenue	$18,243	48%	$12,327	59%	$7,759
Gross margin	4,106	51	2,722	63	1,666
Percentage of net revenue	22.5%		22.1%		21.5%
Operating expenses	$ 2,060	47	$ 1,406	48	$ 952
Percentage of net revenue	11.3%		11.4%		12.3%
Operating income	$ 2,046	56	$ 1,316	84	$ 714
Percentage of net revenue	11.2%		10.7%		9.2%
Net income	$ 1,460	55	$ 944	83	$ 518

Net Revenue

The increase in net revenue for fiscal years 1999 and 1998 was principally due to increased units sold. Unit sales grew 64% and 60% for fiscal years 1999 and 1998, respectively.

Unit sales increased across all product lines during fiscal year 1999. The Company's enterprise systems, which include servers, workstations and storage products, continued to build a substantial presence in the marketplace, with enterprise systems unit sales growing 130% during fiscal year 1999. Notebook computer unit sales increased 108%, primarily as the result of aggressive pricing actions and the launch of new products. Desktop computer systems unit sales increased 55% during fiscal year 1999. This increase was primarily attributable to the Company's aggressive market penetration of new and higher-end products.

Unit sales grew during fiscal year 1998, also the result of increased demand for the Company's products across all product lines. During fiscal year 1998, enterprise systems unit sales grew 265%, notebook computer unit sales grew 66% and desktop computer systems unit sales grew 55%, as the Company continued to introduce products utilizing the latest technology.

Average revenue per unit sold in fiscal year 1999 decreased 10% compared to fiscal year 1998, partially offsetting the effects of the increase in unit sales on consolidated net revenue. The decrease was primarily due to price reductions resulting from continued component cost declines.

Average revenue per unit sold in fiscal year 1998 remained relatively stable compared to fiscal year 1997. This was primarily due to aggressive pricing strategies in desktop computer systems, partially offset by increased unit sales in higher-end enterprise systems and higher-platform notebook computers.

The Company experienced growth in net revenue in all geographic segments in both fiscal years 1999 and 1998. The following table summarizes the Company's net revenue by geographic segment for each of the past three fiscal years:

| | Fiscal Year Ended | | | | |
	January 29, 1999	Percentage Increase	February 1, 1998	Percentage Increase	February 2, 1997
			(dollars in millions)		
Net revenue:					
Americas...................	$12,420	46%	$ 8,531	62%	$5,279
Europe....................	4,674	58	2,956	48	2,004
Asia-Pacific and Japan	1,149	37	840	77	476
Consolidated net revenue ...	$18,243		$12,327		$7,759

In the Americas segment, net revenue grew 46% and 62% in fiscal years 1999 and 1998, respectively, as the Company continued its efforts to strengthen its consumer, small-to-medium business and large corporate customer groups. In the European segment, substantially all countries experienced revenue growth in excess of 50% in fiscal years 1999 and 1998, with growth experienced across all customer groups and product lines. As a result, Europe increased net revenue 58% and 48% in fiscal years 1999 and 1998, respectively. Asia-Pacific and Japan revenues increased 37% in fiscal year 1999, compared to a 77% increase in fiscal year 1998.

Management believes that opportunity exists for continued worldwide growth by increasing the Company's market presence in its existing markets, entering new markets and pursuing additional product opportunities. The Company continues to expand its product offerings to meet a variety of customer needs. Also, the Company continues to enhance and improve the reputation, quality and breadth of all of its product lines and services. The Company is continuing its efforts to strengthen its position in enterprise systems by introducing advanced technologies to serve the growing needs for these products. As a result, the Company continues to expand its global manufacturing, sales and service facilities, completing or announcing plans for one million square feet of additional production capacity during fiscal year 1999. To accommodate this growth, the Company added a state-of-the-art manufacturing facility to its operations in Austin, Texas. The Company also added to its regional manufacturing operations in Limerick, Ireland and Xiamen, China.

Gross Margin

The increase in gross margin as a percentage of consolidated net revenue in fiscal year 1999 over fiscal year 1998 was primarily attributable to component cost declines. These component cost declines were generally passed through to customers, resulting in the aforementioned declines in average revenue per unit sold for fiscal year 1999. Also contributing to the increase in gross margin in fiscal year 1999 were overall efficiencies experienced in the Company's manufacturing operations and a continued shift in product mix to the higher-end enterprise systems and notebook computers. The mix of enterprise systems and notebook computers increased to 13% and 23% of system revenue, respectively, compared with 9% and 20%, respectively, during the prior fiscal year.

The gross margin increase as a percentage of consolidated net revenue in fiscal year 1998 from fiscal year 1997 resulted primarily from component cost declines, manufacturing efficiencies and an overall shift in mix to higher-end enterprise systems and notebook computers.

Operating Expenses

The following table presents certain information regarding the Company's operating expenses during each of the last three fiscal years:

	Fiscal Year Ended		
	January 29, 1999	February 1, 1998	February 2, 1997
	(dollars in millions)		
Operating expenses:			
Selling, general and administrative	$1,788	$1,202	$826
Percentage of net revenue	9.8%	9.8%	10.7%
Research, development and engineering	$ 272	$ 204	$126
Percentage of net revenue	1.5%	1.6%	1.6%
Total operating expenses	$2,060	$1,406	$952
Percentage of net revenue	11.3%	11.4%	12.3%

Selling, general and administrative expenses increased in absolute dollar amounts but remained flat as a percentage of consolidated net revenue for fiscal year 1999, and declined for fiscal year 1998. The increase in absolute dollars was due primarily to the Company's increase in staffing and increased infrastructure expenses, including information systems, to support the Company's continued growth. The decline in selling, general and administrative expenses as a percentage of net revenue for fiscal year 1998 resulted from significant net revenue growth.

The Company continues to invest in research, development and engineering activities to support its continued goal of improving and developing efficient procurement, manufacturing and distribution processes, and to develop and introduce new products. As a result, research, development and engineering expenses have increased each year in absolute dollars due to increased staffing levels and product development costs. The Company expects to continue to increase its research, development and engineering spending in absolute dollar amounts.

The Company believes that its ability to manage operating expenses is an important factor in its ability to remain competitive and successful. The Company will continue to invest in personnel, information systems and other infrastructure, and in research, development and engineering activities, to support its continued growth and to continue to develop new, competitive products and more efficient methods of delivery. It is the Company's goal to manage operating expenses, over time, relative to its net revenue and gross margin.

While delivering annual revenue growth of 48% and 59% in fiscal year 1999 and 1998, respectively, the Company has grown operating income by 56% in fiscal year 1999 and 84% in fiscal year 1998. This reflects the Company's ability to manage operating expenses relative to gross margin resulting in increased operating profitability.

Income Taxes

The Company's effective tax rate was 30% for fiscal year 1999 compared to 31% for fiscal year 1998 and 29% for fiscal year 1997. The differences in the effective tax rates among fiscal years result from changes in the geographical distribution of income and losses. The Company's effective tax rate is lower than the U.S. federal statutory rate of 35%, principally resulting from the Company's geographical distribution of income.

. . .

Liquidity and Capital Resources

The following table presents selected financial statistics and information for each of the past three fiscal years:

	Fiscal Year Ended		
	January 29, 1999	February 1, 1998	February 2, 1997
	(dollars in millions)		
Cash and marketable securities	$3,181	$1,844	$1,352
Working capital	2,644	1,215	1,089
Days of sales in accounts receivable	36	36	37
Days of supply in inventory	6	7	13
Days in accounts payable	54	51	54
Cash conversion cycle	(12)	(8)	(4)

During fiscal year 1999, the Company generated $2.4 billion in cash flows from operating activities, which represents the Company's principal source of cash. Cash flows from operating activities resulted primarily from the Company's net income, changes in operating working capital and income tax benefits resulting from the exercise of employee stock options.

Throughout fiscal year 1999, the Company invested a significant portion of its available cash in highly liquid investments with maturities of three months or less at date of acquisition to primarily minimize principal risk and maintain liquidity.

During fiscal year 1999, the Company continued to improve on its efficient asset management. Days of sales in accounts receivable remained flat in fiscal year 1999, while days of supply in inventory decreased one day from fiscal year 1998 to six days. This, combined with a three-day increase in days in accounts payable, resulted in an improvement in the Company's cash conversion cycle to a negative 12 days in fiscal year 1999 from a negative eight days in fiscal year 1998. The Company's return on invested capital, a key indicator of efficient asset management, increased to 195% in fiscal year 1999 from 186% in fiscal year 1998.

During fiscal year 1999, the Company repurchased 149 million shares of common stock for an aggregate cost of $1.5 billion, primarily to manage the dilution resulting from shares issued under the Company's employee stock option and purchase plans. The Company is currently authorized to repurchase up to 200 million additional shares of its outstanding common stock and anticipates that repurchases will constitute a significant use of future cash resources. At January 29, 1999, the Company held equity instrument contracts that entitle it to purchase 49 million additional shares of common stock at an average cost of $14 per share at various times through the third quarter of fiscal year 2000. For additional information regarding the Company's stock repurchase program, see Note 6 of Notes to Consolidated Financial Statements included in "Item 8 — Financial Statements and Supplementary Data."

The Company utilized $296 million in cash during fiscal year 1999 to improve and equip its manufacturing and office facilities as the Company continues to grow. Cash flows for similar capital expenditures for fiscal year 2000 are expected to be approximately $400 million.

The Company maintains master lease facilities providing the capacity to fund up to $820 million. The combined facilities provide for the ability of the Company to lease certain real property, buildings and equipment to be constructed or acquired. At January 29, 1999, $222 million of the combined facilities had been utilized.

In April 1998, the Company issued $200 million in Senior Notes and $300 million in Senior Debentures. For additional information regarding these issuances, see Note 2 of Notes to Consolidated Financial Statements included in "Item 8 — Financial Statements and Supplementary Data."

The Company maintains a $250 million revolving credit facility, which expires in June 2002. At January 29, 1999, this facility was unused.

Management believes that the Company has sufficient resources from cash provided from operations and available borrowings to support its operations and capital requirements for at least the next 12 months.

Market Risk

The Company is exposed to a variety of risks, including foreign currency exchange rate fluctuations and changes in the market value of its investments. In the normal course of business, the Company employs established policies and procedures to manage these risks.

Foreign Currency Hedging Activities

The Company's objective in managing its exposure to foreign currency exchange rate fluctuations is to reduce the impact of adverse fluctuations in earnings and cash flows associated with foreign currency exchange rate changes. Accordingly, the Company utilizes foreign currency option contracts and forward contracts to hedge its exposure on anticipated transactions and firm commitments in most of the foreign countries in which the Company operates. The principal currencies hedged during fiscal year 1999 were the British pound, Japanese yen, German mark, French franc and Canadian dollar. The Company monitors its foreign currency exchange exposures daily to ensure the overall effectiveness of its foreign currency hedge positions. However, there can be no assurance the Company's foreign currency hedging activities will substantially offset the impact of fluctuations in currency exchange rates on its results of operations and financial position.

Based on the Company's foreign currency exchange instruments outstanding at January 29, 1999, the Company estimates a maximum potential one-day loss in fair value of approximately $12 million, using a Value-at-Risk ("VAR") model. The VAR model estimates were made assuming normal market conditions and a 95% confidence level. The Company used a Monte Carlo simulation type model that valued its foreign currency instruments against a thousand randomly generated market price paths. Anticipated transactions, firm commitments, receivables and accounts payable denominated in foreign currencies were excluded from the model. The VAR model is a risk estimation tool, and as such is not intended to represent actual losses in fair value that will be incurred by the Company. Additionally, as the Company utilizes foreign currency instruments for hedging anticipated and firmly committed transactions, a loss in fair value for those instruments is generally offset by increases in the value of the underlying exposure. Foreign currency fluctuations did not have a material impact on the Company's results of operations and financial position during fiscal years 1999, 1998 and 1997.

Euro Conversion

The Company has evaluated the potential impact of the Euro conversion on the Company. The Company identified issues related to the Euro conversion, including issues related to information systems and business processes, and assessed the effect on the Company's results of operations and financial position. Also, the Company introduced www.euro.dell.com to provide the latest information on the Company's Euro initiatives, as well as to provide basic tools to assist the Company's customers in dealing with the Euro conversion. There can be no assurance that all issues related to the Euro conversion have been identified and that any issues will not have a material effect on the Company's results of operations or financial position. However, the Company believes that it has and will continue to take appropriate steps to assess and address Euro conversion issues and currently does not expect that its business will be adversely affected by such conversion in any material respect.

Marketable Securities

The fair value of the Company's investments in marketable securities at January 29, 1999, was approximately $3 billion. The Company's investment policy is to manage its marketable securities portfolio to preserve principal and liquidity while maximizing the return on the investment portfolio through the full investment of available funds. The Company diversifies the marketable securities portfolio by investing in multiple types of investment-grade securities and through the use of different investment brokers. The Company's marketable securities portfolio is primarily invested in short-term securities with at least an investment grade rating to minimize interest rate and credit risk as well as to provide for an immediate source of funds. Based on the Company's marketable securities portfolio and interest rates at January 29, 1999, a 175 basis point increase or decrease in interest rates would result in a decrease or increase of $25 million, respectively, in the fair value of the marketable securities portfolio. Changes in interest rates may affect the fair value of the marketable securities portfolio; however, such gains or losses would not be realized unless the investments are sold.

Factors Affecting the Company's Business and Prospects

There are numerous factors that affect the Company's business and the results of its operations. These factors include general economic and business conditions; the level of demand for personal computers; the level and intensity of competition in the computer industry and the pricing pressures that may result; the ability of the Company to timely and effectively manage periodic product transitions, as well as component availability; the ability of the Company to develop new products based on new or evolving technology and the market's acceptance of those products; the ability of the Company to manage its inventory levels to minimize excess inventory, declining inventory values and obsolescence; the product, customer and geographic sales mix of any particular period; the Company's ability to continue to improve its infrastructure (including personnel and systems) to keep pace with the growth in its overall business activities; and the Company's ability to ensure its products and internal systems and devices will be Year 2000 ready and to assess the Year 2000 readiness and risk to the Company of its third party providers, and implement effective contingency plans where needed. For a discussion of these and other factors affecting the Company's business and prospects, see "Item 1 — Business — Factors Affecting the Company's Business and Prospects."

Year 2000

The following disclosure is a Year 2000 readiness disclosure statement pursuant to the Year 2000 Readiness and Disclosure Act.

State of Readiness

The Company established a formal Year 2000 readiness program in February 1997. The Company's Year 2000 program consists of two separate initiatives, the Millennium Project and the Product Group Y2K Project.

The purpose of the Millennium Project is to assess the Year 2000 readiness of the Company's component and service providers and the Company's internal systems and devices. The Company identified and assessed its internal systems and devices and, where remedial steps were required to make those systems Year 2000 ready, prioritized the remedial steps to be taken. As of March 31, 1999, the Company had completed its assessment and renovation of all mission critical internal systems and devices and believes all are substantially Year 2000 ready. However, because the full ramifications of the Year 2000 issue will not be fully realized until after the Year 2000 date change, the Company can provide no assurances that its internal systems and devices will not be adversely affected by the Year 2000 date change.

The Company has also identified, through the Millennium Project, its critical component and service providers and is contacting each such vendor to assess that vendor's Year 2000 readiness. The Company has assigned each such vendor a priority rating based on the criticality of the function it provides to the Company. The Company is assessing the Year 2000 readiness of each critical vendor. Through March 31, 1999, the Company had received written responses from approximately 50% of its critical vendors, and expects to complete a review of all of its critical vendors by no later than June 30, 1999. Because the Company is relying on information provided to it by third parties to assess the Year 2000 readiness of such vendors, the Company cannot provide assurances that all of its critical vendors are or will be Year 2000 ready. Therefore, the Company cannot provide assurances that the Company will not be adversely affected by the Year 2000 date change.

Through the Product Group Y2K Project, the Company is analyzing the Year 2000 readiness status of the computer hardware manufactured by the Company, to provide an effective means of communicating the readiness status to customers, and to implement an ongoing testing and monitoring program to help enable all new Dell computer hardware offerings to meet the Company's Year 2000 readiness standards. The Company has analyzed and continues to analyze the Year 2000 status of the computer hardware manufactured by the Company. All Dell-branded hardware products shipped after January 1, 1997 meet the Company's Year 2000 readiness standards. Dell-branded hardware manufactured prior to that time can generally be updated to meet the Company's Year 2000 readiness standards through BIOS upgrades or software patches. The Company has created a Web site at www.dell.com/year2000, which contains detailed information about the Year 2000 issue, the Company's Year 2000 readiness standards and its Year 2000 program. Through the Web site, customers can assess the Year 2000 readiness of their hardware and can obtain software patches and BIOS upgrades from the Company, free of charge, to help prepare the hardware for the Year 2000 rollover. Customers without Internet access may request free copies of the software patches and BIOS upgrades by telephone or mail. The Company's Year 2000 readiness program applies only to Dell-branded hardware manufactured and Dell-branded software developed by the Company. Although the Company has attempted to ascertain the Year 2000 status of third party software and peripherals loaded on or distributed with Company computer systems, it does not and cannot guarantee the Year 2000 status of any software or peripherals provided by third parties.

Costs

The Company currently does not expect that the total costs of its Year 2000 readiness program will be material to its financial condition or results of operation. All costs are charged to expense as incurred, and do not include potential costs related to any customers or other claims or the cost of internal software and hardware replaced in the normal course of business.

Risks/Contingency Plans

The Company believes that the most likely worst case scenarios would involve the interruption of crucial suppliers as a result of infrastructure failures or third party vendor failures. As a result, the Company is developing contingency plans that will address each of the most likely worst case scenarios. Such contingency plans are expected to be completed no later than September 30, 1999. The Company believes that it is taking appropriate steps to assess and address its Year 2000 issues and currently does not expect that its business will be adversely affected by the Year 2000 issue in any material respect. Nevertheless, achieving Year 2000 readiness is dependent on many factors, some of which are not completely within the Company's control. Should either the Company's internal systems and devices or the internal systems and devices of one or more critical vendors fail to achieve Year 2000 readiness, the Company's business and its results of operations could be adversely affected.

Recently Issued Accounting Pronouncements

In June 1998, the Financial Accounting Standards Board issued Statement of Financial Accounting Standards No. 133, "Accounting for Derivative Instruments and Hedging Activities." See Note 1 of Notes to Consolidated Financial Statements included in "Item 8 — Financial Statements and Supplementary Data."

ITEM 7A — QUANTITATIVE AND QUALITATIVE DISCLOSURES ABOUT MARKET RISK

Response to this item is included in "Item 7 — Management's Discussion and Analysis of Financial Condition and Results of Operations — Market Risk."

ITEM 8 — FINANCIAL STATEMENTS AND SUPPLEMENTARY DATA

INDEX TO CONSOLIDATED FINANCIAL STATEMENTS

All other schedules are omitted because they are not applicable.

REPORT OF INDEPENDENT ACCOUNTANTS

To the Board of Directors and Stockholders of
Dell Computer Corporation

In our opinion, the consolidated financial statements listed in the accompanying index present fairly, in all material respects, the financial position of Dell Computer Corporation and its subsidiaries at January 29, 1999 and February 1, 1998, and the results of their operations and their cash flows for each of the three fiscal years in the period ended January 29, 1999, in conformity with generally accepted accounting principles. In addition, in our opinion, the financial statement schedule listed in the accompanying index, presents fairly, in all material respects, the information required to be set forth therein when read in conjunction with the consolidated financial statements. These financial statements and financial statement schedule are the responsibility of the Company's management; our responsibility is to express an opinion on these financial statements and financial statement schedule based on our audits. We conducted our audits of these statements in accordance with generally accepted auditing standards, which require that we plan and perform the audit to obtain reasonable assurance about whether the financial statements are free of material misstatement. An audit includes examining, on a test basis, evidence supporting the amounts and disclosures in the financial statements, assessing the accounting principles used and significant estimates made by management, and evaluating the overall financial statement presentation. We believe that our audits provide a reasonable basis for the opinion expressed above.

PRICEWATERHOUSECOOPERS LLP

Austin, Texas
February 16, 1999

DELL COMPUTER CORPORATION

CONSOLIDATED STATEMENT OF FINANCIAL POSITION
(in millions)

ASSETS

	January 29, 1999	February 1, 1998
Current assets:		
Cash	$ 520	$ 320
Marketable securities	2,661	1,524
Accounts receivable, net	2,094	1,486
Inventories	273	233
Other	791	349
Total current assets	6,339	3,912
Property, plant and equipment, net	523	342
Other	15	14
Total assets	$6,877	$4,268

LIABILITIES AND STOCKHOLDERS' EQUITY

	January 29, 1999	February 1, 1998
Current liabilities:		
Accounts payable	$2,397	$1,643
Accrued and other	1,298	1,054
Total current liabilities	3,695	2,697
Long-term debt	512	17
Other	349	261
Commitments and contingent liabilities	—	—
Total liabilities	4,556	2,975
Stockholders' equity:		
Preferred stock and capital in excess of $.01 par value; shares issued and outstanding: none	—	—
Common stock and capital in excess of $.01 par value; shares issued and outstanding: 2,543 and 2,575, respectively	1,781	747
Retained earnings	606	607
Other	(66)	(61)
Total stockholders' equity	2,321	1,293
Total liabilities and stockholders' equity	$6,877	$4,268

The accompanying notes are an integral part of these consolidated financial statements.

DELL COMPUTER CORPORATION

CONSOLIDATED STATEMENT OF INCOME
(in millions)

	Fiscal Year Ended		
	January 29, 1999	February 1, 1998	February 2, 1997
Net revenue	$18,243	$12,327	$7,759
Cost of revenue	14,137	9,605	6,093
Gross margin	4,106	2,722	1,666
Operating expenses:			
Selling, general and administrative	1,788	1,202	826
Research, development and engineering	272	204	126
Total operating expenses	2,060	1,406	952
Operating income	2,046	1,316	714
Financing and other	38	52	33
Income before income taxes and extraordinary loss	2,084	1,368	747
Provision for income taxes	624	424	216
Income before extraordinary loss	1,460	944	531
Extraordinary loss, net of taxes	—	—	(13)
Net income	$ 1,460	$ 944	$ 518
Basic earnings per common share (in whole dollars):			
Income before extraordinary loss	$ 0.58	$ 0.36	$ 0.19
Extraordinary loss, net of taxes	—	—	(0.01)
Earnings per common share	$ 0.58	$ 0.36	$ 0.18
Diluted earnings per common share (in whole dollars)	$ 0.53	$ 0.32	$ 0.17
Weighted average shares outstanding:			
Basic	2,531	2,631	2,838
Diluted	2,772	2,952	3,126

The accompanying notes are an integral part of these consolidated financial statements.

DELL COMPUTER CORPORATION

CONSOLIDATED STATEMENT OF CASH FLOWS
(in millions)

	Fiscal Year Ended		
	January 29, 1999	February 1, 1998	February 2, 1997
Cash flows from operating activities:			
Net income	$ 1,460	$ 944	$ 518
Adjustments to reconcile net income to net cash provided by operating activities:			
Depreciation and amortization	103	67	47
Tax benefits of employee stock plans	444	164	37
Other	11	24	29
Changes in:			
Operating working capital	367	365	622
Non-current assets and liabilities	51	28	109
Net cash provided by operating activities	2,436	1,592	1,362
Cash flows from investing activities:			
Marketable securities:			
Purchases	(16,459)	(12,305)	(9,538)
Maturities and sales	15,341	12,017	8,891
Capital expenditures	(296)	(187)	(114)
Net cash used in investing activities	(1,414)	(475)	(761)
Cash flows from financing activities:			
Purchase of common stock	(1,518)	(1,023)	(495)
Issuance of common stock under employee plans	212	88	57
Proceeds from issuance of long-term debt, net of issuance costs	494	—	—
Cash received from sale of equity options and other	—	37	—
Repurchase of 11% senior notes	—	—	(95)
Net cash used in financing activities	(812)	(898)	(533)
Effect of exchange rate changes on cash	(10)	(14)	(8)
Net increase in cash	200	205	60
Cash at beginning of period	320	115	55
Cash at end of period	$ 520	$ 320	$ 115

The accompanying notes are an integral part of these consolidated financial statements.

DELL COMPUTER CORPORATION

CONSOLIDATED STATEMENT OF STOCKHOLDERS' EQUITY
(in millions)

	Common Stock and Capital in Excess of Par Value		Retained Earnings	Other	Total
	Shares	Amount			
Balances at January 28, 1996..............	2,990	$ 430	$ 570	$(27)	$ 973
Net income.............................	—	—	518	—	518
Stock issuance under employee plans, including tax benefits	25	65	—	(18)	47
Purchase and retirement of 246 million shares	(246)	(22)	(388)	—	(410)
Purchase and reissuance of 76 million shares for employee plans and preferred stock conversion	—	—	(55)	(6)	(61)
Reclassification of put options	—	(279)	—	—	(279)
Other	—	1	2	15	18
Balances at February 2, 1997	2,769	195	647	(36)	806
Net income.............................	—	—	944	—	944
Stock issuance under employee plans, including tax benefits	84	274	—	(11)	263
Purchase and retirement of 278 million shares	(278)	(39)	(984)	—	(1,023)
Reclassification of put options	—	279	—	—	279
Other	—	38	—	(14)	24
Balances at February 1, 1998	2,575	747	607	(61)	1,293
Net income.............................	—	—	1,460	—	1,460
Stock issuance under employee plans, including tax benefits	117	1,092	—	(7)	1,085
Purchase and retirement of 149 million shares	(149)	(60)	(1,458)	—	(1,518)
Other	—	2	(3)	2	1
Balances at January 29, 1999...............	2,543	$1,781	$ 606	$(66)	$ 2,321

The accompanying notes are an integral part of these consolidated financial statements.

DELL COMPUTER CORPORATION

NOTES TO CONSOLIDATED FINANCIAL STATEMENTS

NOTE 1 — Description of Business and Summary of Significant Accounting Policies

Description of Business — Dell Computer Corporation, a Delaware corporation (including its consolidated subsidiaries, the "Company") designs, develops, manufactures, markets, services and supports a wide range of computer systems, including desktop computer systems, notebook computers and enterprise systems (includes servers, workstations and storage products), and also markets software, peripherals and service and support programs. The Company is managed on a geographic basis with those geographic segments being the Americas, Europe and Asia-Pacific and Japan regions. The Company markets and sells its computer products and services under the Dell® brand name directly to its various customer groups. These customer groups include large corporate, government, medical and education accounts, as well as small-to-medium businesses and individuals. The Company conducts operations worldwide through wholly owned subsidiaries; such operations are primarily concentrated in the North America, Europe and Asia-Pacific and Japan regions.

Fiscal Year — During fiscal year 1999, the Company changed its fiscal year from the 52 or 53 week period ending on the Sunday nearest January 31 to the Friday nearest January 31. The change in fiscal year had no material effect on the Company's consolidated financial statements.

Principles of Consolidation — The accompanying consolidated financial statements have been prepared in accordance with generally accepted accounting principles and include the accounts of the Company. All significant intercompany transactions and balances have been eliminated.

Use of Estimates — The preparation of financial statements in accordance with generally accepted accounting principles requires the use of management's estimates. These estimates are subjective in nature and involve judgements that affect the reported amounts of assets and liabilities, the disclosure of contingent assets and liabilities at fiscal year end and the reported amounts of revenues and expenses during the fiscal year. Actual results could differ from those estimates.

Marketable Securities — The Company's marketable securities are classified as available-for-sale securities and are reported at fair value. Unrealized gains and losses are reported, net of taxes, as a component of stockholders' equity. Unrealized losses are charged against income when a decline in fair value is determined to be other than temporary. The specific identification method is used to determine the cost of securities sold. Gains and losses on marketable securities are included in Financing and Other when realized. The Company accounts for highly liquid investments with maturities of three months or less at date of acquisition as marketable securities and reflects the related cash flows as investing cash flows. As a result, a significant portion of its gross marketable securities purchases, maturities and sales activity disclosed as investing cash flows is related to highly liquid investments.

Inventories — Inventories are stated at the lower of cost or market with cost being determined on a first-in, first-out basis.

Property, Plant and Equipment — Property, plant and equipment are carried at depreciated cost. Depreciation is provided using the straight-line method over the estimated economic lives of the assets, which range from 10 to 30 years for buildings and two to five years for all other assets. Leasehold improvements are amortized over the shorter of five years or the lease term.

Foreign Currency Translation — The majority of the Company's international sales are made by international subsidiaries which have the U.S. dollar as their functional currency. International subsidiaries which have the U.S. dollar as the functional currency are remeasured into U.S. dollars using current rates of exchange for monetary assets and liabilities and historical rates of exchange for nonmonetary assets. Gains and losses from remeasurement are included in Financing and

Other. The Company's subsidiaries that do not have the U.S. dollar as their functional currency translate assets and liabilities at current rates of exchange in effect at the balance sheet date. The resulting gains and losses from translation are included as a component of stockholders' equity. Items of revenue and expense for the Company's international subsidiaries are translated using the monthly average exchange rates in effect for the period in which the items occur.

Foreign Currency Hedging Instruments — The Company enters into foreign currency exchange contracts to hedge its foreign currency risks. These contracts are designated at inception as a hedge and measured for effectiveness both at inception and on an ongoing basis. Realized and unrealized gains or losses and premiums paid on foreign currency purchased option contracts that are designated and effective as hedges of probable anticipated, but not firmly committed, foreign currency transactions are deferred and recognized in income as a component of net revenue, cost of revenue and/or operating expenses in the same period as the hedged transaction. Forward contracts designated as hedges of probable anticipated or firmly committed transactions are accounted for on a mark-to-market basis, with realized and unrealized gains or losses recognized in the accompanying consolidated statement of income.

Equity Instruments Indexed to the Company's Common Stock — Proceeds received upon the sale of equity instruments and amounts paid upon the purchase of equity instruments are recorded as a component of stockholders' equity. Subsequent changes in the fair value of the equity instrument contracts are not recognized. If the contracts are ultimately settled in cash, the amount of cash paid or received is recorded as a component of stockholders' equity.

Revenue Recognition — Sales revenue is recognized at the date of shipment to customers. Provision is made for an estimate of product returns and doubtful accounts and is based on historical experience. Revenue from separately priced service and extended warranty programs is deferred and recognized over the extended warranty period.

Warranty and Other Post-sales Support Programs — The Company provides currently for the estimated costs that may be incurred under its initial warranty and other post-sales support programs.

Advertising Costs — Advertising costs are charged to expense as incurred. Advertising expenses for fiscal years 1999, 1998 and 1997 were $199 million, $137 million and $87 million, respectively.

Stock-Based Compensation — The Company applies the intrinsic value method in accounting for its stock option and employee stock purchase plans. Accordingly, no compensation expense has been recognized for options granted with an exercise price equal to market value at the date of grant or in connection with the employee stock purchase plan.

Income Taxes — The provision for income taxes is based on income before taxes as reported in the accompanying consolidated statement of income. Deferred tax assets and liabilities are determined based on the difference between the financial statement and tax basis of assets and liabilities using enacted tax rates in effect for the year in which the differences are expected to reverse.

Earnings Per Common Share — Basic earnings per share is based on the weighted effect of all common shares issued and outstanding, and is calculated by dividing net income by the weighted average shares outstanding during the period. Diluted earnings per share is calculated by dividing net income by the weighted average number of common shares used in the basic earnings per share calculation plus the number of common shares that would be issued assuming conversion of all potentially dilutive common shares outstanding. The following table sets forth the computation of basic and diluted earnings per share for each of the past three fiscal years:

| | Fiscal Year Ended | | |
	January 29, 1999	February 1, 1998	February 2, 1997
	(in millions, except per share data)		
Net income	$1,460	$ 944	$ 518
Weighted average shares outstanding:			
Basic	2,531	2,631	2,838
Employee stock options and other	241	321	288
Diluted	2,772	2,952	3,126
Earnings per common share(a):			
Basic	$ 0.58	$ 0.36	$ 0.18
Diluted	$ 0.53	$ 0.32	$ 0.17

(a) Includes extraordinary loss of $0.01 basic per common share for fiscal year 1997.

Comprehensive Income — The Company adopted Statement of Financial Accounting Standards ("SFAS") No. 130, "Reporting Comprehensive Income," in the fiscal year ended January 29, 1999. The Company's comprehensive income is comprised of net income, foreign currency translation adjustments and unrealized gains and losses on marketable securities held as available-for-sale investments. Comprehensive income of $1,459 million, $923 million and $517 million, respectively, for fiscal years 1999, 1998 and 1997, was not materially different from reported net income.

Segment Information — The Company adopted SFAS No. 131, "Disclosures about Segments of an Enterprise and Related Information," in the fiscal year ended January 29, 1999. SFAS No. 131 supersedes SFAS No. 14, "Financial Reporting for Segments of a Business Enterprise," replacing the "industry segment" approach with the "management" approach. The management approach designates the internal organization that is used by management for making operating decisions and assessing performance as the source of the Company's reportable segments. SFAS No. 131 also requires disclosures about products and services, geographic areas and major customers. The adoption of SFAS No. 131 did not affect the Company's results of operations or financial position, but did affect the disclosure of segment information as illustrated in Note 11.

Recently Issued Accounting Pronouncement — In June 1998, the Financial Accounting Standards Board ("FASB") issued SFAS No. 133, "Accounting for Derivative Instruments and Hedging Activities," which establishes accounting and reporting standards for derivative instruments and hedging activities. SFAS No. 133 requires that an entity recognize all derivatives as either assets or liabilities in the statement of financial position and measure those instruments at fair value. SFAS No. 133 is effective for all fiscal quarters of fiscal years beginning after June 15, 1999. The Company is assessing the impact of SFAS No. 133 on its consolidated financial statements.

Reclassifications — Certain prior year amounts have been reclassified to conform to the fiscal year 1999 presentation.

NOTE 2 — Financial Instruments

Disclosures About Fair Values of Financial Instruments

The fair value of marketable securities, long-term debt and related interest rate derivative instruments has been estimated based upon market quotes from brokers. The fair value of foreign currency forward contracts has been estimated using market quoted rates of foreign currencies at the applicable balance sheet date. The estimated fair value of foreign currency purchased option contracts is based on market quoted rates at the applicable balance sheet date and the Black-Scholes options pricing model. Considerable judgment is necessary in interpreting market data to develop estimates of fair value. Accordingly, the estimates presented herein are not necessarily indicative of the amounts that the Company could realize in a current market exchange. Changes in assumptions could significantly affect the estimates.

Cash, accounts receivable, accounts payable and accrued and other liabilities are reflected in the accompanying consolidated statement of financial position at fair value because of the short-term maturity of these financial instruments.

Marketable Securities

The following table summarizes by major security type the cost of the Company's holdings of marketable securities, which approximates fair value on both dates.

	January 29, 1999	February 1, 1998
	(in millions)	
Mutual funds, principally invested in debt securities	$1,298	$ 800
Preferred stock	270	172
Debt securities:		
U.S. corporate and bank debt	689	307
State and municipal securities	328	190
U.S. government and agencies	33	40
International corporate and bank debt	43	15
Total debt securities	1,093	552
Total marketable securities	$2,661	$1,524

At January 29, 1999, debt securities with a carrying amount of $831 million mature within one year; the remaining debt securities mature within five years. The Company's gross realized gains and losses on the sale of marketable securities for fiscal years 1999, 1998 and 1997, were not material.

Foreign Currency Instruments

The Company uses foreign currency purchased option contracts and forward contracts to reduce its exposure to currency fluctuations involving probable anticipated, but not firmly committed, transactions and transactions with firm foreign currency commitments. These transactions include international sales by U.S. dollar functional currency entities, foreign currency denominated purchases of certain components and intercompany shipments to certain international subsidiaries. The risk of loss associated with purchased options is limited to premium amounts paid for the option contracts. Foreign currency purchased options generally expire in 12 months or less. At January 29, 1999, the Company held purchased option contracts with a notional amount of $1 billion, a net asset value of $48 million and a combined net realized and unrealized deferred loss of $21 million. At February 1, 1998, the Company held purchased option contracts with a notional amount of $2 billion, a net asset value of $69 million and a combined net realized and unrealized deferred loss of $2 million. The risk of loss associated with forward contracts is equal to the exchange rate differential from the time the contract is entered into until the time it is settled. Transactions with firm foreign currency commitments are generally hedged using foreign currency forward contracts for periods not exceeding three months. At January 29, 1999, the Company held forward contracts with a notional amount of $1 billion, a net liability value of $24 million and a combined net realized and unrealized deferred gain of $1 million. At February 1, 1998, the Company held forward contracts with a notional amount of $800 million, a net asset value of $26 million and a net realized and unrealized deferred gain of $10 million.

Long-term Debt and Interest Rate Risk Management

In April 1998, the Company issued $200 million 6.55% fixed rate senior notes due April 15, 2008 (the "Senior Notes") and $300 million 7.10% fixed rate senior debentures due April 15, 2028 (the "Senior Debentures"). Interest on the Senior Notes and Senior Debentures is paid semi-annually. The Senior Notes and Senior Debentures are redeemable, in whole or in part, at the election of the Company for principal, any accrued interest and a redemption premium based on the present value of interest to be paid over the term of the debt agreements. The Senior Notes and Senior Debentures generally contain no restrictive covenants, other than a limitation on liens on the Company's assets and a limitation on sale-leaseback transactions.

Concurrent with the issuance of the Senior Notes and Senior Debentures, the Company entered into interest rate swap agreements converting the Company's interest rate exposure from a fixed rate to a floating rate basis to better align the associated interest rate characteristics to its cash and marketable securities portfolio. The interest rate swap agreements have an aggregate notional amount of $200 million maturing April 15, 2008 and $300 million maturing April 15, 2028. The floating rates are based on three-month London interbank offered rates ("LIBOR") plus .40% and .79% for the Senior Notes and Senior Debentures, respectively. As a result of the interest rate swap agreements, the Company's effective interest rates for the Senior Notes and Senior Debentures were 6.08% and 6.44%, respectively, for fiscal year 1999.

The Company has designated the issuance of the Senior Notes and Senior Debentures and the related interest rate swap agreements as an integrated transaction. Accordingly, the differential to be paid or received on the interest rate swap agreements is accrued and recognized as an adjustment to interest expense as interest rates change.

During fiscal year 1997, the Company repurchased $95 million of its outstanding $100 million 11% senior notes due August 15, 2000. As a result of the repurchase, the Company recorded an extraordinary loss of $13 million (net of tax benefit of $7 million).

The difference between the Company's carrying amounts and fair value of its long-term debt and related interest rate swaps was not material at January 29, 1999 and February 1, 1998.

NOTE 3 — Income Taxes

The provision for income taxes consists of the following:

	Fiscal Year Ended		
	January 29, 1999	February 1, 1998	February 2, 1997
	(in millions)		
Current:			
Domestic	$567	$362	$252
Foreign	86	41	34
Deferred	(29)	21	(70)
Provision for income taxes	$624	$424	$216

Income before income taxes and extraordinary loss included approximately $529 million, $309 million and $191 million related to foreign operations in fiscal years 1999, 1998 and 1997, respectively.

The Company has not recorded a deferred income tax liability of approximately $263 million for additional taxes that would result from the distribution of certain earnings of its foreign subsidiaries, if they were repatriated. The Company currently intends to reinvest indefinitely these undistributed earnings of its foreign subsidiaries.

The components of the Company's net deferred tax asset (included in other current assets) are as follows:

	Fiscal Year Ended		
	January 29, 1999	February 1, 1998	February 2, 1997
		(in millions)	
Deferred service contract revenue	$118	$124	$107
Inventory and warranty provisions	45	24	21
Provisions for product returns and doubtful accounts	25	20	31
Other	(51)	(62)	(26)
Net deferred tax asset.................................	$137	$106	$133

The effective tax rate differed from statutory U.S. federal income tax rate as follows:

	Fiscal Year Ended		
	January 29, 1999	February 1, 1998	February 2, 1997
U.S. federal statutory rate	35.0 %	35.0 %	35.0 %
Foreign income taxed at different rates	(7.0)%	(4.6)%	(6.2)%
Other	2.0 %	0.6 %	0.2 %
Effective tax rates.....................................	30.0 %	31.0 %	29.0 %

NOTE 4 — Financing Arrangements

The Company maintains a $250 million revolving credit facility, which expires in June 2002. At February 1, 1998, the Company had a $150 million receivables securitization facility. The receivables securitization facility was cancelled during fiscal year 1999. Commitment fees for both facilities are payable quarterly and are based on specific liquidity requirements. Commitment fees paid in fiscal years 1999, 1998 and 1997 were not material to the Company. At January 29, 1999 and February 1, 1998, these facilities were unused.

NOTE 5 — Preferred Stock

Authorized Shares — The Company has the authority to issue five million shares of preferred stock, par value $.01 per share. At January 29, 1999 and February 1, 1998, no shares of preferred stock were issued or outstanding.

Series A Junior Participating Preferred Stock — In conjunction with the distribution of Preferred Share Purchase Rights (see Note 8 — Preferred Share Purchase Rights), the Company's Board of Directors designated 200,000 shares of preferred stock as Series A Junior Participating Preferred Stock ("Junior Preferred Stock") and reserved such shares for issuance upon exercise of the Preferred Share Purchase Rights. At January 29, 1999 and February 1, 1998, no shares of Junior Preferred Stock were issued or outstanding.

. . .

Reports on Form 8-K

On December 21, 1998, the Company filed a Current Report on Form 8-K reporting a change in the fiscal year end of the Company under "Item 8 — Change in Fiscal Year." No financial statements were included in such filing.

SIGNATURES

Pursuant to the requirements of Section 13 or 15(d) of the Securities Exchange Act of 1934, the Registrant has duly caused this Report to be signed on its behalf by the undersigned, thereunto duly authorized.

DELL COMPUTER CORPORATION

By: _____ /s/ MICHAEL S. DELL _____

Michael S. Dell,
Chairman of the Board,
Chief Executive Officer
and Director

Date: April 27, 1999

Pursuant to the requirements of the Securities Exchange Act of 1934, this Report has been signed below by the following persons on behalf of the Registrant and in the capacities and on the dates indicated.

Name	Title	Date
/s/ MICHAEL S. DELL Michael S. Dell	Chairman of the Board, Chief Executive Officer (principal executive officer) and Director	April 27, 1999
/s/ DONALD J. CARTY Donald J. Carty	Director	April 27, 1999
/s/ PAUL O. HIRSCHBIEL, JR. Paul O. Hirschbiel, Jr.	Director	April 27, 1999
/s/ MICHAEL H. JORDAN Michael H. Jordan	Director	April 27, 1999
/s/ THOMAS W. LUCE, III Thomas W. Luce, III	Director	April 27, 1999
/s/ KLAUS S. LUFT Klaus S. Luft	Director	April 27, 1999
/s/ CLAUDINE B. MALONE Claudine B. Malone	Director	April 27, 1999
/s/ ALEX J. MANDL Alex J. Mandl	Director	April 27, 1999
/s/ MICHAEL A. MILES Michael A. Miles	Director	April 27, 1999
* Mary Alice Taylor	Director	
/s/ THOMAS J. MEREDITH Thomas J. Meredith	Senior Vice President and Chief Financial Officer (principal financial officer)	April 27, 1999
/s/ JAMES M. SCHNEIDER James M. Schneider	Senior Vice President — Finance (principal accounting officer)	April 27, 1999

* Ms. Taylor did not become a director of the Company until fiscal year 2000. Accordingly, Ms. Taylor did not participate in the preparation or review of this Report related to fiscal year 1999.

THE QUARTERLY FILING (FORM 10-Q)

Form 10-Q must be filed with the SEC by a publicly traded company at the end of each of the first three quarters of its fiscal year. The filing deadline is 45 days after the end of the quarter.

Form 10-Q contains only quarterly information. Just as with a company's published quarterly reports to stockholders, the quarterly financial statements contained in the 10-Q need not have been audited; they must only have been reviewed by the company's CPAs (the difference between an audit and a review is discussed in Chapter 9).

The contents of Form 10-Q are:

Part 1: Financial Information

Item 1   Quarterly financial statements.
Item 2   Management's discussion of the company's financial condition, changes that have occurred in financial condition, and the results of operations.

Part 2: Other Information

Item 1   A description of any legal proceedings in which the company is involved.
Item 2   Changes in securities.
Item 3   Defaults on senior securities.
Item 4   A discussion of matters that have been voted on by the shareholders.
Item 5   Other information.
Item 6   Exhibits and reports on Form 8-K.

Figure 10-3 contains excerpts from the May 2, 1999 10-Q report for Home Depot, Inc. (This 10-Q was obtained from the SEC Internet site http://www.FreeEDGAR.com.)

THE FILING OF SIGNIFICANT CHANGES (FORM 8-K)

Form 8-K is the form most commonly used to report any significant changes in the information the company has filed with the SEC. Filing of the 8-K must take place within 15 days of a significant change. Because the filing reports change so quickly, Form 8-K does not contain audited data. Much of the value of the Form 8-K information is its timeliness.

Examples of changes reported on Form 8-K are changes in the company's controlling ownership interest, major purchases or sales of assets, filing for bankruptcy or receivership, a change in the company's auditors, and resignations of directors.

FIG. 10-3 *Excerpts from the May 2, 1999 10-Q Report for Home Depot, Inc. obtained from the SEC Internet site.*

HOME DEPOT, INC.

Filing Type:	10-Q
Description:	Quarterly Report
Filing Date:	Jun 3, 1999
Period End:	May 2, 1999
Primary Exchange:	New York Stock Exchange
Ticker:	HD

Table of Contents
Created by FreeEDGAR.com, Inc.

10-Q

10-Q
Page 1 of 15
UNITED STATES SECURITIES AND EXCHANGE COMMISSION
WASHINGTON, D.C. 20549
FORM 10-Q

QUARTERLY REPORT PURSUANT TO SECTION 13 OR 15(d) OF THE
SECURITIES EXCHANGE ACT OF 1934

For the quarterly period ended May 2, 1999

- OR -

TRANSITION REPORT PURSUANT TO SECTION 13 OR 15(d) OF THE
SECURITIES EXCHANGE ACT OF 1934

For the transition period from   to
Commission file number 1-8207

THE HOME DEPOT, INC.

(Exact name of registrant as specified in its charter)

Delaware	95-3261426
(State or other jurisdiction of incorporation or organization)	(I.R.S. Employer Identification Number)

2455 Paces Ferry Road	Atlanta, Georgia	30339
(Address of principal executive offices)		(Zip Code)

(770) 433-8211

(Registrant's telephone number, including area code)

(Former name, former address and former fiscal year, if changed since last report.)

Indicate by check mark whether the registrant (1) has filed all reports required to be filed by Section 13 or 15(d) of the Securities Exchange Act of 1934 during the preceding 12 months (or for such shorter period that the registrant was required to file such reports), and (2) has been subject to such filing requirements for the past 90 days. Yes   X   No

APPLICABLE ONLY TO CORPORATE ISSUERS:

Indicate the number of shares outstanding of each of the issuer's classes of common stock, as of the latest practicable date.

$.05 par value 1,481,685,346 Shares, as of May 28, 1999

THE HOME DEPOT, INC. AND SUBSIDIARIES
INDEX TO FORM 10-Q

May 2, 1999

THE HOME DEPOT, INC. AND SUBSIDIARIES
CONSOLIDATED STATEMENTS OF EARNINGS
(Unaudited)

(In Millions, Except Per Share Data)	Three Months Ended	
	May 2, 1999	May 3, 1998
Net Sales	$ 8,952	$ 7,123
Cost of Merchandise Sold	6,386	5,155
Gross Profit	2,566	1,968
Operating Expenses:		
Selling and Store Operating	1,584	1,268
Pre-Opening	22	19
General and Administrative	150	121
Total Operating Expenses	1,756	1,408
Operating Income	810	560
Interest Income (Expense):		
Interest and Investment Income	3	7
Interest Expense	(8)	(11)
Interest, Net	(5)	(4)
Earnings Before Income Taxes	805	556
Income Taxes	316	219
Net Earnings	$ 489	$ 337
Weighted Average Number of Common Shares Outstanding	1,478	1,466
Basic Earnings Per Share	$ 0.33	$ 0.23
Weighted Average Number of Common Shares Outstanding Assuming Dilution	1,558	1,539
Diluted Earnings Per Share	$ 0.32	$ 0.22

See accompanying notes to consolidated condensed financial statements.

THE HOME DEPOT, INC. AND SUBSIDIARIES
CONSOLIDATED CONDENSED BALANCE SHEETS
(Unaudited)

(In Millions, Except Share Data) ASSETS	May 2, 1999	January 31, 1999
Current Assets:		
Cash and Cash Equivalents	$ 604	$ 62
Short-Term Investments	—	—
Receivables, Net	502	469
Merchandise Inventories	4,955	4,293
Other Current Assets	150	109
Total Current Assets	6,211	4,933
Property and Equipment, at cost	9,937	9,422
Less: Accumulated Depreciation and Amortization	(1,342)	(1,262)
Net Property and Equipment	8,595	8,160
Long-Term Investments	15	15
Notes Receivable	29	26
Cost in Excess of the Fair Value of Net Assets Acquired	274	268
Other	75	63
	$15,199	$13,465
LIABILITIES AND STOCKHOLDERS' EQUITY		
Current Liabilities:		
Accounts Payable	$ 2,592	$ 1,586
Accrued Salaries and Related Expenses	465	395
Sales Taxes Payable	263	176
Other Accrued Expenses	599	586
Income Taxes Payable	289	100
Current Installments of Long-Term Debt	8	14
Total Current Liabilities	4,216	2,857
Long-Term Debt, Excluding Current Installments	1,319	1,566
Other Long-Term Liabilities	238	208
Deferred Income Taxes	85	85
Minority Interest	12	9
Stockholders' Equity:		
Common Stock, Par Value $0.05.		
Authorized: 2,500,000,000 Shares;		
Issued and Outstanding—		
1,479,491,000 Shares at 5/2/99		
and 1,475,452,000 Shares at 1/31/99	74	74
Paid-in Capital	2,972	2,854
Retained Earnings	6,321	5,876
Accumulated Other Comprehensive Income	(33)	(61)
	9,334	8,743
Less Shares Purchased for Compensation Plans	(5)	(3)
Total Stockholders' Equity	9,329	8,740

See accompanying notes to consolidated condensed financial statements.

THE HOME DEPOT, INC. AND SUBSIDIARIES
CONSOLIDATED STATEMENTS OF CASH FLOWS
(Unaudited)

(In Millions)	Three Months Ended	
	May 2, 1999	May 3, 1998
Cash Provided from Operations:		
Net Earnings	$ 489	$ 337
Reconciliation of Net Earnings to Net Cash Provided by Operations:		
Depreciation and Amortization	107	87
(Increase) Decrease in Receivables, Net	(31)	74
Increase in Merchandise Inventories	(654)	(404)
Increase in Accounts Payable and Accrued Expenses	1,198	818
Increase in Income Taxes Payable	241	171
Other	(47)	(23)
Net Cash Provided by Operations	1,303	1,060
Cash Flows from Investing Activities:		
Capital Expenditures	(550)	(424)
Proceeds from Sales of Property and Equipment	19	12
Purchase of Remaining Interest in The Home Depot Canada	—	(261)
Purchases of Investments	—	(1)
Proceeds from Maturities of Investments	—	2
Repayments of Advances Secured by Real Estate, Net	(3)	3
Net Cash Used in Investing Activities	(534)	(669)
Cash Flows from Financing Activities:		
Repayments of Commercial Paper Obligations, Net	(246)	—
Principal Repayments of Long-Term Debt	(6)	(4)
Proceeds from Sale of Common Stock, Net	63	47
Cash Dividends Paid to Stockholders	(44)	(36)
Minority Interest Contributions to Partnership	5	8
Net Cash (Used in) Provided by Financing Activities	(228)	15
Effect of Exchange Rate Changes on Cash and Cash Equivalents	1	—
Increase in Cash and Cash Equivalents	542	406
Cash and Cash Equivalents at Beginning of Period	62	172

See accompanying notes to consolidated condensed financial statements.

THE HOME DEPOT, INC. AND SUBSIDIARIES
CONSOLIDATED STATEMENTS OF COMPREHENSIVE INCOME
(Unaudited)

(In Millions)	Three Months Ended	
	May 2, 1999	May 3, 1998
Net Earnings	$ 489	$ 337
Other Comprehensive Income:		
Foreign Currency Translation Adjustments	28	5

THE HOME DEPOT, INC. AND SUBSIDIARIES
NOTES TO CONSOLIDATED CONDENSED FINANCIAL STATEMENTS
(Unaudited)

1. Summary of Significant Accounting Policies:

   Basis of Presentation — The accompanying consolidated condensed financial statements have been prepared in accordance with the instructions to Form 10-Q and do not include all of the information and footnotes required by generally accepted accounting principles for complete financial statements. In the opinion of management, all adjustments (consisting of normal recurring accruals) considered necessary for a fair presentation have been included. These statements should be read in conjunction with the consolidated financial statements and notes thereto included in the Company's Annual Report on Form 10-K for the year ended January 31, 1999, as filed with the Securities and Exchange Commission (File No. 1-8207).

THE HOME DEPOT, INC. AND SUBSIDIARIES

Item 2.   MANAGEMENT'S DISCUSSION AND ANALYSIS
OF RESULTS OF OPERATIONS AND FINANCIAL CONDITION

The data below reflect selected sales data, the percentage relationship between sales and major categories in the Consolidated Statements of Earnings and the percentage change in the dollar amounts of each of the items.

	Three Months Ended		
	May 2, 1999	May 3, 1998	Percentage Increase (Decrease) in Dollar Amounts
Selected Consolidated Statements of Earnings Data			
Net Sales	100.0%	100.0%	25.7%
Gross Profit	28.7	27.6	30.4
Operating Expenses:			
Selling and Store Operating	17.7	17.8	24.9
Pre-Opening	0.2	0.2	15.8
General and Administrative	1.7	1.7	24.0
Total Operating Ex	19.6	19.7	24.7
Operating Income	9.1	7.9	44.6
Interest Income (Expense):			
Interest and Investment Income	0.0	0.1	(57.1)
Interest Expense	(0.1)	(0.2)	(27.3)
Interest, Net	(0.1)	(0.1)	25.0
Earnings Before Income Taxes	9.0	7.8	44.8

Income Taxes	3.5	3.1	44.3
Net Earnings	5.5%	4.7%	45.1
Selected Consolidated Sales Data			
Number of Transactions (000's)	185,200	156,209	18.6%
Average Sale Per Transaction	$ 47.97	$ 45.19	6.2
Weighted Average Weekly Sales Per Operating Store (000's)	$ 878	$ 854	2.8

Weighted Average Sales

THE HOME DEPOT, INC. AND SUBSIDIARIES

MANAGEMENT'S DISCUSSION AND ANALYSIS
OF RESULTS OF OPERATIONS AND FINANCIAL CONDITION
(CONTINUED)

FORWARD-LOOKING STATEMENTS

Certain written and oral statements made by The Home Depot, Inc. and subsidiaries (the "Company") or with the approval of an authorized executive officer of the Company may constitute "forward-looking statements" as defined under the Private Securities Litigation Reform Act of 1995. Words or phrases such as "should result," "are expected to," "we anticipate," "we estimate," "we project," or similar expressions are intended to identify forward-looking statements. These statements are subject to certain risks and uncertainties that could cause actual results to differ materially from the Company's historical experience and its present expectations or projections. These risks and uncertainties include, but are not limited to, unanticipated weather conditions, stability of costs and availability of sourcing channels, our ability to attract, train and retain highly qualified associates, conditions affecting the availability, acquisition, development and ownership of real estate, year 2000 problems, general economic conditions, the impact of competition and regulatory and litigation matters. Caution should be taken not to place undue reliance on any such forward-looking statements, since such statements speak only as of the date of the making of such statements. Additional information concerning these risks and uncertainties is contained in the Company's Annual Report on Form 10-K for the year ended January 31, 1999, as filed with the Securities and Exchange Commission.

RESULTS OF OPERATIONS

Sales for the first quarter of fiscal 1999 increased 25.7% to $8.952 billion from $7.123 billion for the first quarter of fiscal 1998. The sales increase for the period was primarily attributable to 141 new stores (total of 797 stores at the end of the first quarter of fiscal 1999 compared with 656 at the end of the first quarter of fiscal 1998) and a comparable store-for-store sales increase of 9% for the first quarter of fiscal 1999.

Gross profit as a percent of sales was 28.7% for the first quarter of fiscal 1999 compared with 27.6% for the first quarter of fiscal 1998. The gross profit rate increase for the period was primarily attributable to sales mix changes and to lower costs of merchandise resulting from continued product line reviews and other merchandising initiatives including direct sourcing of imports.

Total operating expenses as a percent of sales decreased to 19.6% for the first quarter of fiscal 1999 from 19.7% for the first quarter of fiscal 1998. Selling and store operating expenses as a percent of sales decreased to 17.7% for the first quarter of fiscal 1999 from 17.8% for the first quarter of fiscal 1998. Net advertising expenses decreased as a percent of sales due to increased national advertising, cost leverage achieved from opening new stores in existing markets, and higher vendor co-op

THE HOME DEPOT, INC. AND SUBSIDIARIES

MANAGEMENT'S DISCUSSION AND ANALYSIS
OF RESULTS OF OPERATIONS AND FINANCIAL CONDITION
(CONTINUED)

RESULTS OF OPERATIONS — (Continued)

advertising support. Partially offsetting this decrease were higher credit card discounts due to higher penetrations of credit sales and increases in non-private label credit card discount rates. Pre-opening expenses as a percent of sales were 0.2% for the first quarter of both fiscal 1999 and fiscal 1998. The Company opened 37 new stores and relocated 1 store during the first quarter of fiscal 1999 compared with 32 new stores opened during the first quarter of fiscal 1998. General and administrative expenses as a percent of sales were 1.7% for the first quarter of both fiscal 1999 and fiscal 1998. Certain variable G&A expenses were lower than last year as a percent of sales, which offset increased cost of staffing and investments for various growth initiatives.

Net interest expense as a percent of sales was 0.1% for the first quarter of both fiscal 1999 and fiscal 1998. As a percent of sales, interest and investment income for the first quarter of fiscal 1999 decreased to 0.0% from 0.1% for the first quarter of fiscal 1998, primarily due to lower investment balances. Interest expense as a percent of sales decreased to 0.1% for the first quarter of fiscal 1999 from 0.2% for the comparable period of fiscal 1998. The decrease was primarily attributable to leverage achieved from higher sales in fiscal 1999 and to higher capitalized interest expense during fiscal 1999.

The Company's combined federal and state effective income tax rate decreased to 39.2% for the first quarter of fiscal 1999 from 39.3% for the comparable period of fiscal 1998. During the fourth quarter of fiscal 1998, an adjustment was made to lower the annual effective tax rate to 39.2%.

Net earnings as a percent of sales increased to 5.5% for the first quarter of fiscal 1999 from 4.7% for the first quarter of fiscal 1998. The increase as a percent of sales for fiscal 1999 was primarily attributable to higher gross margin rates and lower selling and store operating expenses as described above.

Diluted earnings per share was $0.32 for the first quarter of fiscal 1999 compared to $0.22 for the first quarter of fiscal 1998.

LIQUIDITY AND CAPITAL RESOURCES

Cash flow generated from store operations provides the Company with a significant source of liquidity. Additionally, a significant portion of the Company's inventory is financed under vendor credit terms. During the first quarter of fiscal 1999, the Company opened 37 stores, relocated 1 store and temporarily closed 1 store, which will be reopened on the same site during the third quarter of fiscal 1999. During the remainder of fiscal 1999, the Company plans to open approximately 130 new stores and relocate 6 stores, for a growth rate of approximately 22%. It is currently anticipated that approximately 85% of these locations will be owned, and the remainder will be leased.

During the last three fiscal years, the Company entered into two operating lease agreements totaling $882 million for the purpose of financing construction costs of certain new stores. Under the operating lease agreements, the lessor purchases the properties, pays for the construction costs and subsequently leases the facilities to the Company. The leases provide for substantial residual value guarantees and include purchase options at original cost on each property.

THE HOME DEPOT, INC. AND SUBSIDIARIES
MANAGEMENT'S DISCUSSION AND ANALYSIS
OF RESULTS OF OPERATIONS AND FINANCIAL CONDITION
(CONTINUED)

LIQUIDITY AND CAPITAL RESOURCES — (Continued)

The Company financed a portion of new stores opened in fiscal 1997 and 1998 under the operating lease agreements and anticipates utilizing these facilities to finance selected new stores in fiscal 1999 and 2000 and an office building in fiscal 1999. In addition, some planned locations for fiscal 1999 will be leased individually, and it is expected that many locations may be obtained through the acquisition of land parcels and construction or purchase of buildings. While the cost of new stores to be constructed and owned by the Company varies widely, principally due to land costs, new store costs are currently estimated to average approximately $13.0 million per location. The cost to remodel and/or fixture stores to be leased is expected to average approximately $3.6 million per store. In addition, each new store will require approximately $3.1 million to finance inventories, net of vendor financing.

During fiscal 1996, the Company issued, through a public offering, $1.1 billion of 3.25% Convertible Subordinated Notes due October 1, 2001 (the "3.25% Notes"). The 3.25% Notes were issued at par and are convertible into shares of the Company's common stock at any time prior to maturity, unless previously redeemed by the Company, at a conversion price of $23.0417 per share, subject to adjustment under certain conditions. The 3.25% Notes may be redeemed by the Company, at any time on or after October 2, 1999, in whole or in part, at a redemption price of 100.813% of the principal amount and after October 1, 2000, at 100% of the principal amount. The Company used the net proceeds from the offering to repay outstanding commercial paper obligations, to finance a portion of the Company's capital expenditure program, including store expansions and renovations, and for general corporate purposes.

The Company has a commercial paper program that allows borrowings up to a maximum of $800 million. During the first quarter of fiscal 1999 the Company repaid $246 million outstanding under the commercial paper program and as of May 2, 1999, there were no borrowings outstanding under the program. In connection with the program, the Company has a back-up credit facility with a consortium of banks for up to $800 million. The credit facility, which expires in December 2000, contains various restrictive covenants, none of which is expected to materially impact the Company's liquidity or capital resources.

As of May 2, 1999, the Company had $604 million in cash and cash equivalents, as well as $15 million in long-term investments. Management believes that its current cash position, the proceeds from long-term investments, internally generated funds, funds available from its $800 million commercial paper program, funds available from the operating lease agreements, and the ability to obtain alternate sources of financing should enable the Company to complete its capital expenditure programs, including store openings and renovations, through the next several fiscal years.

YEAR 2000

The Company is currently addressing a universal situation commonly referred to as the "Year 2000 Problem." The Year 2000 Problem relates to the inability of certain computer software programs to properly recognize and process date-sensitive information relative to the year 2000 and beyond. During fiscal 1997, the Company developed a plan to devote the necessary resources to identify and modify internal systems impacted by the Year 2000 Problem, or implement new systems to become

THE HOME DEPOT, INC. AND SUBSIDIARIES

MANAGEMENT'S DISCUSSION AND ANALYSIS
OF RESULTS OF OPERATIONS AND FINANCIAL CONDITION
(CONTINUED)

YEAR 2000 — (Continued)

year 2000 compliant in a timely manner. This compliance plan consists of four major areas of focus: systems, desktops, facilities and supplier management. The total cost of executing this plan is estimated at $13 million, and as of May 2, 1999, the Company had expended approximately $9.6 million to effect the plan.

The Company has substantially completed the systems portion of the compliance plan. In implementing the systems portion of the plan, the Company completed an inventory of all software programs operating on its systems, identified year 2000 problems, and then created an appropriate testing environment. Additionally, as of May 2, 1999, the Company had substantially completed the final phases of the compliance plan, which involve testing and installing year 2000 compliant software in the production environment.

All desktop applications critical to the Company's overall business have been inventoried and evaluated under the method described above, and as of January 31, 1999, this process was complete. The compliance plan for desktop infrastructure was also substantially complete at the end of the first quarter of fiscal 1999.

Substantially all critical facilities systems, including, but not limited to, security systems, energy management, material handling, copiers and faxes, have been inventoried and are being tested. As of May 2, 1999, this process was over 60% complete. The Company anticipates completing the facilities systems portion of its compliance plan before the end of the second quarter of fiscal 1999.

The Company is assessing the year 2000 compliance status of its suppliers, many of which participate in electronic data interchange ("EDI") or similar programs with the Company. The Company will conduct substantial testing with EDI merchandise suppliers and transportation carriers. With respect to merchandise suppliers participating in EDI programs with the Company, the Company is conducting point-to-point testing of these EDI systems for year 2000 compliance.

The Company's risks involved with not solving the Year 2000 Problem include, but are not limited to, the following: loss of local or regional electrical power, loss of telecommunication services, delays or cancellations of merchandise shipments, manufacturing shutdowns, delays in processing customer transactions, bank errors and computer errors by suppliers. Because the Company's year 2000 compliance is dependent upon certain third parties (including infrastructure providers) also being year 2000 compliant on a timely basis, there can be no assurance that the Company's efforts will prevent a material adverse impact on its results of operations, financial condition or business.

The Company is modifying its existing disaster recovery plans to include year 2000 contingency planning. Also, the Company is identifying critical activities that would normally be conducted during the first two weeks of January 2000, which may be completed instead in December 1999. The Company expects its year 2000 contingency planning to be substantially complete by the end of the second quarter of fiscal 1999 and to test and modify contingency plans throughout the remainder of 1999.

THE HOME DEPOT, INC. AND SUBSIDIARIES
MANAGEMENT'S DISCUSSION AND ANALYSIS
OF RESULTS OF OPERATIONS AND FINANCIAL CONDITION
(CONTINUED)

IMPACT OF INFLATION AND CHANGING PRICES

Although the Company cannot accurately determine the precise effect of inflation on its operations, it does not believe inflation has had a material effect on sales or results of operations.

Item 3. QUANTITATIVE AND QUALITATIVE DISCLOSURES ABOUT MARKET RISK

The Company has not entered into any transactions using derivative financial instruments or derivative commodity instruments and believes that its exposure to market risk associated with other financial instruments (such as investments) and interest rate risk is not material.

PART II. OTHER INFORMATION

Item 4. SUBMISSION OF MATTER TO A VOTE OF SECURITY HOLDERS

During the first quarter of fiscal 1999, no matters were submitted to a vote of security holders.

Item 5. OTHER INFORMATION

On May 13, 1999, the Board of Directors appointed William S. Davila to serve as a member of the Board. Mr. Davila's term will expire at the Annual Meeting of Stockholders in 2001. Mr. Davila is the retired President and Chief Operating Officer of The Vons Companies, Inc., and he serves on the Boards of Directors of Wells Fargo Bank, Pacific Gas & Electric Corporation and Hormel Foods Corporation.

Item 6. EXHIBITS

- 3.1 Restated Certificate of Incorporation of The Home Depot, Inc., as amended
- 11.1 Computation of Basic and Diluted Earnings Per Share
- 27. Financial Data Schedule (only submitted to SEC in electronic format)

SIGNATURES

Pursuant to the requirements of the Securities Exchange Act of 1934, the Registrant has duly caused this report to be signed on its behalf by the undersigned thereunto duly authorized.

THE HOME DEPOT, INC.
(Registrant)
By: /s/ Arthur M. Blank
Arthur M. Blank
President & CEO

/s/ Marshall L. Day
Marshall L. Day
Senior Vice President
Finance & Accounting

June 2, 1999

A company required to file financial statements with the SEC must report a change in independent accountants on Form 8-K within five business days. In addition, the company must provide a copy of the 8-K to the former accountants no later than the date of filing with the SEC.

CHAPTER PERSPECTIVE

The SEC seeks to give all investors equal access to information on publicly traded companies. To accomplish this, it requires companies to file a registration statement when stock is issued and to file Form 10-K annually, Form 10-Q quarterly, and Form 8-K whenever significant changes occur in the information that companies have filed with the SEC. The registration statement and Forms 10-K and 10-Q contain financial statements prepared by the companies' accountants; Form 8-K contains information about the changes that have occurred. The accounting data in the registration statement and Form 10-K are audited, but accounting data in Forms 10-Q and 8-K are not.

Ratio Analysis

INTRODUCTION AND MAIN POINTS

Published financial statements and their accompanying notes contain a wealth of information, presented in a uniform manner, consistent from period to period, and comparable (with limitations) from company to company. This chapter introduces you to the ratios used in financial statement analysis and shows you how to use them to evaluate a company's income performance, financial position, and stock. Specific ratios are used to examine a company's liquidity, profitability, activity, and debt-to-equity proportion.

After studying the material in this chapter:

■ You will know what a ratio is and what kind of information it can give.

■ You will begin to understand how to use ratios to evaluate a company using the company's past performance in comparison to others in its industry.

■ You will know which ratios to use to examine a company's profitability.

■ You will know which ratios to use to examine a company's activity.

■ You will know which ratios to use to examine a company's liquidity.

■ You will know which ratios to use to examine a company's debt and equity levels.

RATIO ANALYSIS

To understand ratio analysis—the basic analytical technique used in financial statement analysis—you must understand what it is and how financial analysts and other financial-statement readers use it to gain insight into the content of an annual report. It is also necessary to understand that financial statement analysis—using ratios and other tools—is hard work.

There is a common misunderstanding that learning the tools of financial statement analysis immediately gives you secret knowledge or special insight into annual reports. This is not true. Ratio analysis is a valuable tool for use in understanding financial statements. But it is a tool in the way that a shovel is a tool—once you acquire the tool, hard work and diligence are required to obtain results.

WHAT ARE RATIOS?

First, what is a ratio? A *ratio* is a measure of relative size and is calculated by dividing one number into another.

A ratio can be expressed in a number of ways. All the following describe a ratio of four to three:

4 divided by 3
4/3
4:3
4 to 3
1.33

These expressions all show the ratio of four to three, but they are also the ratio of any other pair of numbers where the first is 1.33 times the second. Thus, they also are the ratio of 400 to 300, or 4 million to 3 million, or 1200 to 900, or 200 to 150, and so on. A ratio describes the relative size of two numbers or quantities but does not tell you the absolute size of the quantities being described. Each of the pairs listed (e.g., 200 to 150), expressed as a fraction, reduces to 4/3 or, divided, equals 1.33. Still, a ratio gives information about the two quantities used to generate the ratio.

Assume the ratio of weight (in pounds) to height (in feet) for Bill Jones is 45:1. Can you make judgments about Bill based only on this ratio? Would Bill be a good pick for a basketball team? Well, let's see. If Bill weighs 225 pounds, he is 5 feet tall (225/5 reduces to 45/1, or the ratio we expressed as 45:1). At 6 feet tall, Bill would have to weigh 270 pounds ($6 \times 45 = 270$) to have a weight-to-height ratio of 45:1. So Bill is probably not a good pick for a basketball team. However, he may be a great pick for a football lineman. You cannot tell for sure, because you do not know the absolute values for his weight or height, but you can begin to form judgments from the relative measure of weight to height. Bill is a better pick for a football lineman, for instance, than is Ted Jones, a boy whose weight-to-height ratio is 35:2. At 6 feet tall, Ted would weigh only 105 pounds ($35 \times 6/2 = 105$).

Ratios can be used to make assessments regarding financial statements. Assume a company has assets of $10 million and liabilities of $6 million. The ratio of assets to liabilities is therefore 5:3 (10:6 reduces to 5:3). What judgments can you make from this ratio? Is the company solvent? Yes, the company is solvent, for assets are greater than liabilities (the ratio of assets to liabilities is greater than one). But does the company have an ideal level of debt? Should the company have more debt? Less debt? Without a standard of comparison, you cannot tell. In the example above, the terms "basketball team" and "football lineman" provided a standard of reference for judging Bill and Ted. The same is true of ratio analysis for companies. If you know the ratio for assets to liabilities for the company's industry (a standard of reference) or for its major competitor (a comparison), you can make a judgment as to the desirability of an asset-to-liability ratio of 5:3.

A ratio for a company can be compared to each of the following:
1. The company's industry average or standard
2. Another company in the same industry
3. The same ratio for the company in prior years.

Composite ratios for different industries are published by Dun and Bradstreet, Standard and Poor's Corporation, Robert Morris and Associates, and the Federal Trade Commission. These references can be found in most public or college libraries. An example of industry ratios published by Robert Morris is shown in Figure 11-1.

A comparison with ratios of prior years gives a different perspective than does a comparison with ratios for the company's industry or competitors. A comparison with prior years may disclose a pattern in the company's functioning. Assume, for instance, that the ratio of assets to liabilities for a company has gone from 5:2 to 2:1 to 5:3 during the last three years. Debt is increasing—from 40 percent to 50 percent to 60 percent of total assets. Depending on other factors, this may be a cause of great concern.

Interpreting Ratios

It is important to note several points about ratios. First, financial ratios are only a starting point in analyzing a company's performance. Ratios do not give answers, but they do provide clues to what might be expected from the company's future performance. Second, ratios often give conflicting signals. For instance, on one hand, the more cash a company has, the better it is able to pay its debts. But having too much cash is bad because cash in the bank earns a limited, or no, return; the company could probably generate additional profits by investing its cash.

Income Data

Net Sales	100.0
Gross Profit	26.0
Operating Expenses	22.3
Operating Profit	3.7
All Other Expenses (Net)	1.6
Profit Before Taxes	2.1

Ratios

Current	2.2 1.7 1.4
Quick	1.5 .8 .6
Sales/Receivables	13.1 8.4 6.7
Cost of Sales/Inventory	7.8 5.5 3.7
Cost of Sales/Payables	14.7 9.2 8.2

FIG. 11-1 *Recent industry ratios and income statement data for the metal household furniture industry (published by Robert Morris and Associates).*

Finally, you should note that more than one ratio is needed to assess the financial statements in a company's annual report. Ratios are available that help in analyzing profitability, solvency, activity, and liquidity. A company's solvency ratios may be ideal, but if ratios that help analyze profitability and activity are bad (i.e., profits are down and sales are stagnant), a financial analyst would be concerned. You learn to use ratios in financial statement analysis only by diving in and doing a bit of hard work.

Additionally, financial-statement analysts use ratios for different purposes, because analysts' relationships to the company differ. For example, vendors generally have loans to the company of relatively short duration (under six months, perhaps a year); hence, they are concerned about the company's current debt-paying ability. Vendors want to know the likelihood that a company will be able to pay its obligations in the near future. On the other hand, banks, insurance companies, and pension funds, which make relatively long-term commitments ranging from one to 30 years, are concerned with the company's long-term solvency, rather than its short-term outlook. (They are concerned with the short term only because the company cannot get to the long term without surviving the short term.) Long-term creditors are interested in financial stability, overall financial strength, and earnings prospects. Their analysis is more difficult to do than that of a short-term investor.

Stockholders have the most difficult analytical task. A company can pay both its short-term debt and its long-term debt and still not earn enough to justify an investor's purchasing its common stock. Stockholders are concerned with profitability, earnings, dividends, and increases in the market price of a company's shares, in addition to liquidity and solvency.

There are five basic types of financial ratios, each of which measures a different aspect of company performance. In the remainder of this chapter, we discuss these ratios:

1. Profitability ratios
2. Activity ratios
3. Liquidity ratios
4. Cash-flow ratios
5. Overall (debt and equity) ratios

PROFITABILITY RATIOS

Profitability ratios are concerned primarily with income statement and stock performance and provide clues as to how well the company's managers are able to turn each dollar in sales into profit and support the price of the company's stock.

Profitability ratios are primarily "return on" ratios, in which some measure of profit (net income or gross margin, for example) is divided by some significant financial statement item. Profitability ratios measure some aspect of management's operating efficiency or stock performance. When measuring management's operating efficiency, the numerator of a profitability ratio is usually some measure of net income or profit, and the denominator is some aspect of management's responsibility.

Management Performance

Profitability ratios relate profit to some particular aspect of management performance, such as employing assets profitably, creating a return on owners' investment, or generating a profit on sales. Profitability ratios that measure management's performance on these three areas follow.

To measure employing assets profitability:

$$\text{return on assets} = \frac{\text{net income}}{\text{total assets}}$$

To measure the creation of a return on owners' investment:

$$\text{return on equity} = \frac{\text{net income}}{\text{owners' equity}}$$

To evaluate the profit generated on sales:

$$\text{gross profit ratio} = \frac{\text{gross profit (sales minus cost of goods sold)}}{\text{sales}}$$

$$\text{operating ratio} = \frac{\text{operating profit (sales minus operating expenses)}}{\text{sales}}$$

$$\text{return on sales} = \frac{\text{net income (sales minus all expenses)}}{\text{sales}}$$

Analysts draw conclusions based on these clues. For example, if the gross profit ratio is high while the operating ratio is low, an analyst might conclude that the company is using a high-priced promotion strategy. A high gross profit ratio indicates either high selling prices or low cost of goods sold; a low operating ratio (coupled with a high gross profit ratio) indicates high operating expenses, such as expensive advertising or promotion. However, other explanations are possible for high gross margin and low operating ratios, such as high administrative expenses, and the analyst must do a great deal more work before reaching the conclusion we did.

Stock Ratios

Another class of profitability ratios relates the earnings reported by the company to the dividend pattern established by management or to the price of the company's stock.

Dividend Ratios. Investors receive their return on investment from dividends and increases in the market value of their shares, rather than from earnings per share. The *dividend yield ratio* is the percentage of a share's market value paid annually in dividends; the *dividend payout ratio* is the percentage of common share earnings paid out in dividends.

$$\text{dividend yield} = \frac{\text{dividend per share}}{\text{market price per share}}$$

$$\text{dividend payout ratio} = \frac{\text{dividend per common share}}{\text{earnings per common share}}$$

Investors compare dividend yields to other investment opportunities but sometimes accept a lower yield if management is plowing back earnings into the company with the expectation that reinvestment will lead to increased earnings and dividends in the future. In general, high-growth companies have relatively low dividend yields and payout ratios because they reinvest cash that could otherwise be used for dividends; investors who purchase stock in such companies are not looking for dividends as much as for increases in the market price of the stock. Because these increases may or may not occur, investing in high-growth companies is generally riskier than investing in companies that pay relatively high, stable dividends.

Price Earnings Ratio. Investors expect a return on their investment through dividends and share appreciation. If investors expect that earnings and dividends will increase, they will be willing to pay a higher price for the stock. The *price earnings (PE) ratio* relates these two factors:

$$\text{price earnings (PE) ratio} = \frac{\text{common stock market price}}{\text{earning per common share}}$$

If the market prices of Lake Company and Brown Company stock are $20 and $16, respectively, and earnings per share are $4 and $2, we might conclude that the Lake Company stock is worth more (sells at a higher price) and the company is doing better (i.e., has higher earnings) than Brown Company. However, the PE ratios are:

$$\text{Lake Company } \frac{\$20}{\$4} = 5 \qquad \text{Brown Company } \frac{\$16}{\$2} = 8$$

Based on the PE ratio, stockholder expectations regarding growth in earnings and dividends will be higher for Brown Company than for Lake Company, and investors will be willing to pay relatively more for a given amount of the earnings of Brown Company than of Lake Company.

Stock ratios are important to analysts. The price earnings ratio helps an analyst decide if the stock is overpriced or underpriced in the marketplace based on the income the company is reporting. The dividend payout ratio helps an analyst determine what management is doing with the earnings produced by operations. Both ratios are important in establishing the price of the company's stock in the market.

ACTIVITY RATIOS

Activity ratios, which measure management's effectiveness in using assets, generally measure the relationship between some asset and some indicator of management's ability to employ the investment in the asset effectively.

The key to understanding activity ratios is to note that the general form of these ratios is an asset divided into the best measure of that asset's activity. The general form is:

$$\text{activity ratio} = \frac{\text{best measure of asset activity}}{\text{asset}}$$

For the asset accounts receivable, the best measure of asset activity is sales. The less money management is forced to tie up in uncollected accounts for a given volume of sales, the better. Assume, for example, that for annual sales of $1 million, management has $500,000 in accounts receivable at the end of the year. Management's performance would be improved if more sales dollars could be collected and accounts receivable reduced to $100,000.

Activity ratios are usually referred to as turnover ratios. Accounts receivable of $100,000 is said to have turned over ten times if annual sales are $1 million. For a company that does credit business, all sales go through accounts receivable. If sales pass through accounts receivable $100,000 at a time (the average balance), accounts receivable "turn over" ten times. The activity ratio *"accounts receivable (AR) turnover"* is:

$$\text{AR turnover} = \frac{\text{sales}}{\text{accounts receivable}}$$

In this example, the turnover ratio is calculated as $1 million divided by $100,000, or ten. When the turnover of accounts receivable is known, the average collection period (average time funds are tied up in the asset) can be calculated. If accounts receivable turn over 10 times in a 360-day year (a banker's year), the average collection period is 360 divided by ten, or 36 days.

$$\text{average turnover period} = \frac{360}{\text{asset turnover}}$$

This relationship can also be used to calculate the number of days funds are tied up in any other asset once the asset turnover is known. (The number of days funds are invested in inventory is frequently of interest to financial analysts.)

Other common activity or turnover ratios are these:

$$\text{inventory turnover} = \frac{\text{cost of goods sold}}{\text{inventory}}$$

$$\text{fixed assets turnover} = \frac{\text{sales}}{\text{fixed assets}}$$

$$\text{total asset turnover} = \frac{\text{sales}}{\text{total assets}}$$

The DuPont Method

Frequently the return on sales ratio is combined with the asset turnover ratio so that the components of the return on assets profitability ratio can be studied. The combination of these equations is called the DuPont method of financial analysis.

Return on Sales × Asset Turnover = Return on Assets

$$\frac{\text{net income}}{\text{sales}} \times \frac{\text{sales}}{\text{assets}} \times \frac{\text{net income}}{\text{assets}}$$

Depending on the firm and the industry, a company may stress either the return (or margin) on sales or the turnover and still generate the same return on assets. Imagine two car dealerships: a large dealership with high turnover and low prices and a small dealership with low turnover and high prices. Both might generate the same return on total assets:

Return on Sales × Asset Turnover = Return on Assets

| large dealership: | .05 | × | 6 | = | .30 |
| small dealership: | .15 | × | 2 | = | .30 |

LIQUIDITY RATIOS

Liquidity is a measure of a company's ability to pay its short-term debts. High liquidity is evidenced by high current assets relative to current liabilities and by a high proportion of current assets in cash and receivables (as opposed to inventory or prepaid expenses). (Current assets, remember, are short-term assets that either are cash or will become cash in one year. Examples are receivables that will be collected in 90 days or inventory on hand that will be sold in the next quarter. Current liabilities are short-term debts that must be paid in one year or less. Any part of a long-term debt which comes due in the next year is also a current liability. Accounts payable or next year's installment on a 40-year mortgage are examples of current liabilities.)

Working capital—the difference between current assets and current liabilities—is a crude measure of liquidity; a decrease in working capital is not always a sign of decreased liquidity. Working capital is a dollar amount, not a ratio, and is difficult to evaluate in the absence of additional information on the company's activities.

$$\text{working capital} = \text{current assets} - \text{current liabilities}$$

Big Company and Little Company, according to the figures below, both have the same dollar amount of working capital, but Big Company obviously has less of a safety buffer available to pay its short-term debts (current liabilities) than does Little Company. The fact that both companies have $5,000 in working capital, by itself, means little.

	Current Assets	Current Liabilities	Working Capital
Big Company	$25,000	$20,000	$5,000
Little Company	$10,000	$ 5,000	$5,000

Because different accounting methods (such as LIFO or FIFO) result in differing inventory amounts on the balance sheet, comparisons of working capital liquidity measures between companies are not valid. The use of different inventory cost-flow assumptions also affects intercompany comparisons of the current ratio (discussed below). This changes the focus to trend analysis for individual companies rather than direct comparisons among companies.

There are only two liquidity ratios in common use, the *current ratio* and the *quick ratio*. Both of these ratios are designed to evaluate the company's ability to pay its short-term obligations.

Current Ratio

The current ratio is simply the relationship between current assets and current liabilities.

$$\text{current ratio} = \frac{\text{current assets}}{\text{current liabilities}}$$

The difference in liquidity between Big Company and Little Company (see previous section) is evident when we calculate the current ratios for these two companies. By expressing the relative sizes of current assets and liabilities, the current ratio shows that Big Company clearly has a smaller safety buffer available to pay its short-term debts than does Little Company.

	Current Assets	Current Liabilities	Current Ratio
Big Company	$25,000	$20,000	1.25
Little Company	$10,000	$ 5,000	2

Quick Ratio

One major problem that arises with the quick or acid-test ratio (as with any ratio) is composition. The use of broad-based totals (e.g., current assets and current liabilities) masks information about individual account components (e.g., cash and receivables) and fails to disclose vital information, such as how soon the current assets can be converted into cash and used to pay current liabilities or how soon the current liabilities are due for payment. The financial-statement analyst obtains a general idea of the potential magnitude of the composition problem by reviewing the balance sheet to see the extent to which current assets are composed of relatively liquid items.

The quick ratio is current assets minus inventory divided by current liabilities.

$$\text{quick ratio} = \frac{\text{current assets} - \text{inventory}}{\text{current liabilities}}$$

In the quick ratio, inventory is removed from current assets because inventory is usually not directly convertible to cash. Generally, inventory is sold to create an account receivable; the receivable must be collected before cash is available to pay short-term creditors.

The rule of thumb for the current ratio is 2:1 and for the quick ratio is 1:1. These rules of thumb are often cited but are, in fact, quite useless. To have meaning, a ratio must either be compared to that for other companies in the same industry or be viewed as part of a trend for a particular company. An analyst must ask questions: Is the company's liquidity (current ratio) increasing or decreasing? Are any changes appropriate for the economic climate in the company's industry?

CASH-FLOW RATIOS

The amount of cash generated by a company's operations is as important as its reported net income. The choice of accounting methods, the timing of certain activities, and improper manipulation by management can increase a company's net income but have no effect on its cash flows. Analysts judge the quality of a company's earnings by the extent to which earnings is accompanied by cash flow. Earnings that are not accompanied by cash flows (e.g., earnings much higher than cash flow from operations) are thought to be of low quality. Earnings accompanied by an equal or greater amount of cash flow are thought to be of high quality.

Analysts have developed three ratios that help to assess a company's cash flow relative to its earnings.[1] All three ratios address two fundamental questions:

1. How much cash flow is embedded in reported earnings?
2. Do the two measures move in the same direction?

$$\text{cash return on sales} = \frac{\text{cash flow from operations}}{\text{sales}}$$

$$\text{cash flow to net income} = \frac{\text{cash flow from operations}}{\text{net income}}$$

$$\text{free cash flow} = \frac{\text{cash flow from operations minus capital expenditures}}{\text{net income}}$$

Cash return on sales and the cash flow to net income ratio help analysts determine if the company's sales and earnings are matched by appropriate cash flows. The free cash-flow ratio tells analysts how much cash (relative to earnings) is available to support future earnings after the year's capital expenditures are made. These measures help investors determine the quality of the company's earnings.

OVERALL (DEBT AND EQUITY) RATIOS

Overall (debt and equity) ratios are sometimes called solvency ratios. While liquidity ratios assist analysts in examining a company's short-term debt-paying ability, overall or solvency ratios assist the analyst in determining the relative size of the claims of long-term creditors compared to the claims or property rights of owners.

The existence of too much long-term debt places restrictions on management and increases risk to stockholders, because large amounts of long-term debt increase the fixed charges against income

---

[1]For discussion of ratios used to analyze cash flows, see Lloyd Brant, Jr., Joseph R. Danos, and J. Herman Brasseaux, "Financial Statement Analysis: Benefits and Pitfalls" (Part Two), *The Practical Accountant,* June 1989, pp. 69–78.

in each reporting period. The times-interest-earned and the fixed-charge-coverage ratios described below assist analysts in evaluating the burden of fixed interest and other periodic charges, such as lease payments. These ratios are similar to the rules of thumb that say a consumer's house payment, or house and car payments, should not exceed a certain percent of the consumer's income. The proportion of company income that should be used to meet interest and other fixed charges, however, varies from industry to industry.

Another effect of high levels of long-term debt is added risk to creditors. As levels of long-term debt rise, creditors are reluctant to continue to loan the company money; eventually, funds will no longer be available or will be available only at very high interest rates.

The more common ratios used to evaluate a company's solvency or overall debt and equity position are these:

$$\text{times-interest-earned} = \frac{\text{earnings before interest and taxes}}{\text{interest expense}}$$

$$\text{fixed-charge-coverage} = \frac{\text{earnings before interest and taxes}}{\text{interest expense} + \text{lease payments}}$$

$$\text{debt-to-total-assets} = \frac{\text{debt}}{\text{total assets}}$$

$$\text{debt-to-total-equity} = \frac{\text{debt}}{\text{total liabilities} + \text{stockholders' equity}}$$

$$\text{debt-to-stockholders'-equity} = \frac{\text{debt}}{\text{stockholders' equity}}$$

How Much Is Too Much Debt?

Because too much long-term debt can be bad because of its claim on a company's earnings, readers of annual reports may have a bias against long-term debt. But companies do not borrow without the desires of stockholders in mind; quite the contrary. Managers use long-term debt to increase returns to common stockholders through financial leverage (see Chapter 12). Long-term debt is not of itself bad, any more than using a mortgage to purchase a home is bad. The danger in both instances is in an excessive level of total indebtedness and the burden imposed by the resulting fixed payments.

CHAPTER PERSPECTIVE

This chapter has discussed ratios, what they are, and how they are used. Ratios express only the relative size of two amounts; from a ratio alone, we cannot tell how large either of the amounts is. A single ratio is of little use; ratios should be used in combinations. The DuPont system of financial analysis is an example of the use of several ratios in combination to analyze the source of a company's return of investment. Wise judgments can be made only when several ratios are used to evaluate relationships.

Ratios are used to examine four different areas of company performance and financial condition: liquidity, profitability, activity, and overall debt to owners' equity. The next chapter continues our discussion and adds to our arsenal of financial statement analysis techniques.

Analyzing Financial Statements

INTRODUCTION AND MAIN POINTS

Chapter 11 introduced the ratios most commonly used in financial-statement analysis. This chapter introduces more tools used in the analysis and interpretation of financial statements.

After studying the material in this chapter:

■ You will know how to analyze financial statements using common size statements.

■ You will know how to analyze financial statements using trend analysis and comparative statements.

■ You will understand how a company can use operating leverage and will know the risks involved.

■ You will understand how a company can use financial leverage and will know the risks involved.

■ You will understand why a calculated ratio is neither good nor bad; its value depends on circumstances.

■ You will see how the information contained in the statement footnotes can help in financial statement analysis.

MAKING JUDGMENTS ABOUT THE FUTURE

The principal purpose of financial analysis is to form judgments about the future: Will the company be able to repay a loan or increase dividends? Will its income grow? Is the debt level likely to rise? To fall? Is the market price of the stock too high or too low? Some amounts listed in financial statements reflect management's expectations; the allowance for doubtful accounts is an example. For the most part, however, the financial statement analyst works with historical information and assumes, unless there is other information to the contrary, that historical trends will continue.

Still, a company may be hurt by some event it cannot control: A competitor may bring out an improved product, a strike may paralyze production, or a major product may become obsolete. Financial analysts watch for developments that indicate that the future will not be like the past. Because good management is critical to success, one of the major questions that the financial analyst seeks to answer is whether the managers are running the company efficiently and effectively.

Financial-statement analysis focuses not only on financial and quantitative information but on nonfinancial and qualitative information as well. Other sources of information that assist in financial-statement analysis are the financial press (for example, *The Wall Street Journal*), reports to the Securities and Exchange Commission, and business service publications such as *Value Line* and *Dun & Bradstreet.*

COMMON-SIZE STATEMENTS

Financial analysts sometimes use a variation of ratio analysis, called *common-size statements,* that looks at all the financial statement components. This method presents every item in a statement as a percentage of the largest item in the statement. The procedure may sound confusing but in fact common-size statements are quite useful and easy to understand.

Both the income statement and the balance sheet can be converted to common size statements.

Income Statement

The largest item in the income statement is sales; therefore, when the income statement is converted to a common size statement, all items in the income statement are expressed as percentages of sales. For instance, if cost of goods sold is 40 percent of sales, gross profit is then 60 percent of sales. An illustration of a simple income statement converted to a common size statement is shown below.

INCOME STATEMENT

	Dollar Amounts	Common Size
Sales Percent	$200,000	100
Cost of Goods Sold	80,000	40
Gross Profit	120,000	60
Selling Expense	30,000	15
Administrative Expense	50,000	25
Operating Profit	40,000	20
Income Taxes	20,000	10
Net Income	$ 20,000	10

Balance Sheet

The largest item in the balance sheet is total assets or total equities; when a balance sheet is converted to a common-size format, all components are expressed as percentages of total assets or total equities. For instance, current assets may be 40 percent of total assets; bonds payable may be 30 percent of total equities. (Remember that total assets and total equities are equal. Either may be used.) An illustration of a simple balance sheet converted to common size is shown below.

BALANCE SHEET

	Assets Dollar Amounts	Common Size Percent Amounts
Current assets:		
Cash	$ 50,000	10
Accounts receivable	75,000	15
Inventories	75,000	15
Total Current Assets	200,000	40
Plant, property, and equipment		
(net of depreciation)	250,000	50
Investment	50,000	10
Total Assets	$500,000	100

	Equities Dollar Amounts	Common Size Percent Amounts
Current liabilities:		
Accounts payable	$ 75,000	15
Notes payable	25,000	5
Total Current Liabilities	100,000	20
Long-term liabilities:		
Bonds payable	150,000	30
Mortgage payable	50,000	10
Total Long-term liabilities	200,000	40
Stockholders' equity:		
Common stock	150,000	30
Retained earnings	50,000	10
Total Stockholders' Equity	200,000	40
Total Equities	$500,000	100

Side-by-Side Analysis

Common-size statements highlight the relationship of all the statement components and are especially useful when comparing the company's performance for two years side by side or when comparing two companies of different size.

When two years' figures for the same company are being examined in common-size form, changes in the relative size of the components are readily apparent to the analyst—changes that might have been missed by examining the absolute dollar amounts. For example, if sales have increased, an analyst might not notice that gross profit has decreased by several percentage points or that selling costs have risen sharply as a percent of sales dollars. When the two years are converted to common-size statements, both of those changes become obvious.

Analyzing the financial statements of two companies of different size is more confusing than analyzing two years' statements of the same company. Large differences in the dollar amounts for various expense items tend to camouflage differences in the relationship of the income statement components, and large differences in the proportion of the sales dollars spent on administrative expenses or debt service may go unnoticed if the statements are not converted to a common-size format.

HORIZONTAL ANALYSIS

A frequently used variation of common-size statements is constructed by using the financial statements of some prior year as the base and expressing the components of a future year as percentages of each component in the base year. This is called *horizontal common-size* or *horizontal analysis* because it deals with the changes in financial statements from period to period. This analysis answers questions such as: Are sales, gross profit, expenses, and net income increasing or decreasing over time? What was the change in sales from last year? Has cash increased or decreased over the last two years?

Trend Analysis

Trend analysis is a type of horizontal analysis in which a base year is selected and comparisons are made to the base year by the use of percentages. Sometimes the dollar change from one period to the next period in a particular account is not sufficient by itself to make an informed decision regarding that account; trend analysis can be useful in comparing financial statements over several time periods because it discloses changes occurring over time and it can provide information as to the direction in which a company is moving.

For instance, suppose advertising in the base year was $10,000 and advertising in the next three years was $11,000, $12,000 and $20,000, respectively. Expressed in horizontal common size as a percentage of the base year amount of $10,000, a trend analysis in advertising appears as:

	Year 4	Year 3	Year 2	Year 1
Dollar Amount	$20,000	$12,000	$11,000	$10,000
Common-Size Amount	200%	120%	110%	100%

The jump to 200 percent in year 4 appears significant—something that might warrant additional study. But the large percentage increase may be misleading—what if advertising is a $20,000 expense for a company with total expenses of $800,000? In such case, the small dollar amount involved—while representing a large percentage increase—may be immaterial, and investigation is therefore a waste of time.

Comparative Statements

Developing comparative statements—a form of horizontal analysis using financial statements for two years—shows the dollar and percentage change from year to year. (A two-year analysis of the current assets section of the balance sheets of the Snow Company is shown in Figure 12-1.) This analysis requires two steps. First, you must compute the dollar amount of the change from the base year (the year against which you are making the comparison); second, you must divide the dollar amount of the change by the base-year amount.

Horizontal analysis allows us to study the changes in accounts year by year, examining both the absolute amount of the change and its relative (percentage) amount. Note in our example that Snow's largest percentage increase is for prepaid expenses (100 percent) but that the absolute dollar amount of the change in prepaid expenses is not significant. Percentage changes must be viewed from the perspective of the item's relative dollar value significance.

Increase (Decrease) 2000 over 1999 Assets	2000	1999	Amount	Percent
Current assets:				
Cash	$ 32,000	$ 38,000	$ (6,000)	(15.8)
Accounts receivable, net	123,000	153,000	(30,000)	(19.6)
Inventories	94,000	81,000	13,000	16.0
Prepaid expenses	600	300	300	100.0
Total current assets	249,600	272,300	(22,700)	(8.3)

FIG. 12-1 *Snow Company comparative balance sheets December 31, 1999 and 2000*

LEVERAGE

Leverage is frequently a subject for physics courses. When a lever is properly placed across a fulcrum, downward pressure on the handle results in a greatly magnified upward force on the other end; ten pounds of downward pressure may be sufficient to lift a hundred-pound weight, enabling a small child to lift a large boulder. When a child lifts a rock with a lever, leverage gives the child a mechanical advantage.

Business managers use leverage to increase the profitability of a business to its owners. Business managers may employ two kinds of leverage: operational leverage and financial leverage. Both are very similar in principle to a child lifting a rock with a lever.

Operating Leverage

A company uses operating leverage to its advantage by balancing the type of costs in its operations. Assume a company manufactures a product that it sells for $10. The labor and raw material costs for each unit of product total $8. (Labor and raw materials are called variable costs because the total amount of these costs varies directly with the number of units produced. Each additional unit produced causes more labor and raw material costs to be incurred.)

Because the company uses a lot of labor, it can manufacture the product with nonvariable or fixed costs (largely related to machinery) of only $20,000 per year. Total fixed costs do not vary when additional units are produced; producing additional units does not, for example, increase the cost of a leased machine. The $20,000 fixed cost remains the same regardless of the number of units produced. With this balance of fixed costs and variable costs, each unit of product contributes $2 to covering the fixed cost of machinery and building profits. For each unit:

Selling price	$10
Labor and Raw Material	8
Contribution per unit	$ 2

Assume now that the company's managers decide to automate several previously manual operations. The annual fixed machinery cost increases to $50,000 and the cost of labor and raw materials per unit decreases to $6. Now each unit contributes $4 to covering fixed charges and building profit.

Selling price	$10
Labor and Raw Material	6
Contribution per unit	$ 4

Leverage increases the impact of a change in sales volume on the company profits. Let us consider the contribution to profits of a 1,000-unit increase in sales.

Manual Operation		Automated Operation	
Selling price	$10	Selling price	$10
Labor and		Labor and	
Raw Material	8	Raw Material	6
Contribution per unit	$ 2	Contribution per unit	$ 4
Increased units	× 1,000	Increased units	× 1,000
Contribution	$ 2,000	Contribution	$ 4,000

Changing the variable labor cost of operations to a fixed machinery cost has increased the contribution of sales of 1,000 units from $2,000 to $4,000. The automation has "leveraged" the effect of a sales increase on company profit.

Increased Risk. Despite its beneficial effect, operating leverage can also have a downside. For instance, assume that instead of a 1,000-unit increase in sales, the company has a 1,000-unit decrease in sales volume. The effect in terms of dollar amount is still the same, but now the $2,000 and $4,000 changes in contribution are decreases rather than increases.

A highly leveraged company has greater fluctuations in profits than a company with low operating leverage. A low leveraged, manual operation does not benefit as much from increases in sales, but neither does it suffer as much from declines. Profits, by and large, remain fairly stable. An automated, highly leveraged company, in contrast, benefits greatly from sales increases and suffers greatly from sales decreases. The contribution lost or gained will be greater, and the pattern of profits less stable.

Higher Breakeven Sales. Another warning about highly leveraged firms: The breakeven sales point for a highly leveraged company is higher than the breakeven point for a less leveraged company. In the example above, for instance, the company has to cover annual fixed charges of $50,000 after automating, but only $20,000 before. Breakeven points for both operating structures are shown below.

Manual operation:
$$\frac{\$20,000 \text{ fixed cost breakeven point}}{\$2 \text{ per unit contribution}} = 10,000 \text{ unit breakeven point}$$

Automated operation:
$$\frac{\$50,000 \text{ fixed cost breakeven point}}{\$4 \text{ per unit contribution}} = 12,500 \text{ unit breakeven point}$$

In summary, operating leverage can improve a company's profits for a given level of sales—but to receive this benefit the company must endure the risk associated with an unstable profit pattern and an increased breakeven sales level.

Financial Leverage

Financial leverage is used to increase the return to owners. The idea is very simple. Assume that investors are forming a company that requires an investment in assets of $100,000. The company is expected to produce earnings of $15,000 per year. If owners supply the entire $100,000, the return on owners' equity will be 15 percent ($15,000/$100,000).

Now assume instead that owners wish to leverage their investment by borrowing half of the $100,000 required to start the business. Funds are available at 12 percent interest. If owners follow this route, investing $50,000 and borrowing $50,000 at 12 percent interest, earnings will be reduced by the $6,000 interest on the borrowed funds ($50,000 × .12) and earnings will be only $9,000. But even these lower earnings will increase the return on owners' equity to 18 percent ($9,000/$50,000).

Increased Risk. All companies use financial leverage to some extent. There is a great body of scholarly thought on what proportion of a company's funding should come from debt and what proportion from owners. Too much debt increases business risk, which in turn leads to higher interest rates on borrowed funds.

When interest rates are high—or returns on assets are low—financial leverage may work against owners. Assume, for instance, that the owners in the illustration above attempt to use financial leverage by borrowing $50,000 but that interest rates rise to 20 percent. If the business does as expected and earns $15,000 before interest, the profit after an interest expense of $10,000 ($50,000 × .20) will be only $5,000 and the return on owners' equity will be only 10 percent ($5,000/$50,000).

Alternatively, assume that owners use financial leverage, borrowing funds as planned at 15 percent, but conditions change and the company earns only $10,000 before paying the interest charges. After paying the $6,000 interest on the debt, profits will be only $4,000 and the return on owners' equity will be only 8 percent ($4,000/$50,000). If owners had not borrowed at all, the return on owners' equity would have been 10 percent ($10,000/$100,000).

Quite simply, if a firm borrows at an interest rate less than the return on assets, the return on owners' equity will be increased. If a firm borrows at a rate greater than the return on assets, the return on owners' equity is reduced. If the rates are equal, the percent return on owners' equity is not affected.

Firms such as public utilities that have relatively stable revenues and expenses can use considerable financial and operating leverage. Leverage is very risky, however, for companies in cyclical businesses such as automobile manufacturing and construction, in which sales fluctuate greatly from year to year. Several consecutive years of low sales can bring a heavily leveraged firm to bankruptcy.

Measuring Leverage

Both operational and financial leverage can be used to benefit stockholders because they maximize the benefit obtained from growth—but both may also maximize the damage that occurs when business conditions sour.

The extent to which a company uses financial leverage can be determined by examining a company's debt structure and profit pattern. Because companies list their costs by function and not by behavior, it is very difficult to measure operating leverage directly. An understanding of operating leverage may be most useful when analyzing investment or other opportunities in industries that differ in their degree of automation or operating leverage. Machinery manufacturing is, for example, more highly leveraged than the restaurant business. An investor wishing to receive the benefits of operating leverage would invest in machinery manufacturing rather than in a restaurant chain.

THE PARADOX IN INTERPRETING RATIOS

Ratios do not always mean what appears obvious at first glance. For instance, a high accounts-receivable turnover generally means that receivables are collected rapidly. Reducing the sales dollars tied up in accounts receivable results in more dollars available for other purposes. On the other hand, a decrease in accounts-receivable turnover (and an increase in days' sales in accounts receivables) suggests that the firm is becoming less efficient in collecting its accounts. Other things being equal, the faster customers pay, the better. All these are reasonable conclusions an analyst might draw.

However, a high turnover ratio might also indicate that credit policies are too strict. Strict credit policies can drive away customers, reduce sales, and damage profitability. There are tradeoffs: If the firm loses sales because of tight credit policies, the advantage of faster collection may be more than offset by the loss of profits due to lower total sales.

A similar analysis can be used with inventories. Inventory turnover is important because the quicker the inventory is sold, the quicker the company converts its investment back to cash. Slow inventory turnover may result in obsolete goods and excess storage costs. On the other hand, if investment turnover is too high, it may indicate that the company does not carry enough inventory to support its sales—stockouts may occur and customers may be lost. Consequently, a company cannot seek continually to increase its inventory turnover ratio but instead must strive to maintain the most profitable ratio, given its sales level, costs of carrying inventory, and risk of experiencing stock-outs.

ADDITIONAL INFORMATION

As we saw in Chapter 2, an annual report contains more than just the financial statements. A thorough understanding of the financial statements requires the analyst to study the information contained in the rest of the annual report. Supplemental schedules and other information are contained in the notes to the financial statements. This section includes disclosures such as the summary of significant accounting policies followed by the company (including inventory and depreciation methods); types of inventory and plant and equipment; information about long-term debt, profit-sharing, and pension plans; litigation involving the company; and research and development project expenditures.

Some annual reports include management's discussion and analysis of financial condition and results of operation. This discussion includes summarized income statement and balance sheet data for the last three years and addresses the company's financial condition and results of operations. It also includes specific information on liquidity, capital resources, and events or uncertainties that might cause future operating results or financial conditions to diverge from those that have prevailed historically.

CHAPTER PERSPECTIVE

This chapter emphasized that judgments can be made only when several ratios are used to evaluate several different relationships and those ratios are compared either to the trend of ratios in prior years or to standard ratios for the industry in which the company operates. It introduced common-size statements, which help the analyst examine all the elements of the financial statements as ratios and perform trend and comparative analysis. We have seen that footnotes can contain information affecting the company's future and the analyst's judgment, and that a calculated ratio is neither good nor bad but depends on circumstances.

Finally, the chapter discussed financial and operating leverage and the ways they can increase a company's profitability and return to owners. We have seen how both techniques, while potentially beneficial, can be dangerous because of the risks they carry.

Working with Budgets

INTRODUCTION AND MAIN POINTS

Although they may not realize it, most people budget to some extent in their daily affairs. We make estimates of the income necessary to cover expenditures such as food, clothing, and housing and limit our expenditures to the income earned in a stipulated time period. Our budget serves as both a planning and a control device in that we plan expenditures on the basis of our estimate of income and control spending in accordance with the plan. An intuitive, personal budget performs the same function for the average person as a formal budget does for a large company.

A budget is management's action plan for the future. Budgets may be for short periods of time, perhaps one quarter, or may extend over several years. Companies spend considerable time and resources establishing a budget because, once completed, the budget is one of the most important management tools used to accomplish the company's goals. The budget is management's formal plan outlining the anticipated results of financial transactions for the forthcoming budget period. It both helps management coordinate and plan the various functional activities (such as production and sales) of the company and, during the budget period, acts as a control device by helping management measure actual performance against planned performance. Deviations from plan can be isolated and action taken to improve future performance.

Because many companies are interested in achieving a desired level of profits, budgeting is sometimes called profit planning. Essentially, profit planning is accomplished through the preparation of a number of integrated individual budgets, resulting in what is known as the master budget.

After reading and studying this chapter:

■ You will understand the definition of budgeting.
■ You will understand the role of the budget as a planning and coordinating device.

■ You will understand the types of budgets.

■ You will understand the major components of the master budget.

BUDGETING DEFINED

Budgets are formal, quantitative plans of action. They can be prepared for an organization as a whole or for any element of the organization. Essentially, the budget quantifies management's expectations of future levels of income, financial position, and cash flows after considering not only the direction the company is taking but also the economic environment in which it operates. The *master* or *static budget,* discussed in detail in this chapter, is a summary of all the objectives and goals of all the various subunits of the company. These goals or targets, which include desired levels for items such as sales, production, selling, financing, and administrative expenses, result in a projected income statement, balance sheet, and statement of cash position. The organization's goals for the future and plans for achieving them are captured by the master budget.

THE ROLE OF BUDGETS

The budget serves as a planning device, but it also serves other functions. The budgeting process aids in evaluating performance; since the budget provides objectives and standards that can be used for the evaluation of performance, it focuses on actual results relative to anticipated ones and allows management to assess deviations from the budget and make necessary changes.

By coordinating activities, budgets promote the ideal that the plans and objectives of individual subunits should be consistent with those of the company as a whole. Coordination also means that all subunits work as one cohesive unit so that the company's overall objectives can be met; for example, the purchasing department should integrate its plans with the production department, which in turn then bases its requirements on the sales budget for the period. In practice, however, coordination is difficult to achieve because of "empire building" or simply because people act in their own self-interest. Sometimes this might be unintentional; for example, segment managers may get wrapped up in their own activities. Budgets are helpful, but they depend on the people who implement the plans of the budget by their actions.

As a motivational tool, budgets communicate to managers and employees what is expected of them. For managers, the process provides a way for them to standardize their planning efforts in an attempt to meet the company's goals. It also forces managers to plan. For employees, knowing what is expected helps reduce anxiety.

TYPES OF BUDGETS
Time Frame of Budgets

The normal time frame for a budget is one year, although some budgets, such as those for purchases of plant and equipment, are prepared for up to ten years. The annual budget is usually broken down into quarters; the first quarter is then broken down into months and the next three quarters are carried as quarterly totals. Each quarter is broken down into months as the company moves through the year. The budgeted data are altered if new information indicates that changes are warranted; hence, the budgeting process requires constant scrutiny and modification when conditions change from what was initially expected.

Continuous or *rolling* budgets have gained increased popularity in recent years. This type of budget uses a 12-month period as its time frame. However, as the year progresses, one month is constantly added so that a twelve-month budget is always prepared. This forces management continually to look into the future in its planning function. The major advantage of this type of budget is that a greater degree of accuracy is achieved because the budget has been recently prepared. However, a disadvantage is that this process requires a substantial commitment of resources in terms of people, time, and money. Management needs to assess whether the benefits of a budget requiring frequent evaluation are greater than the cost.

Categories of Budgets

Among the many forms of budgets are:

▬ Flexible budgets that compare actual operations with budgeted operations at the actual level of output. Such budgets are discussed in Chapter 14.

▬ The capital budget, a long-term budget for planning the purchase and retirement of long-lived productive assets, that is used in preparing the master budget.

▬ The master budget, which is divided into two sections: the operating budget and the financial budget. The *operating budget,* which reflects the planned future costs of operating the company, consists of a number of detailed budgets. They are:

1. Sales budget
2. Production budget
3. Direct materials budget
4. Direct labor budget
5. Factory overhead budget
6. Selling and administrative expense budget
7. Budgeted income statement

The *financial budget* consists of the cash budget, the capital budget, and the budgeted balance sheet. Figure 13-1 illustrates the relationship between the various budgets that make up the master budget.

PREPARING THE MASTER BUDGET

Preparing a master budget is a complex process that takes into account the goals of the company and the economic environment in which it operates. The steps involved in developing a master budget are:

1. Preparing a sales forecast
2. Calculating the expected production for the period
3. Estimating the costs of direct material, direct labor, factory overhead, and operating expenses
4. Estimating cash flows
5. Preparing the projected income statement and balance sheet

The preparation of the master budget begins with the development of a broad set of assumptions regarding the economy in general, the industry the company operates within, and specific goals that the firm expects to meet. Many times economists are employed in this process. From the assumptions management develops strategies relating to expected sales, production scheduling, anticipated inventory levels, projected expenses, and so on. After analysis of these relevant factors, management quantifies its expectations for the coming budget period.

Basic data are presented in Figure 13-2 for the Hypothetical Company, manufacturers of plastic decoy ducks, as it prepares its annual budget. The operating budget is prepared first.

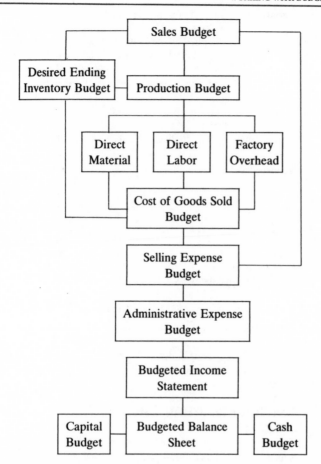

FIG. 13-1 *A Master Budget*

Direct materials	1 pound of plastic raw material cost $3.00
Direct labor	$6.00 per hour
Factory overhead	is applied on the basis of direct labor hours used. That is, for every hour of direct labor used in the manufacturing of a duck, one hour of factory overhead is added to the cost of the unit

Each finished decoy requires:

Direct material	2 pounds of raw material
Direct labor	1 hour
Factory overhead	1 hour (applied on the basis of direct labor)

	Finished Decoys
Anticipated sales for the year	10,000 units
Selling price	$22.00
Beginning inventory	1,000 units $18,000
Desired ending inventory	1,500 units

	Direct Materials
Beginning inventory	3,000 pounds $9,000
Desired ending inventory	5,000 pounds
Factory overhead estimate	$65,100
Selling and distribution expenses	$24,200

FIG. 13-2 *Hypothetical Company Budget Data*

Preparation of the master budget involves a series of interdependent steps, starting with the sales forecast.

THE MASTER BUDGET: THE OPERATING SECTION
Sales Forecasting

The sales budget, which shows expected sales for the coming period in dollars as well as in units, is prepared from the sales forecast, which is affected by such factors as past experience, industry market conditions, economic indicators, and competition. The sales forecast is the starting point for the master budget because production costs and inventory levels are a function of sales volume. Figure 13-3 shows the sales budget for Hypothetical Company; obviously, a company selling multiple products would have a much more detailed sales budget.

$$\frac{\text{Units}}{10,000} \times \frac{\text{Selling Price}}{\$22.00} = \frac{\text{Total Sales}}{\$220,000}$$

FIG. 13-3 *Hypothetical Company Sales Budget for the Period Ending December 31, 2000*

Production Budget

After the sales budget is prepared, the production budget can be prepared. The number of units to be produced is a function of anticipated sales and also of the change in inventories from the beginning of the year to the end of the year. Management needs to decide how much inventory it wants remaining at the end of the year. The decision as to anticipated inventory levels takes into consideration the possibility of unexpected high demand and the possibility of a stock-out (not enough units on hand), as well as the costs of carrying excessive amounts of inventory, such as interest. Another input in this decision process is the effective utilization of production personnel and facilities. From Figure 13-1, we see that management wishes to have 1,500 decoys on hand at the end of the year. This figure was determined after consideration of the aforementioned factors. Figure 13-4 presents the production budget.

Budgeted sales in units (from Figure 13-3)	10,000 units
Add: Desired ending inventory of finished decoys	1,500
Total needed	11,500
Less: Beginning inventory of finished decoys	1,000
Total units to be produced	10,500

FIG. 13-4 *Hypothetical Company Production Budget for the Period Ending December 31, 2000*

Direct Materials Budget

After the production budget is completed, the company calculates the direct materials to be used. This enables the company to determine its direct materials purchases for the year. Figure 13-5 presents these calculations.

Production units (from Figure 13-4)	10,500
Multiplied by 2 pounds per unit	× 2 lbs.
Total pounds of direct material to be used	21,000
Cost per pound	× $3.00
Total cost of direct material to be used	$63,000
Total pounds needed in production	21,000
Add: Desired ending inventory (from Figure 13-2)	5,000
Total direct material needed	26,000
Less: Beginning inventory (from Figure 13-2)	3,000
Direct material to be purchased	23,000
Multiplied by the cost per pound	× $3.00
Cost of purchased direct material	$69,000

FIG. 13-5 *Hypothetical Company Direct Materials Budget for the Period Ending December 31, 2000*

Direct Labor Budget

The direct labor shown in Figure 13-6 is a function of the various labor rates and labor methods used by a company. Hypothetical Company has only one labor rate.

Finished decoy units to be produced (from Figure 13-4)	10,500 units
Multiplied by the direct labor hours needed per unit	× 1 hour
Total direct labor hours required	10,500
Multiplied by the cost per direct labor hour	× $6.00
Total cost of direct labor hours	$63,000

FIG. 13-6 *Hypothetical Company Direct Labor Budget for the Period Ending December 31, 2000*

Factory Overhead Budget

Next, the factory overhead budget is prepared. Factory overhead includes all costs of production other than direct materials and direct labor. The costs are broken down by cost behavior pattern. That is, the budget consists of the estimated variable and fixed overhead for the coming period. The budget is necessary in order to apply overhead to the finished decoys. The factory overhead budget for the Hypothetical Company appears in Figure 13-7. Notice that the total estimated factory overhead is $65,100, which is the estimate from Figure 13-2.

Variable Overhead:	
Utilities	$ 6,000
Fringe benefits	10,500
Supplies	9,000
Indirect labor	21,000
Total variable overhead	$46,500
Fixed Overhead:	
Depreciation	11,300
Insurance	6,000
Property taxes	1,300
Total fixed overhead	18,600
Total factory overhead (from Figure 13-2)	$65,100

FIG. 13-7 *Hypothetical Company Factory Overhead Budget for the Period Ending December 31, 2000*

Factory overhead rate is $65,100/10,500 direct labor hours or $6.20 per direct labor hour.

Ending Inventory Budget

Ending inventory figures were used in Figures 13-4 and 13-5 for the production budget and the direct materials budget. These figures are also needed for the projected income statement and balance sheet as displayed in Figure 13-8.

Finished Goods

	Required		Cost per Unit		
Direct material	2 pounds	×	$3.00	=	$ 6.00
Direct labor	1 hour	×	6.00	=	6.00
Factory overhead	1 hour	×	6.20	=	6.20
Total cost per unit					$18.20

	Units		Cost per Unit		Total Cost
Desired ending Finished Goods inventory	1,500	×	$18.20	=	$27,300
Direct Materials: Desired ending direct materials inventory	5,000 lbs.	×	$3.00	=	15,000
Total ending inventory					$42,300

FIG. 13-8 *Hypothetical Company Ending Inventory Budget for the Period Ending December 31, 2000*

Cost of Goods Sold Budget

Using the information from Figures 13-5 through 13-8, the cost of goods sold budget can be prepared. This budget is presented in Figure 13-9.

Beginning finished goods inventory (from Figure 13-2)		$18,000
Add: Direct materials used (from Figure 13-5)	$63,000	
Direct labor (from Figure 13-6)	$63,000	
Factory overhead (from Figure 13-7)	65,100	191,100
Cost of goods manufactured		209,100
Less: Ending finished goods inventory (from Figure 13-8)		27,300
Cost of goods sold		$181,800

FIG. 13-9 *Hypothetical Company Cost of Goods Sold Budget for the Period Ending December 31, 2000*

Sales and Distribution Expenses Budget

The sales and distribution expenses budget takes into consideration all selling, general, administrative, and other necessary operating expenses. Some of these expenses, such as sales commissions, are a function of other budgetary items; others are estimated based upon historical patterns taking into consideration anticipated future price changes. The sales and distribution expense budget for Hypothetical Company is shown in Figure 13-10.

Sales commissions and salaries	$ 8,000
Advertising	7,400
Supplies	5,200
Travel	5,200
Total sales and distribution expenses (Figure 13-2)	$25,800

FIG. 13-10 *Hypothetical Company Sales and Distribution Expense Budget for the Period Ending December 31, 2000*

The Budgeted Income Statement

Hypothetical Company's budgeted income statement (presented in Figure 13-11) is simplified compared to what one would expect in the budget of a large manufacturing firm, where greater detail would be provided along with a larger number of supporting schedules. If the number of revenue and/or expense items is very large (as it is with a large manufacturing company), separate budgets might be necessary for each item. That is, expected revenues other than sales, such as interest, and other anticipated expenses would be submitted by the manager or managers responsible for the individual items.

Sales (from Figure 13-3)	$220,000
Cost of goods sold (from Figure 13-9)	181,800
Gross margin	38,200
Selling and distribution expenses (from Figure 13-10)	24,200
Net income	$ 14,000

FIG. 13-11 *Hypothetical Company Budgeted Income Statement for the Period Ending December 31, 2000*

THE MASTER BUDGET: THE FINANCIAL BUDGET

The financial budget is prepared next. For our purposes several key assumptions need to be made in order to demonstrate its preparation. First, assume that Hypothetical Company had the balance sheet at January 1, 2000, shown in Figure 13-12.

ASSETS	
Current Assets	
Cash	$110,000
Accounts receivable (net)	20,000
Inventory	27,000
Total current assets	157,000
Noncurrent Assets	
Property	200,000
Plant & equipment (net)	350,000
Total noncurrent assets	550,000
Total assets	$707,000
LIABILITIES AND STOCKHOLDERS' EQUITY	
Liabilities	
Accounts payable	26,000
Bonds payable	140,000
Total liabilities	166,000
Stockholders' Equity	
Common stock	200,000
Retained earnings	341,000
Total stockholders' equity	541,000
Total liabilities and stockholders' equity	$707,000

FIG. 13-12 *Hypothetical Company Balance Sheet at December 31, 2000*

Further assume that Hypothetical had the capital budget appearing in Figure 13-13 relating to purchases of plant, property, and equipment in the forthcoming year.

	Property	Plant & Equipment	Depreciation Accumulated	Net Amount
Beginning balance	$200,000	$450,000	$100,000	$350,000
Add: Purchase of property	$ 15,000			
Purchase of equipment		$ 20,000		
Less: Depreciation ($11,300 from Figure 13-7)			11,300	
Ending balance	$215,000	$470,000	$111,300	$573,700

FIG. 13-13 *Hypothetical Company Capital Budget for the Period Ending December 31, 2000*

Other assumptions are these:

1. The company will collect all of the beginning balance of accounts receivable during the coming year.
2. The company will collect 90 percent of its sales in cash during the coming year.
3. The company will pay for purchases of property, plant, and equipment with the proceeds of a $100,000 bond that it will issue during the year.
4. The balance of accounts payable will be paid during the year.
5. At the end of the year, one-half of the direct materials purchased during the year will still be on account.
6. There will be no changes in the common-stock account.
7. All other purchases and expenses will be for cash.

Using the previous information, the cash budget and the budgeted balance sheet (presented in Figures 13-14 and 13-15) can be prepared.

Beginning cash balance (from Figure 13-12)	$110,000
Add: Receipts from sales ($220,000 from Figure 13-13 × .90 assumption 2 above)	$198,000
and accounts receivable (from Figure 13-12 and assumption 1 above)	20,000
	218,000
Proceeds from issuance of bond (from assumption 3 above)	100,000
Total cash inflows	428,000
Less: Disbursements	
Purchase of property (from Figure 13-13)	15,000
Purchase of equipment (from Figure 13-13)	20,000
Purchase of direct materials (from Figure 13-5) only 50% paid for in cash	34,500
Payment of direct labor costs (from Figure 13-6)	63,000
Payment of factory overhead costs less $11,300 of depreciation (from Figure 13-7)	53,800
Payment of sales and distribution expenses (from Figure 13-10)	24,200
Payment of beginning balance of accounts payable (from Figure 13-12 and assumption 4 above)	26,000
Total cash outflows	236,500
Ending cash balance (from Figure 13-15)	$191,500

FIG. 13-14 *Hypothetical Company Cash Budget for the Period Ending December 31, 2000*

ASSETS
Current Assets

Cash (from Figure 13-14)	$191,500
Accounts receivable (net) ($20,000 − $20,000 + $220,000 − $198,000)	22,000
Inventory (from Figure 13-8)	42,300
Total current assets	255,800

Noncurrent Assets

Property (from Figure 13-13)	215,000
Plant & equipment (net) (from Figure 13-13)	358,700
Total noncurrent assets	573,700
Total assets	$829,500

LIABILITIES AND STOCKHOLDERS' EQUITY
Liabilities

Accounts payable (50% of direct material purchases from Figure 13-14)	34,500
Bonds payable ($140,000 + $100,000)	240,000
Total liabilities	274,500

Stockholders' Equity

Common stock	200,000
Retained earnings ($341,000 + $14,000 net income from Figure 13-11)	355,000
Total stockholders' equity	555,000
Total liabilities and stockholders' equity	$829,500

FIG. 13-15 *Hypothetical Company Budgeted Balance Sheet at December 31, 2000*

CHAPTER PERSPECTIVE

Our discussion centered on the budget as a formal financial plan. Most companies budget in order to force planning, set a standard for performance evaluation, and provide a means for all functional areas to coordinate their activities.

Budgets can be prepared for any time period; the most common is a single year. Some budgets, particularly capital budgets, may be prepared for extended periods, such as ten years. Companies decide on a time period based on the degree of control they have over operating activities and on the cost/benefit trade-off with the resources that must be committed to the budget process.

The master budget is a collection of budgets, divided into two sections: the operating budget and the financial budget. The operating budget consists of the sales, production, direct materials, direct labor, factory overhead, inventory, cost of goods sold, and the sales and distribution expense budgets; these form the basis of the budgeted income statement. The financial budget consists of a capital budget, a budgeted balance sheet, and a cash budget.

Standard Costs, Variances, and Budgets

INTRODUCTION AND MAIN POINTS

Responsibility Accounting refers to a system of gathering and communicating revenue and expense information to divisions, departments, and individuals by areas of responsibility. An important aspect of responsibility accounting is establishing standard costs in order to assist management in evaluating performance. In a standard-cost system, production activities are maintained at both standard and actual costs, and the difference between standard and actual costs assists management in judging performance.

After studying the material in this chapter:

■ You will understand the development, types, and uses of standard costs.

■ You will understand how standard cost variances are computed and reported.

■ You will understand how budget variances are computed and used for budgetary control purposes.

DEVELOPMENT, TYPES, AND USES OF STANDARD COSTS
Development of Standard Costs

Standard costs are predetermined costs, usually expressed on a per unit basis, of what costs should be under normal operating conditions. They are carefully determined, often using engineering and time and motion studies. However, standards are not always based on rigid specifications. Because the primary purpose of standard costing is to aid management in judging performance, a less formal, nonscientific approach to standard-setting can also result in useful standard costs.

Physical standards are developed by analyzing the types and amounts of material, labor, and overhead necessary in the production of a unit. The standard cost of a unit is obtained by multiplying the standard prices of material, labor, and overhead by the physical standards.

Conceptually, responsibility for setting standards lies primarily with the personnel directly involved with the task; those who negotiate with their respective managers regarding the relative tightness of the budget. However, many times management uses a "top-down" approach to the standard-setting process and establishes standards without participation from the personnel involved; this approach can lead to a significant amount of friction between management and the workers and can prove to be counterproductive.

The accountant's primary responsibilities in regard to standards is to convert physical standards, such as pounds or yards, into dollars and to prepare performance reports that compare actual and standard costs.

Types of Standards

Perfect or *ideal* standards reflect the absolute minimum costs attainable under only the best operating conditions. They contain no provision for breakdowns, lost time, or work stoppages. Many managers feel that the use of perfect standards suggests to employees that they must constantly strive to improve their performance and efficiency. However, the use of perfect or ideal standards can be counterproductive; their use tends to discourage workers since it is impossible to meet ideal standards. Furthermore, deviations or *variances* from these standards cannot be interpreted because they contain ordinary or expected inefficiencies as well as abnormal inefficiences. Therefore, it becomes impossible to isolate and bring the abnormal efficiencies to management's attention.

On the other hand, *practical standards* (also called *currently attainable standards*) are those that can be obtained under normal efficient operating conditions. The standards set are "tight" but not unreasonable and include normal allowances for such items as machine breakdowns, lost personnel time, spoilage, and waste.

Practical standards are more useful than ideal standards for motivating personnel, budgetary control, and product costing because they allow for normal inefficiencies. Employees are more highly motivated when they know that the standards being used for evaluative purposes can be attained by a reasonable but still efficient effort. Better budgetary control and product costing can also be achieved with practical standards because, by taking into consideration normal production inefficiencies, realistic budget figures and product costs can be used for planning, forecasting, pricing, and control. Ideal standards should not be used because they result in impractical and unreasonable figures.

Uses of Standards Costs

Basic uses of standard costs include:

1. Motivating employees to improve performance by encouraging a course of corrective action. In many instances, improved employee performance can lead to cost reductions.

2. Monitoring the costs associated with planning and control and by directing attention to situations where conditions or operations are not within the limits or standards set by management. This mechanism of "red-flagging" potential problems is called *management by exception.*

3. Enhancing performance measurement by affixing responsibility to the individual or department responsible for any variations from the standards. Responsibility over cost control can then be evaluated through performance reports.

4. Inventory valuation.

5. Budgetary planning and decision making.

6. Setting selling, transfer prices, and bid prices on contracts. Serving as organizational goals or targets.

7. Transfer prices are necessary when products and/or services are exchanged between operating divisions of a firm.

8. Streamlining the accounting system and reducing clerical costs. The accumulation of actual costs takes place over an extended time period, while the use of standard costs allows the costing and pricing of products to be made on a timely basis.

THE GENERAL MODEL FOR VARIANCE ANALYSIS

Our general model for variance analysis separates standards into two categories: price and quantity variances. The general model, representing variable manufacturing costs, is shown in Figure 14-1.

(1)	(2)	(3)
Actual Quantity of Inputs, at Actual Price $(AQ \times AP)$	Actual Quantity of Inputs, at Standard Price $(AQ \times SP)$	Standard Quantity Allowed for Output, at Standard Price $(SQ \times SP)$

Price Variance	Quantity Variance
(1) − (2)	(2) − (3)
Materials price variance	Materials quantity variance
Labor rate variance	Labor efficiency variance
Variable overhead spending variance	Variable overhead efficiency variance

Total Variance

FIG. 14-1 *General Model for Variance Analysis Variable Manufacturing Costs*

A *price variance* is defined as the difference between the actual price of a unit and the standard price of the unit multiplied by the actual quantity of the unit used or purchased. The variance measures the difference between actual unit prices and the standard unit prices for the actual quantity used or purchased.

The *quantity variance* is defined as the difference between the actual quantity of a unit and the standard quantity of a unit multiplied by the standard quantity used. This variance measures the difference between the quantity of units actually used (such as pounds of material) and the quantity of units that should have been used, multiplied by the standard price.

As a general rule, separation or isolation of variances should be done as early as possible. Separation of the total variance into two components gives management the ability to identify the party responsible for control of that variance. For example, the purchasing manager may be responsible for a material price variance, while the production foreman may have responsibility for a quantity (usage) variance.

Material Price and Quantity Variances

In monitoring material price and quantity variances, attention is normally focused on situations in which the cost or quantity of inputs exceeds the standards set. This condition results in unfavorable variances.

What are some of the causes of unfavorable materials price variances? One obvious cause may be improper setting of the standard. Another possible cause is the inability of the purchasing department or manager to seek the lowest price possible. Of course, the unfavorable variance may simply be the result of material prices increases and the unavailability of a suitable replacement material. Inefficient operation of the purchasing department may be another factor causing an unfavorable price variance.

Unfavorable quantity variances can also arise as a result of incorrect standards. In order to conserve cash, a company might buy a lower quality raw material; this, in turn, might cause higher usage of the material, resulting in an unfavorable variance. If workers are not adequately trained or instructed, the result may be excessive material usage or waste and an unfavorable variance. Machinery and equipment need to be properly adjusted and maintained and prescribed production procedures should be followed; failure to do so can also lead to unfavorable material quantity variances because of the use of abnormal quantities of material.

Figure 14-2 demonstrates the calculation of material price and quantity variances. Baker Company uses a standard costing system and has established the following standards for material used in making Product X:

For each unit of Product X, 2.0 pounds of raw material should be used. The standard cost of one pound of raw material is $4.00. During the month, 7,500 pounds of raw material were purchased at a cost of $3.90. All 7,500 pounds were used in the production of 3,000 units of Product X.

(1) Actual Quantity of Inputs, at Actual Price (AQ × AP)	(2) Actual Quantity of Inputs, at Standard Price (AQ × SP)	(3) Standard Quantity Allowed for Output, at Standard Price (SQ × SP)
7,500 lbs. × $3.90 = $29,250	7,500 lbs. × $4.00 = $30,000	2 lbs. per unit × 3,000 units × $4.00 = $24,000

Price Variance =	30,000 29,250 $750 Favorable	Quantity Variance =	24,000 30,000 $6,000 Unfavorable

Total Variance = 6,000 − 750 = $5,250 Unfavorable

FIG. 14-2 *Baker Company Calculation of Material Price and Quantity Variances*

(1) Actual Quantity of Inputs, at Actual Price[1] (AQ × AP)	(2) Actual Quantity of Inputs, at Standard Price (AQ × SP)	(3) Standard Quantity Allowed for Output, at Standard Price (SQ × SP)
8,500 lbs. × $3.90 = $33,150	8,500 × $4.00 = $34,000	2 lbs. per unit × 3,000 units × $4.00 = $24,000

Price
Variance =

$34,000
33,150
850F

7,500 × $4.00
= $30,000

Quantity
Variance =

$30,000
24,000
6,000 U

FIG. 14-3 *Baker Company Calculation of Material Price and Quantity Variances Using the Quantity of Materials Purchased*

[1]The material purchase price variance was computed using the 8,500 pounds purchased while the material quantity variance was computed using the 7,500 pounds used in production. Because of this difference, a total variance cannot be computed.

Note that in our example we assumed that the amount purchased was the same amount put into production. If this were not the case, that is, if the amount put into production were less than the amount purchased, the material price variance would be computed using the amount purchased. In this instance a total variance could be computed because of the difference. (Most firms do compute the price variance when materials are purchased rather than when they are placed into production.)

Labor Rate and Efficiency Variances

Labor variances are measured or isolated when labor is used in the production process. They are computed in the same manner as the material price and quantity variances, and the three column model can be used. The only difference is that the terms "rate" and "efficiency" are substituted for "price" and "quantity."

Unfavorable rate variances can arise from misallocation of the work force; for example, highly paid skilled workers being substituted for lower-skilled workers who are paid a lower hourly wage. Favorable rate variances occur when the reverse happens. Overtime pay also results in unfavorable labor rate variances. Finally, an increase in wages without a corresponding change in the standard creates an unfavorable rate variance.

Causes of unfavorable labor rate variances include poor supervision, poorly trained workers, and the use of substandard machinery that leads to breakdowns and work stoppages. Another possible cause is the use of low-grade materials, which can require extra processing time.

Figure 14-4 demonstrates the calculation of labor rate and efficiency variances, assuming the following information for the Baker Company:

Each unit of Product X requires 1.5 hours of direct labor. The standard cost for direct labor is $12 per direct labor hour. There were 3,000 units produced. The actual direct labor cost was $13.50 per hour and the actual number of direct labor hours was 4,200.

(1) Actual Hours of Input, at Actual Rate (AH × AR)	(2) Actual Hours of Input, at Standard Rate (AH × SR)	(3) Standard Hours Allowed for Output, at Standard Rate (SH × SR)
4,200 hrs. × $13.50 = $56,700	4,200 hrs. × $12.00 = $50,400	1.5 hrs. per unit × 3,000 units × $12,000 = $54,000

Rate Variance	=	56,700 − 50,400 $6,300 U	Efficiency Variance =	54,000 − 50,400 $3,600 F

Total Variance = 6,300 − 3,600 = $2,700 U

FIG. 14-4 *Baker Company Calculation of Labor Rate and Efficiency Variances*

Variable Overhead Spending and Efficiency Variances

Variances arising from deviations from the standard cost of variable overhead items are normally the responsibility of the production department. The calculation of these variances is very similar to that of the labor rate and efficiency variances, with the difference that "spending" is substituted for "rate."

The variable overhead spending variance measures the difference between what was spent for variable overhead items, such as utilities, and what should have been spent as required by the standard, or the actual amount of variable overhead minus the expected amount. The variable overhead efficiency variance is the difference between the actual activity (in hours) and the standard activity (in hours) allowed. Variable overhead normally fluctuates in proportion to some measure of production, such as machine hours or direct labor hours. In this case, we can say that what the efficiency variance really measures is the excess variable overhead incurred or saved because the measure of production (for example, direct labor hours) differed from the standard.

In evaluating variable overhead variances, the two categories of spending and efficiency are different from the material and labor variances. This is due to the fact that variable overhead consists of many types of costs, such as utilities, fringe benefits, and repairs. The best way to evaluate these variances is to observe the difference between the actual cost and the standard cost for each individual item of variable overhead.

Unfavorable variable overhead spending variances can arise because of incorrect setting of standards, waste and carelessness, and increases in the prices of variable overhead items. Since indirect labor is normally a component of variable overhead, increases in the wage rate can also cause an unfavorable spending variance.

Causes of unfavorable variable overhead efficiency variances include poor quality materials and supplies, lack of supervision, and poorly trained workers. Work stoppages and defective machinery and equipment can also lead to unfavorable efficiency variances.

Using the Baker Company example, Figure 14-5 presents the calculation of the variable overhead spending and efficiency variances. We assume that Baker Company applies overhead to Product X on a direct labor hour basis; that is, variable overhead is allocated to Product X on the same basis as direct labor.

Again assume that each unit of Product X requires 1.5 hours of direct labor and, therefore, 1.5 hours of variable overhead. The standard variable overhead rate is $10 per hour. Actual variable overhead incurred for the production of 3,000 units of Product X amounted to $46,000. The actual number of direct labor hours was 4,200.

(1) Actual Hours of Input, at Actual Rate (AH × AR)	(2) Actual Hours of Input, at Standard Rate (AH × SR)	(3) Standard Hours Allowed for Output, at Standard Rate (SH × SR)
$46,000*	4,200 hrs. × $10.00 = $42,000	1.5 hrs. per unit × 3,000 units × $10.00 = $45,000

	46,000		45,000
Rate	− 42,000	Efficiency	− 42,000
Variance	= $4,000 U	Variance	= $3,000 F

Total Variance = 4,000 − 3,000 = $1,000 U

FIG. 14-5 *Baker Company Calculation of Variable Overhead Spending and Efficiency Variances*

Notice that the variable overhead efficiency variance and the labor efficiency variance (Figure 14-4) are both favorable. Again, this

---

* The actual variable overhead rate could be computed by dividing the actual cost by the actual direct labor hours since variable overhead is applied on the same basis ($46,000/4,200 = $10.952).

is because variable overhead has been allocated on the basis of direct labor hours. Because we were efficient in our usage of direct labor, we used less variable overhead. This relationship always occurs when variable overhead is allocated based upon some production measure such as labor hours. The key is to pick the best production measure; that is, the one that has the closest relationship to the incurrence or variable overhead. This measure of activity is sometimes referred to as a cost driver and may not be labor cost since in recent years many companies have moved from being labor intensive to machine intensive. Computer time or machine hours might be a more appropriate cost driver for use in applying variable overhead.

Variances for Fixed Overhead

Unlike materials, labor, and variable overhead costs, fixed variable overhead are set at the beginning of the period and are then spread over the units of production during the period. Variances arise because the actual amount of fixed overhead differs from that which was anticipated at the beginning of the period. Unlike materials, labor, and variable overhead costs, fixed overhead costs are beyond the control of production personnel. They normally cannot be changed quickly; as a result, analysis of these variances is of dubious value to the production department manager. Therefore, we forgo any further discussion of the fixed overhead variance.

Reporting of Variances

We said earlier that one of the keys to variance analysis is to isolate the variance as soon as possible. Computer-integrated manufacturing systems allow immediate feedback regarding variances and allow management to take corrective actions that minimize the variances and assist in controlling costs. A decisive advantage is that the corrective action can take place during production rather than after production ceases.

Variances can be formally integrated into the accounting system and separately isolated and accounted for. In such cases, variances are accumulated in accounts on a daily, weekly, or monthly basis. Variance reports are prepared accordingly and distributed to the appropriate level of management for action. There is no prescribed form of report for variance analysis; each report is tailored to meet the needs of the intended user.

VARIANCE ANALYSIS AND BUDGETARY CONTROL: FLEXIBLE BUDGETING

We introduced the master budget in Chapter 13, discussing how the budget is prepared as the first step in the planning and control process. In this chapter, we presented standard costing and ways the system can be used to plan and control the costs of materials, labor, and variable overhead. We now turn to the concept of *flexible budgeting,* which also assists management in the planning and control phase of the budgeting process.

Budgeted Costs and Standard Costs

Budgeted costs and standard costs are not necessarily the same. Budgeted costs usually refers to total costs; for example, we budget for $100,000 of total variable cost for a particular fiscal period. Normally, standard cost relates to *unit* cost rather than *total* cost. In our previous discussion we referred to the standard cost per unit of material; you might view standard cost as the budgeted *cost per unit.* Standard costs do not differ from budgeted costs if the standards are reasonably attainable; in such cases they can be used in the preparation of budgets.

Static Budgets

The master budget, the budgetary technique discussed in Chapter 13, was essentially based upon past expenditures. The process also took into account existing asset and liability levels, possible changes in costs to the firm, and changes in economic environment. This type of budget is sometimes referred to as a *static* budget, since each item in the budget is a single figure that is not adjusted for alternate levels of activity. A static budget is prepared prior to the beginning of the period and is necessary for management to plan future operations and to set predetermined overhead rates for product costing purposes. Such a budget appears in Figure 14-6 for the Baker Company for 2000. (The comparison of actual and budgeted results is an example of a *performance report,* discussed in Chapter 16.)

	Actual Results	Static Budget	Variance
Number of Units	80,000	100,000	20,000 U
Sales	$280,000	$300,000	$20,000 U
Variable Expenses:			
Direct materials	22,000	36,000	14,000 F
Direct labor	43,000	42,000	1,000 U
Overhead	21,400	20,000	1,400 U
Selling	57,600	72,000	14,400 F
Total Variable Expenses	144,000	170,000	26,000 F
Fixed Expenses:			
Overhead	63,000	60,000	3,000 U
Selling	15,000	10,000	5,000 U
Total Fixed Expenses	78,000	70,000	8,000 U
Operating Income	$ 58,000	$ 60,000	$ 2,000 U

FIG. 14-6 *Baker Company Performance Report for the Period Ending December 31, 2000*

One problem in analyzing this report is that the number of units sold is not equal to the number initially budgeted. It is therefore difficult to determine whether the $2,000 unfavorable variance in operating income is the result of increased fixed expenses, a decrease in the sales volume, or a combination of these. This is especially puzzling because total variable expenses were lower than expected. That is, in Figure 14-6, total fixed expenses were in excess of the amount budgeted. Also, actual sales were lower than budgeted sales and could have contributed to the unfavorable variance. On the other hand, total variable expenses were less than the amount budgeted. What caused the $2,000 unfavorable budget variance? We cannot make this determination by comparing the actual costs at 80,000 units with the budgeted costs at 100,000 units.

Flexible Budgets

To permit a more detailed and helpful analysis, companies prepare *flexible* or *variable* budgets for various activity levels. Figure 14-7 shows a flexible budget for three different activity levels. Note that the amounts for 100,000 units are those from the static budget in Figure 14-6.

Number of Units	Amount Per Unit	70,000	100,000	130,000
Sales	$3.00	$210,000	$300,000	$390,000
Variable Expenses:				
Direct materials	.36	25,200	36,000	46,800
Direct labor	.42	29,400	42,000	54,600
Overhead	.20	14,000	20,000	26,000
Selling	.72	50,400	72,000	93,600
Total Variable Expenses	$1.70	119,000	170,000	221,000
Fixed Expenses:				
Overhead		60,000	60,000	60,000
Selling		10,000	10,000	10,000
Total Fixed Expenses		70,000	70,000	70,000
Operating Income		$ 21,000	$ 60,000	$ 99,000

FIG. 14-7 *Baker Company Flexible Budget 2000*

In reviewing Figure 14-7, note two things. First, the cost per unit is calculated by taking the amount of a particular budget item and dividing that amount by the activity level from the static budget level.

For example, the static budget amount for direct materials is $36,000. Dividing this amount by 100,000 units results in a cost per unit of $0.36. At an activity level of 70,000 units, total direct material cost would be $25,200 (70,000 units × $0.36). Also note that since fixed costs do not fluctuate with volume changes, they are expressed as total amounts rather than on a per unit basis.

Flexible Budget Formula

Using the data from Figure 14-7, we can construct a flexible budget formula, which will allow us to compute a budget at any level of activity.

Revenues	− Variable Expenses	− Fixed Expenses	= Operating Income (or Loss)
Units Sold × Selling Price Per Unit	− Units Sold × Variable Costs Per Unit	− Fixed Expenses	= Operating Income (or Loss)

Using this formula, Baker Company's flexible budget formula is:

$$\$3.00X + \$1.70X + \$70,000$$

where X is the chosen activity level. You can confirm the amounts of operating income from Figure 14-6 by substituting 70,000, 100,000, and 130,000 units for "X" in Baker Company's flexible budget formula.

Analysis of Baker Company's Actual Results

Using the static budget, the flexible budget, and the actual results, we can isolate the variances from planned results for Baker Company. Figure 14-8 presents this analysis.

	(A) Actual Results (Based on Actual Activity Level)	(B) Flexible Budget Variances	(C) Flexible Budget (Based on Actual Activity Level)	(D) Sales Volume Variance	(E) Static Budget
Units Sales	80,000	-0-	80,000	20,000	100,000
Variable Expenses:	$280,000	$40,000 F	$240,000	$60,000 U	$300,000
Direct materials	22,000	6,800 F	28,800	7,200 F	36,000

Direct labor	43,000	9,400 U	33,600	8,400 F	42,000
Overhead	21,400	5,400 U	16,000	4,000 F	20,000
Selling	57,600	-0-	57,600	14,400 F	72,000
Total Variable Expenses	144,000	8,000 U	136,000	34,000 F	170,000
Fixed Expenses:					
Overhead	63,000	3,000 U	60,000	-0-	60,000
Selling	15,000	5,000	10,000	-0-	10,000
Total Fixed Expenses	78,000	8,000 U	70,000	-0-	70,000
Operating Income	$58,000	$24,000 F	$34,000	$26,000 U	$60,000

Flexible Budget Variance = $24,000 F
Sales Volume Variance = $26,000 U
Total Variance from Static Budget = $2,000 U

FIG. 14-8 *Baker Company Report on Actual vs. Budgeted Performance for the Period Ended December 31, 2000*

The actual results for 2000 in Column A are from Figure 14-6. Column C is the flexible budget based upon the activity level used in Column A. Column E is the static budget from Figure 14-6 prepared prior to the beginning of the fiscal year.

The *sales volume variance* is isolated in Column D. This variance results from the differences between the static and flexible budget amounts for revenues, expenses, and operating income. In our example, the targeted amount of sales of 100,000 units was not achieved. This might have been caused by environmental factors outside the control of Baker Company, an overly optimistic sales forecast, or inefficiencies of the sales staff. Obviously, detailed analysis would have to be conducted to determine the cause and to plan any necessary corrective action. As you might expect, operating at an activity level lower than anticipated lowers total variable expenses. The sales volume variance for 2000 for Baker Company is $26,000 and is unfavorable.

The *flexible budget variance* for Baker is a favorable $24,000 (see column B in Figure 14-8). This result was caused by selling 80,000 units at a price greater than that initially budgeted and incurring $16,000 more in variable and fixed expenses than budgeted for at an activity level of 80,000 units. Each unit was sold at an average selling price of $3.50

(total sales of $280,000 divided by 80,000 units). Market forces, such as a lack of competition, may have indicated to management that an increase in selling price was warranted. (It may also have been a contributing factor in failing to reach the desired sales level of 100,000 units.) Management will certainly want to know why variable expenses were higher than budgeted. Examining the components of variable expenses, similar to our previous discussion concerning standard costs (price and efficiency variances), might answer these questions. Fixed expenses exceeded the budget by $8,000; this variance also needs to be investigated on an item-by-item basis. (That is, the components of fixed overhead and selling expenses have to be reviewed individually.) The favorable flexible budget variance of $24,000 subtracted from the unfavorable sales volume variance of 26,000 equals the total unfavorable budget variance of $2,000 presented in Figures 14-6 and 14-8.

Cost control is important if a company is to be profitable. The flexible budget approach is one way to control costs by providing management with a signal when actual amounts differ from budgeted amounts at a given activity level.

CHAPTER PERSPECTIVE

According to our discussion of standard costs, standard costs are predetermined costs that management believes should be attainable under normal but efficient operations. Standard costing systems monitor and isolate differences between standard and actual costs.

The price variance for direct materials measures the difference between what was actually paid for materials and what was called for by the standard. The efficiency variance indicates how well the production manager utilizes materials. Similarly, the labor rate variance measures the effect of changing actual labor rates from standard rates. The labor efficiency variance can be a signal indicating the inefficient use of labor.

Variances arising from the application of variable overhead items are categorized as spending and efficiency variances. Their isolation and calculation is similar to that of the labor variances; however, their interpretation is more difficult because of the many items included in variable overhead.

Static budgets are prepared prior to the beginning of the fiscal year and relate to only one level of activity. The interpretation of operating results can be difficult when actual operations differ from the activity level used in the preparation of the static budget. Flexible budgets are used to present budgetary figures at any activity level. The flexible budget formula allows management to make meaningful comparisons of actual and budgeted amounts at the same activity level, as well as to take corrective action when actual amounts exceed budgeted amounts.

Business Plans and Loan Applications

INTRODUCTION AND MAIN POINTS

Companies that seek credit are frequently required to prepare a business plan as part of a loan application; but managers often file the plan away once the loan is secured. However, the business plan has potentially much wider use than just satisfying lender requirements. The business plan contains projected financial statements and resource requirements that managers can use in several ways to help control the business. This chapter discusses the importance of the business plan as part of the loan application package and the uses managers may make of the business plan; it also presents a detailed outline of its composition. The chapter ends with a brief discussion of personal loan applications, also frequently part of the loan application of a small, privately owned company.

After studying the material in this chapter:

■ You will understand the importance of a good business plan in securing business loans.

■ You will see how managers can use a business plan to monitor and control operations, examine the feasibility of proposed projects, and choose between alternative projects.

■ You will know the components that make up a comprehensive business plan.

■ You will understand how a business plan is used as part of a business loan application.

■ You will know the items requested on most personal loan applications and how such applications are used as a component of a business loan application for a small, privately held company.

THE ROLE OF A BUSINESS PLAN

A business plan is a comprehensive document that describes a company's past, current, and projected operations and operating results and includes a statement of the strategy, tactics, and resources that will be used to achieve the projected results. Business plans are often required by lenders as part of a loan application, but they are also useful—perhaps essential—in managing and directing a business.

A business plan is an invaluable working guide and reference tool. The plan requires a company's goals to be formally and quantitatively stated and allows managers to measure performance, evaluate alternative courses of action, and coordinate the activities necessary to carry out the plan. A carefully thought-out business plan is a repository of information useful to both lenders and owners. Owners use it internally to provide consistent policy, establish operating control, and assure that activities are goal-directed. The plan is used externally by a lender to examine a company's history, status, and potential in order to make a lending decision; lenders want to know precisely a company's strengths and strategy before risking funds in a loan commitment.

Facing the Hard Questions

Preparation of a business plan forces managers to answer hard questions in precise ways. Cash flows, sales, income, and other activity measures must be forecast; financial statements must be prepared and projected for future years; and strategies must be expressed in writing. Enthusiastic managers who only have a "gut feel" and "great optimism" for a new project may find it difficult to justify their beliefs in a formal document. As a result, a major achievement of business plans (as with any budgeting process) is to force managers to plan and evaluate effectively.

Who? What? When?

A business plan forces managers to answer the following basic questions:[1] Who? What? Where? When? Why? How?

WHO will be involved in the activities?

WHAT goals does the company expect to achieve?

WHAT resources (financial and otherwise) will be required to achieve these goals?

WHERE will the goal-directed activities take place?

WHEN will each of the goals be accomplished?

WHY is the company pursuing new goals (or continuing to pursue the old)?

HOW will the goals be achieved?

---

[1] Taken, with modification, from "Your Business Plan," a pamphlet distributed by the Economic Development/Small Business Development Center, Louisiana State University, Baton Rouge, LA.

THE MANAGER'S USE FOR A BUSINESS PLAN

A business plan may be prepared by a manager or an accountant. For a small mom-and-pop business, a business plan prepared by an accountant will cost from a few hundred to several thousand dollars; Small Business Development Centers in many cities will assist small businesses (or prospective entrepreneurs) in preparing a business plan as part of a loan application. Either way, however, the manager must set the goals, make the strategic decisions, and compile the data to be used by the accountant. The accountant can prepare a schedule of cash collections, for instance, but the manager must first decide "credit sales of the new product will be $40,000 next April and we expect customers to pay in 30 days, with an estimated 2% bad-debt loss."

A company benefits from the preparation of a business plan even when no additional financing is needed. Once the plan is prepared, managers of a company will find it invaluable as both a reference and a guide. A business plan is the road map the company can follow to success (it hopes). No prudent person would take a trip without an intended destination and a map showing the route to be followed and the terrain to be encountered. Similarly, no prudent manager should direct a company without a well-thought-out business plan that establishes goals to be reached and the route for reaching them. A business plan, like a road map, helps:

1. Identify and locate a desired destination or goal
2. Evaluate alternative routes to the goal
3. Plan progress toward the goal
4. Compare actual progress toward the goal to planned progress
5. Communicate the goal, the planned route, and the actual progress to others

The data accumulated and the decisions made while preparing a business plan help managers evaluate the feasibility of a new business venture, evaluate alternative ventures, and deal responsibly with lenders by selecting appropriate financing and supporting assertions of creditworthiness.

Evaluating Feasibility

A business plan forces a manager to forecast financial and nonfinancial operating needs for the life of a proposed project (or at least three to five years). The manager must not only be certain that a project will be profitable and return positive cash flows but must also demonstrate that it is reasonable to believe that the cash will be available when the debt and other payments are due. The business plan should state exactly how personnel needs will be met; personnel with adequate skills must be available when needed without depriving other operations. The business plan should also state exactly which facilities will be used and at what cost. It is not enough to say "we will use present employees and existing facilities"; the business plan should state which employees and what portion of existing facilities would be used.

If a suitable, detailed business plan cannot be made, it may signal that the new venture may not be feasible. If management believes, despite the contents of the plan, that the venture is still feasible, at least they make that decision with full knowledge of existing facts. In such a case, managers should decide exactly what factors are encouraging a favorable outlook and reconstruct the plan to reflect those factors. If a convincing business plan cannot be completed for a new venture, it is doubtful that the new venture will be successful.

Evaluating Alternatives

A business plan provides the format not only for evaluating the feasibility of a venture but for preparing cash flow, income, and other projections for two or more alternative projects for comparison. If managers have no other formal method of evaluating alternatives, they can use the business plan format discussed later in the chapter simply by preparing business plans for all alternatives and selecting the proposal that accomplishes management's goals with the least risk.

Projected financial statements can be analyzed using the ratio analysis techniques discussed in Chapters 11 and 12 to determine which alternative yields the most attractive financial results or provides the greatest return on investment to stockholders. Cash flows can be compared to see which alternative requires the least financing or best provides for debt repayment.

Dealing with Lenders

Many lenders require a business plan as part of a company's loan application. The plan assures the lender that company management has carefully studied the activity to be financed and the impact it may have on the company's cash flows, operating results, and financial position. (Continuous monitoring of cash needs also impresses lenders and is discussed in the section that follows.) A well-prepared business plan may enhance the company's prospects of securing financing, casting the application in a much more favorable light than a similar application not so well documented.

In addition to convincing the lender to provide financing, a carefully prepared business plan can help management select the most appropriate source of financing. A business plan provides a format for analyzing the effect of different forms of debt, with different restrictions and repayment schedules (a note versus a mortgage, for instance) and different proportions of owner- and creditor-supplied capital. Financial leverage, discussed in Chapter 12, changes as the interest rate changes; often a larger proportion of debt-to-owner financing leads to higher interest rates as lenders see more and more risk of default.

Monitoring Operations and Cash Flows

A business plan can be updated monthly or quarterly to keep managers alert to potential problems. Projections of cash flows and operating results can be revised as conditions change; projected financial statements can be updated; variables that interact can be watched closely (inventory needs might cause cash shortages, for example). As each succeeding month or quarter approaches, cash needs and the results of operations become less and less uncertain and projections more and more certain. Managers can take steps to avoid problems before they occur.

Monitoring cash flows is particularly useful in relations with lenders. Lenders react much more favorably to managers who detect a cash shortage several periods in advance and make arrangements to borrow than to managers who rush in frantically to solve an immediate, unanticipated crisis. Lenders are much more likely to believe projected repayment schedules when the company's cash position is continuously monitored. How much faith, a lender might ask, should be placed in a projection of cash to be available on a proposed loan repayment date if the same managers were not able to anticipate the need for financing?

THE CONTENTS OF A BUSINESS PLAN

There is no set format for preparing a business plan because each company must tell its own story. Companies in different industries must present their plans in the unique context of their environment; a chemical company might need to install special pollution controls on a new building, for example, while an apparel manufacturer might not. Different companies in the same industry may have different goals— growth versus diversification, perhaps; the same company may pursue different goals at start-up than when it is mature and expanding.

Still, all business plans possess some common elements. The following major sections appear in any business plan:

- Business description
- Products and services
- Sales and marketing plan
- Operating plan
- Financial information (past, present, and projected)

Each of these major sections can be expanded to include additional areas (an analysis of financial data, for instance), and other major sections can be added (a personnel or management development plan might be necessary if a large expansion is intended). The detailed business plan format that follows is based, with modifications, on a client loan package used by the Small Business Development Center at Clemson University.

BUILDING A BUSINESS PLAN

There are three main sections to a business plan. First is an executive summary that contains a brief description of the company, its product, and requirements for additional resources. The second section is the detailed business plan that includes economic, marketing, social, and strategic factors that will impact the plan. This section, which also includes the financial data, is the most comprehensive of this part of the business plan. Preparation of the financial data stresses the importance of making and documenting careful assumptions about the objectives of the business plan. The third section of the business plan includes supporting documentation, such as contracts and personal resumes.

I. Executive Summary (not to exceed two typewritten pages)
   A. Company name, address, and phone number
   B. Name(s), address(es), and phone number(s) of all key personnel
   C. Brief description of the business
   D. Brief overview of the market for your product
   E. Brief overview of the strategic actions you plan to take to make your firm a success
   F. Brief description of the managerial and technical experience of key personnel
   G. Brief statement of what the financial needs are and what lender's money would be used for
II. Detailed Business Plan
   A. Background of the type of business you are in
      1. Brief history of the business
      2. Current situation
   B. Your business
      1. What makes your business unique?
      2. How does it create value for others?
      3. Describe the key factors that will dictate the success of your business (i.e., price competitiveness, quality, durability, dependability, technical features)
   C. Market analysis

1. Who are the potential buyers for your products? (be specific)
2. What is their motivation to buy from you?
3. How many customers does the market contain? (How large is the total market?)
4. What is the potential annual sales volume?
5. What is the nature of the buying cycle?
   a. Is the product a durable good that lasts for years or a product that is repurchased on a regular basis?
   b. Is the product likely to be purchased only during certain seasons of the year?
6. Specify the target market—what do you know about the potential customers in your geographic area?
   c. If yours is a consumer product:
      i. What are the product features you feel influence the consumer's buying decision?
      ii. What, if any, research supports your feeling?
      iii. Does the consumer have a preference as to where he/she purchases products? How strong is the preference?
7. Break-even analysis
   d. What volume of inventory do you need to sell at what price to break even?
   e. How did you set prices?
8. External market influences: How might each of the following affect the sale or profitability of your product?
   Economic Factors
      Recession
      Inflation
      High/low unemployment
   Social Factors
      Age of customers
      Location demographics
      Income levels
      Size of household
      Societal attitudes
D. Competitor analysis
   1. Describe each of the following factors and discuss how they will influence your success:
      a. Existing competitors: Who are they? List major known competitors. Why do you believe the potential customers in your target market buy from them now?

        b. Potential firms that might enter the market: Who are they? When and why might they enter the market? What would be the impact in your target market segment if they enter?

        c. List the strengths and weaknesses of each competitor's business.

E. Strategic plan for your business

    1. How do you plan to market your products to the target market you identified above? Identify your specific marketing strategy on key factors such as pricing, product promotion and advertising, and customer service.

    2. How will your products compare to those presently in the market? Compare on a competitor-by-competitor basis.

F. Specifics of your organization and management

    1. How is your business organized?

        a. Legally (corporation, S corporation, partnership, sole proprietorship)

        b. Functionally

    2. Who are the key people in your business? What are their backgrounds, and what do they bring to the business that will enhance the chance of success?

G. Financial plans (tie the response to this question to your production and marketing plan)

    1. How much money do you need to make this product and your business a long-term success?

    2. What sources (loans, owner investment, etc.) can be used to finance proposed projects?

    3. How will debt be repaid? Include a schedule of projected cash receipts and disbursements by month for the first year and by quarter for the second and third years.

    4. Does your past performance indicate that your future activities will be successful? Include current and prior year financial statements. Balance sheets and income statements, as well as tax returns for the past three years, should be included.

    5. Do you have assets that can be pledged as collateral for the loan? Include a list of market values for assets (including assets to be purchased).

    6. How will proposed projects or expansion affect your financial statements? Include projected income state-

ments and balance sheets for the life of the loan or at least three years, if the term of the loan is shorter. A ratio analysis of current and projected financial statements as discussed in Chapters 11 and 12 may assist a lender in making credit decisions (and demonstrate that you are controlling the business and are aware of its financial condition). Figure 15-1 shows part of a sample business plan for a hypothetical firm.

III. Supporting Documents

    A.   Supporting documents include personal resumes, personal balance sheets, cost of living budget, credit reports, job descriptions, letters of reference, copies of leases, contract obligations, legal documents, and any other items relevant to the plan.

BUSINESS LOAN APPLICATIONS

The business plan is generally an integral part of a commercial loan application package. If you are preparing a first-time loan application for a financial institution that does not know you or your business, the plan should be much more detailed than if it is being submitted to a lender to whom you are already known. If you know the lender or lenders you wish to approach, it is much more efficient to visit and ask for the necessary application requirements and forms; the business plan can then be tailored to each specific lender's requirements and prepared with sufficient detail to meet all requirements.

The specific requirements of a loan application package vary from lender to lender. Still, some requirements are common to nearly all loan application packages. The components below appear in most loan application packages:

Business Loan Application Components

1. Request letter including the amount, purpose, and repayment schedule needed.
2. The Executive Summary of the business plan, and the collateral to be provided.
3. Personal resumes, financial statements (see Chapter 19), credit references, and tax returns for all officers, directors, and major stockholders.
4. Company information and the company's business plan, as outlined above.
5. Projections of profits, cash flows and balance sheets, as described in section II, part G above.

FIG. 15-1

SAMPLE BUSINESS PLAN

Name and Address of Business: Stop and Shop Market
Grand Avenue East #1000
Apex, N.C. 27502

History of Business: The business was established in 1980 by the current owner, Glenn Jones, who is retiring. Mr. Jones will remain with the business for a period of one year to assure smooth transfer of ownership and continued customer support. Sales of the business have been growing slowly and steadily in the past 5 years (at a rate of 10 percent per year), gross profit margins have remained stable, and suppliers are strong.

Plan of Operation: Mr. And Mrs. King have observed the operation of Stop and Shop for the past six months and believe that no major changes in the current operation are warranted.

Sales Plan:
1. Current hours of 7 a.m. thru 10 p.m. will be maintained seven (7) days a week.
2. Product line will be extended slowly to include fresh coffee and lunch sandwiches, more quick-stop items, and larger bread and milk selections.
3. Advertising will be increased, with the help of co-op advertisers.
4. Interior and exterior remodeling will be postponed until ownership transfer is complete and the customers are comfortable with the new ownership.

Cost Reductions:
1. Mr. And Mrs. King will manage the store, thus eliminating the position of store manager for the current time.
2. Gross profit margins will be increased with quantity purchases and special incentive product purchases.
3. Close watch will be maintained on inventory to assure that no stale inventory occurs.

Market Potential: The population growth potential of the five-mile radius surrounding Stop and Shop has been estimated by the local council of governments at 38 percent per year for the next five years. The highway upgrade of the major thoroughfare will enhance Stop and Shop's accessibility. The targeted sales growth of 15 percent per year can be obtained by the projected growth rate in households in the surrounding area.

    The two major competitors of Stop and Shop are located in a less desirable location in the Apex area, one in a deteriorating neighborhood and one whose accessibility will be limited by new highway construction to take place in the next 18 months. Clearly, Stop and Shop will be able to draw some market from these two stores.

Managerial Capacity: Mr. And Mrs. King have previous managerial experience in operating the Hot Spot Convenience Store in Morganton, N.C. for ten (10) years. They served as comanagers for the business, employing a total of seven other employees, handling all facets of this business operation. This included personnel hiring and management; bookkeeping and financial statements; inventory control; and purchasing.

Robert Morris Associates has developed a Business Credit Information Package for use by lenders to request information from prospective borrowers. The RMA package contains five components:

1. A request letter which the bank might use to request information,
2. A borrower questionnaire,
3. A reporting and disclosure checklist for accountants preparing the borrower's financial statements,
4. A prescribed form for the financial statements, and
5. An accountant's report in the specific format recommended by RMA.

Figure 15-2 contains the borrower questionnaire and the reporting and disclosure checklist excerpted from the Robert Morris Associates Business Credit Information Package.

Robert Morris Associates
Business Credit Information Package
Business Borrower Questionnaire

Attach additional sheets if needed to complete any section.

Borrower Name (exact legal title):		
Address:		Tax ID Number:
Prepared by:	Date:	Phone Number:
Accountant:		Phone Number:
Attorney:		Phone Number:
Insurance Agent:		Phone Number:

Describe the company's major products or services, markets, and methods of operation.

Describe any significant changes in earnings and financial condition <u>over the past three years</u> and the reasons they occurred.

Describe significant changes expected <u>in the coming year</u> (e.g., asset purchases, new revenue sources, expense increases).

FIG. 15-2 *Borrower questionnaire and reporting and disclosure checklist excerpted from Robert Morris Associates Business Credit Information Package*

List the company's five largest customers, credit terms offered to each, and the percentage of annual sales to each.

Customer's Name and Address	Credit Terms	% of Sales
1		
2		
3		
4		
5		

List the company's five largest suppliers, credit terms from each, and credit limits from each.

Supplier's Name and Address	Credit Terms	Credit Limit
1		
2		
3		
4		
5		

Are any examinations by taxing authorities for sales, income, excise, or other taxes now in process?
☐ Yes ☐ No If yes, describe: Date of last IRS Audit: _____

Are any tax payments (sales, income, payroll, property, etc.) delinquent?
☐ Yes ☐ No If yes, describe:

Is the company currently involved in any lawsuits or pending litigation?
☐ Yes ☐ No If yes, describe:

Does the company have an ownership succession plan (e.g., buy–sell agreement)?
☐ Yes ☐ No If yes, describe:

INSURANCE COVERAGE	DOLLAR AMOUNT	COMPANY NAME
Inventories		
Fixed Assets		
General Liability		
Business Interruption		
Product Liability		
Key Person Life		
Other:		

List owners/partners/shareholders, the percentage of the company they own, and their compensation from the company for the past two years. Include all amounts paid by the company (salary, bonus, interest, dividends, other amounts on Forms W2 and 1099).

Name	Position/Title	% Owned	Total Compensation 20	20

Are there any amounts due to the company from owners or other related parties?
☐ Yes　　☐ No　　If yes, describe:

Is your company in compliance with applicable federal and state regulations (such as environmental, employment, or safety)?
☐ Yes　　☐ No　　If no, describe:

Has your company ever been cited for a violation of any of these regulations?
☐ Yes　　☐ No　　If yes, describe:

ACCOUNTING POLICIES & PROCEDURES	Yes	No	N/A	Comments
Cash Account Are all bank accounts reconciled monthly?				
Accounts Receivable Are agings prepared monthly?				
Are agings reviewed monthly for possible bad debts? If not monthly, how often? _____				
Are all credit memos approved in writing?				
Are credit memos issued by someone other than the person who posts cash receipts?				
Are unusual sales terms offered (dated billings, bill—and—hold, consignment)?				
Inventory Are perpetual inventory records maintained?				
Are physical inventories taken monthly? If not monthly, how often? _____				
Are inventory turnover rates (cost of sales divided by inventory) calculated for each product type and reviewed at least quarterly?				
Are signed shipping receipts obtained and maintained?				
Accounts Payable Are agings prepared monthly?				
Are payables posted by someone other than the person who disburses funds?				
Taxes Is an outside payroll preparation service used?				
Are accrued payroll taxes set aside at the time payroll checks are issued?				
Are any tax returns (payroll, sales, income, etc.) delinquent?				
Are income tax estimates filed and paid quarterly? If not quarterly, how often? _____				
Leases Are assets leased from owners evidenced by written agreements?				
Loans from Owners Are debts to owners evidenced by signed notes?				
Are debts to owners formally subordinated to other creditors?				
Financial Statements Are financial statements prepared internally on a monthly basis?				
Are cash, accounts receivable, inventory, and accounts payable reconciled to the general ledger on a monthly basis?				

BORROWER'S CERTIFICATION: The responses given in this questionnaire are true, accurate, and complete to the best of my knowledge. Company: _____ By: _____ Date:_____	This questionnaire is designed to provide the minimum financial information necessary to bankers in making commercial lending decisions when the prospective borrower's financial statements are compiled, but do not contain full GAAP disclosures. Bankers may require additional information and will consider other factors that are not part of this questionnaire. The bank's receipt of this completed questionnaire does not guarantee that a loan request will be approved.

Robert Morris Associates
Business Credit Information Package
<u>Reporting and Disclosure Checklist</u>

Solely for Accountant's Workpapers

Full GAAP compilations (i.e., financial statements with all required note disclosures) are always preferable. If the client's banker permits the RMA Business Credit Information Package selected disclosure alternative, the Prescribed Form requires the <u>amounts</u> in the financial statements be presented in accordance with GAAP rules for recognition and measurement but permits omission of certain disclosures except those identified in this Reporting and Disclosure Checklist. Any material GAAP measurement departures or departures from the 11 disclosures require that the accountant's report be modified, as required by Statement on Standards for Accounting and Review Services No. 3, "Compilation Reports on Financial Statements Included in Certain Prescribed Forms" (SSARS No. 3).

Check off as considered

FINANCIAL STATEMENTS

1. GAAP is the basis to be used for recognition and measurement purposes _____

2. Two year comparative statements (not applicable retroactively) for fiscal year-end statements:
   a. Balance sheet _____
   b. Income statement _____
   c. Statement of changes in owners equity _____
   d. Statement of cash flows* _____

3. If the income statement is condensed, supplementary schedules are included for:
   a. Cost of goods sold _____
   b. Operating expenses _____

4. Each page in the financial statements includes a reference to the accountant's compilation report _____

ACCOUNTANT'S REPORT

1. Compilation report in compliance with SSARS No. 3 _____

2. Supplementary information is provided _____

3. Any material departures from GAAP recognition and measurement or disclosures required by the BCIP are disclosed (See paragraph 4, SSARS No. 3) _____

4. Report is dated and signed _____

---

* RMA recognizes that both the direct and indirect method are permitted by GAAP; however, as explained in RMA's publication titled *Financial Statements for Bank Credit Purposes,* the direct method provides superior and uniquely valuable information for the bank lender's purposes. Consequently, and especially in situations where lenders do not have full GAAP disclosures, the direct method presentation is preferred.

Check off as considered

REQUIRED DISCLOSURES (Footnotes)

1. Organization and nature of business _____
2. Summary of significant accounting policies:
    a. Basis of accounting _____
    b. Revenue recognition method _____
    c. Inventory composition, basis of valuation, and cost determination method _____
    d. Depreciation methods and estimated useful lives of depreciable assets _____
    e. Method used to account for income taxes _____
3. Allowance for bad debts _____
4. Marketable equity securities—aggregate cost and market values with identification of which is carrying value _____
5. Debt
    a. Repayment terms, interest rates, maturity dates, and collateral _____
    b. Lines of credit—committed amounts, maturity dates, and unused availability _____
    c. Minimum annual maturities for the next five years _____
6. Leases
    a. General description of leasing arrangements _____
    b. Future minimum rental payments required as of the date of the latest balance sheet in aggregate and for each of the five succeeding fiscal years _____
7. Related party transactions
    a. Description of the transaction and nature of the relationship _____
    b. Dollar amount of transactions _____
    c. Amounts due to or from related parties _____
8. Pension plans
    a. Description of the plans including employee groups covered _____
    b. Pension expense for period presented and how calculated _____
    c. Unfunded pension liability _____
9. Income tax expense _____
10. Interest and income taxes paid—either as a footnote or on the face of the statement of cash flows _____
11. Significant subsequent events _____

PERSONAL LOAN APPLICATIONS

The owner's personal loan application is required as part of many small-business loan applications. The lender depends on the credit-worthiness of the company's owner and expects repayment from the owner if the business is unable to repay the loan. If the company is a corporation, legally limiting the owner's liability, the lender will require the owner to cosign with the company and accept legal liability for the debt. (The owners of unincorporated businesses are liable for the debts of their companies without cosigning.)

A personal loan application generally requires a personal balance sheet and a personal income and expense sheet. A personal balance sheet asks for all personal assets and liabilities so that the lender can determine the applicant's net worth. (Chapter 19 discusses personal financial statements in great detail and includes a comprehensive example of the preparation of personal financial statements for a hypothetical loan applicant.) An example of a bank loan application form requiring a personal balance sheet and personal income and expenses is shown in Figure 15-3.

FIG. 15-3 *Bank loan application form requesting personal balance sheet and income/expense data*

EACH APPLICANT OTHER THAN SPOUSE NEEDS TO COMPLETE A SEPARATE APPLICATION

Please check the appropriate box
☐ Individual Applying for credit in your own name and based solely on your own credit worthiness
☐ Joint Credit Applying for joint credit with another person based on combined credit worthiness. Names of other applicants _____
☐ Business Credit ☐ Proprietorship ☐ Partnership ☐ Corporation

| LOAN PURPOSE: | | | | | | REQUESTED LOAN AMOUNT $ | |

SECTION A

PRINT FULL NAME	FIRST	MIDDLE	LAST	SR JR	DATE OF BIRTH		SOCIAL SECURITY NUMBER

PRESENT STREET ADDRESS	CITY		STATE	ZIP	HOW LONG THERE YEARS MONTHS

HOME PHONE NUMBER	NUMBER OF DEPENDENTS	DRIVER'S LICENSE NO	STATE

PREVIOUS STREET ADDRESS	CITY		STATE	ZIP	HOW LONG THERE YEARS MONTHS

PRESENT EMPLOYER	TIME ON JOB YEARS MONTHS	OCCUPATION

MONTHLY INCOME FROM EMPLOYMENT	NET $	GROSS $	DEPARTMENT OR SUPERVISOR	WORK PHONE NUMBER

PREVIOUS EMPLOYER	TIME ON JOB YEARS MONTHS	OCCUPATION

OTHER INCOME OF APPLICANT (ALIMONY, CHILD SUPPORT, OR SEPARATE MAINTENANCE INCOME NEED NOT BE REVEALED IF YOU DO NOT WISH TO HAVE IT CONSIDERED AS A BASIS FOR REPAYING THIS DEBT.) SOURCE OR KIND ____ RECEIVED FROM ____ NET $ ____ GROSS $ ____

TWO NEAREST RELATIVES (NOT LIVING IN HOUSEHOLD)	RELATIONSHIP	STREET ADDRESS	CITY	STATE	PHONE NUMBER
1					
2	RELATIONSHIP	STREET ADDRESS	CITY	STATE	PHONE NUMBER

INFORMATION APPLICABLE TO SPOUSE Complete Section B if:
• Spouse will also be contractually liable for repayment.
• Applicant is relying on income of spouse for approval of credit.

SECTION B

PRINT FULL NAME	FIRST	MIDDLE	LAST	SR JR	DATE OF BIRTH		SOCIAL SECURITY NUMBER

PRESENT EMPLOYER	TIME ON JOB YEARS MONTHS	OCCUPATION	DRIVER'S LICENSE NO

MONTHLY INCOME FROM EMPLOYMENT	NET $	GROSS $	DEPARTMENT OR SUPERVISOR	WORK PHONE NUMBER

PREVIOUS EMPLOYER	TIME ON JOB YEARS MONTHS	OCCUPATION

OTHER INCOME OF APPLICANT (ALIMONY, CHILD SUPPORT, OR SEPARATE MAINTENANCE INCOME NEED NOT BE REVEALED IF YOU DO NOT WISH TO HAVE IT CONSIDERED AS A BASIS FOR REPAYING THIS DEBT.) SOURCE OR KIND ____ RECEIVED FROM ____ NET $ ____ GROSS $ ____

NEAREST RELATIVE (NOT LIVING IN HOUSEHOLD)	RELATIONSHIP	STREET ADDRESS	CITY	STATE	PHONE NUMBER

CREDIT REFERENCES Include finance companies, banks, credit cards, charge accounts. Show the name(s) under which credit was given if other than above. Attach additional pages if necessary.

SECTION C

	NAME AND ADDRESS OF MORTGAGE HOLDER OR LANDLORD	PURCHASE PRICE	ORIGINAL AMOUNT	RENT/MORTGAGE PMT
☐ OWN HOME ☐ RENTING ☐ OTHER: _____		1ST MTG INTEREST RATE ☐ FIXED ☐ ADJUSTABLE	PRESENT BALANCE	VALUE OF HOME

NAME OF CREDITOR/ADDRESS/BRANCH	ACCOUNT NUMBER (SECURED BY)	ORIGINAL BALANCE/LIMIT	BALANCE OWING	NO PAYMENT AMOUNT

OTHER OBLIGATIONS: ALIMONY, CHILD SUPPORT, SEPARATE MAINTENANCE, CO-MAKER, GUARANTOR, ETC.
DESCRIBE ____ $ ____ PER ____

FINANCIAL INSTITUTION & ACCOUNT NUMBER	BRANCH OR ADDRESS	TYPE OF ACCOUNT ☐ SAVINGS ☐ CHECKING

EVER TAKEN BANKRUPTCY? ☐ NO ☐ YES Attach Explanation	EVER HAD SUITS, JUDGMENTS, TAX LIENS OR REPOSSESSIONS? ☐ NO ☐ YES Attach Explanation

SIGNATURE OF APPLICANT	DATE	SIGNATURE OF SPOUSE (IF APPLICABLE)	DATE

DETAILS OF TRANSACTION   DEALER OR BRANCH USE ONLY
COLLATERAL TITLED IN NAME OF

SECTION D

PURCHASE

	YEAR	MAKE	MODEL	CASH PRICE	
☐ NEW ☐ USED				CASH DOWN PAYMENT	
# CYLINDERS	VEHICLE IDENTIFICATION NUMBER	MILEAGE		REBATES	
				TRADE-IN ALLOWANCE	
EQUIPMENT	☐ AUTO/TRANS ☐ AIR COND	☐ 4 X 4 ☐ OTHER		OWING ON TRADE	
				NET TRADE-IN	

TRADE

YEAR	MAKE		MODEL	TOTAL DOWN PAYMENT	
FINANCED BY				UNPAID BALANCE OF CASH PRICE	
ADDRESS				OTHER CHARGES TO BE FINANCED	
TERM OF CONTRACT		DEALER NAME		TOTAL AMOUNT FINANCED	
(MOS)	@$	PER MONTH		NADA AVG TRADE-IN $	INVOICE AMT $

Generally, when the borrower has collateral to back up the loan application, the following loan-to-value guidelines establish the upper limits on the amounts lent to both individuals and companies.

Asset	Loan to Value Ratio (upper limit)
Developed real estate	75–80%
Undeveloped real estate	50–80%
Inventory (of real property)	35–50%
New equipment	70–90%
Used equipment	0–50%
Accounts receivable	70–75%

CHAPTER PERSPECTIVE

The general contents of a comprehensive business plan include a business description, a discussion of products and services, a sales and marketing plan, an operating plan, and detailed financial information, including past, present, and projected financial statements. Each of these sections can be expanded to include additional areas, and other sections, such as a personnel or management development plan, can be added. This chapter has discussed the business plan both as a vital element in a business loan application and as a tool that allows management to monitor and control operations, examine the feasibility of proposed projects, and choose between alternative projects. The chapter ended with a brief discussion of personal loan applications, often required of the owner as part of the loan application for a small, privately held business. A personal loan application generally requires a personal balance sheet and an itemized statement of personal income and expenses.

Performance Reports: Evaluation and Analysis

INTRODUCTION AND MAIN POINTS

In Chapters 13 and 14 we covered budgeting and standard costing, two managerial tools used for profit planning and control. Chapter 13 dealt with the preparation of a master budget detailing a company's plans and goals for the future; Chapter 14 discussed the use of standard costing and flexible budgeting in evaluating and controlling actual costs incurred during the period and introduced the performance report in the context of comparing actual and budgeted costs.

However, as companies become more decentralized, it becomes essential for management to be able to evaluate performance on a departmental or divisional level. In this chapter we discuss some of the methods and guidelines used to evaluate the performance of a company's departments or divisions.

After reading and studying this chapter:

▬ You will understand the purpose and structure of performance reports.

▬ You will understand the definition and advantages of responsibility accounting and be able to identify responsibility centers.

▬ You will understand how segments of an organization are evaluated using the contribution approach, return on investment, and residual income.

PURPOSE AND STRUCTURE OF PERFORMANCE REPORTS

In Chapter 13 we introduced the master budget, management's quantitative plan of action to achieve company objectives. *Performance reports* present the assessment of performance of a company's operational activities. Many times these reports consist of comparisons of budgeted and actual results. In Chapter 14 we presented the *flexible budget,* a comparison of budgeted to actual results, as an example of a performance report. We noted at that time that the comparison of budgeted goals to actual results was an important factor in evaluating performance and identifying the need for corrective action. A simplified flexible budget performance report comparing budgeted amounts to actual results appears in Figure 16-1.

	Actual	Budgeted	Variance
Sales	$100,000	$150,000	($50,000) U
Variable Expenses	60,000	97,500	37,500) F
Fixed Expenses	18,000	16,000	(2,000) U
Total Expenses	78,000	113,500	(35,500) U
Operating Income	$ 22,000	$ 36,500	($14,500) U

FIG. 16-1 *Income Statement Performance Report for the Period Ended September 30, 1999*

Variances, described as favorable or unfavorable, are highlighted when actual activities differ from initial expectations. Since actual sales were $50,000 less than budgeted sales (an unfavorable variance), there was a decrease in net income, about which management should be concerned. The marketing department needs to be concerned as to whether the budget figure was unrealistic or whether sales personnel did an inadequate job of selling the company's products. Actual variable expenses were less than budgeted, resulting in a favorable variance. This variance might have been caused by reduced sales; if this is the case, the variance is really not favorable. Fixed expenses exceeded the budget by $2,000; management needs to examine the elements of both fixed and variable expenses to decide what action, if any, needs to be taken.

This simplified example demonstrates how management uses performance reports to monitor operations and identify areas requiring corrective action. The performance report on budget to actual results is used as a planning and control device to guide the company in its efforts to improve profitability. Other forms of performance reports used in the evaluation of the operating processes of a company will be discussed in this chapter.

Some employees have negative feelings toward the budgetary process because they fear performance evaluations. Employees, as well as managers, should be made aware of the purpose of performance evaluations; that is, their preparation is designed to identify areas needing management's attention. They are not designed to assess blame or fault. The central idea is to identify problem areas and turn unfavorable variances into favorable ones.

To be of any use, performance reports must be prepared and disseminated in a timely fashion. If too long a time elapses before issuance of the report, corrective action may not be feasible and unfavorable variances will not be eliminated in the future.

Characteristically, a performance report focuses on *management by exception,* a strategy in which attention is directed only to activities that deviate from expectations on the assumption that managers have little time to waste examining operations that are running smoothly. Therefore, attention is directed only to those areas not performing according to plan.

Performance reports involve layers of summary data; a manager receives detailed information on performance below his or her level, but summarized data for higher management levels. Figure 16-2 presents a performance report showing the effects of this summarization process. As we move up the chain of command there is a greater summarization of the results of operations.

Refer to the report for the Chicago store manager in the bottom third of the exhibit. A basic question regarding this report is "What items should the store manager be held accountable for?" Should the manager be held responsible for noncontrollable costs such as depreciation, insurance, and property taxes? Many management authorities believe that if a manager cannot influence these types of costs in the short run, then he or she should not be held accountable for these costs. These experts advocate including in the performance report only those costs that are controllable by the manager in the short run. Others favor a more inclusive approach to the preparation of performance reports; they feel that by including all costs in the preparation of a performance report, managers are made more aware of the fact that in the final analysis both controllable and noncontrollable costs need to be recovered in order for the company to be profitable. Both formats are used in practice, and one is not necessarily better than the other. The choice is one of personal preference and should be made on the basis of which format is consistent with the goals and objectives of the company's responsibility accounting system.

Soft Hackle Company

Operating Income of Branches and District	Midwest District Manager Performance Report		
Direct Expenses:	Budget	Actual	Variance
Illinois Branch	$110,000	$111,000	$ 1,000 F
Iowa Branch	97,000	84,600	12,400 U
Nebraska Branch	103,400	105,500	2,100 F
District Office			
Expenses	(67,600)	(69,000)	1,400 U
Operating Income	$242,800	$232,100	$10,700 U

Operating Income of Stores and Branch	Illinois Branch Manager Performance Report		
Direct Expenses:	Budget	Actual	Variance
Chicago Store	$ 16,500	$ 14,800	$ 1,800 U
Moline Store	46,200	48,000	1,800 F
Springfield Store	67,300	69,700	2,400 F
Branch Office			
Expenses	(20,000)	(21,500)	1,500 U
Operating Income	$110,100	$111,000	$ 900 F

Operating Income of Chicago Store:	Chicago Store Manager Performance Report		
Revenue	$30,300	$28,000	$2,300 U
Selling Expenses	4,700	5,600	900 U
Repairs Expense	500	200	300 F
General Expense	1,600	1,300	300 F
Property Taxes and Insurance Expense	2,000	2,000	-0-
Depreciation Expense	3,000	3,000	-0-
Wages Expense	2,000	1,100	900 F
Operating Income	$16,500	$14,800	$1,700 U

FIG. 16-2 *Performance Report for the Period Ended July 31, 1999*

RESPONSIBILITY ACCOUNTING

Responsibility accounting refers to a system of gathering revenue and expense information and communicating it to divisions, departments, and individuals by areas of responsibility. Using the responsibility accounting system that incorporates budgeting, standard costs, and variance analysis, top management can delegate decision-making authority to lower management levels and then evaluate performance based on projections.

Benefits of Responsibility Accounting

Perhaps first and foremost, responsibility accounting allows managers to apply the management by exception principle (see Chapter 14), focusing attention only on those activities not proceeding according to plan and spending more time on other broader issues affecting the organization. Responsibility accounting allows managers to delegate authority because it provides management with a method for guiding performance as well as evaluating that performance. Managers are better able to set objectives when they know that the objectives will be used as the yardstick by which their performance will be measured.

Responsibility Centers

Companies that use responsibility accounting develop budgets and performance reports for every component of the company, each of which is called a *responsibility center.* Each responsibility center is a unit that management has decided needs control over its costs, revenues, and/or investment and has its own individual budget. Responsibility centers can be *cost centers, profit centers,* or *investment centers.*

A *cost center* is a unit that is responsible for and reports only costs. Examples include accounting and purchasing departments. These units are not responsible for generating revenue; thus the focus is on control of costs. Performance reports for cost centers report only costs; normally, variance analysis, using standard costs and flexible budgets, is used to measure performance. For example, an accounting department might be evaluated on the cost of processing a certain number of transactions.

Units that are responsible for selling a product can be either profit or investment centers. A *profit center* is responsible for and reports revenues, expenses, and income. Examples include the men's or jewelry departments of a large department store. The unit reports revenues less expenses and is normally evaluated using the contribution margin approach (revenues − controllable expenses). (The contribution margin approach is discussed later in this chapter.)

An *investment center* is responsible for and reports revenues, expenses, and income, as well as the investment in assets required to support its operations. The Chevrolet division of General Motors and the corporate headquarters division of IBM Corporation are examples of investment centers. In addition to revenues and expense, investment is reported so that a return on investment can be computed. Return on investment and residual income, discussed in the following sections, are the two most popular methods of measuring the performance of an investment center.

SEGMENT ANALYSIS

Most companies measure performance of major segments, which can be divisions, categories of customer, sales territories, or product lines. Decentralization within companies results in the delegation of decision-making to units and individuals at lower levels of the organization. Particular segment managers have varying degrees of autonomy. If a manager has control over only revenue and expenses, the profit center concept is used; on the other hand, if the manager has control over revenues, expenses, and the assets of the segment, the investment center concept is used.

Evaluation Criteria of a Profit Center

Figure 16-3 presents the segment income statement for the Corvis Company, maker of custom fly fishing rods. Corvis makes both bamboo and graphite fly fishing rods and also repairs damaged rods.

	Bamboo Division	Graphite Division	Repair Division	Total for Company
Sales	$230,000	$190,000	$80,000	$500,000
Less: Variable Expenses	168,000	140,000	62,000	370,000
Contribution Margin	62,000	50,000	18,000	130,000
Less: Direct Fixed Expenses	30,000	20,000	10,000	60,000
Segment Margin	$ 32,000	$ 30,000	$ 8,000	70,000
Less: Unallocated Common Fixed Expenses				45,000
Net Income				$ 25,000

FIG. 16-3 *Corvis Company Segment Income Statement for the Period Ended May 31, 1999*

Profit centers such as the Bamboo Division are best evaluated using the *contribution margin approach,* which focuses on the behavior patterns of variable or fixed costs and their controllability by the division. Variable and fixed expenses are separated in Figure 16-3. This is done because fixed expenses generally do not fluctuate with changes in volume and are much less controllable in the short run than variable expenses. *Direct fixed expenses* are those expenses that can be specifically identified with a segment; *common fixed expenses—*

those that cannot be specifically associated with a segment—are expenses that would continue to be incurred even if a division were to be closed or eliminated, such as the salary of the president of the Corvis Company. In Figure 16-3, these common fixed expenses are identified as unallocated. Any allocation of these costs could significantly change the operating net income of each of the divisions, and most allocation schemes are arbitrary. However, some companies do attempt to allocate common fixed expenses even though division managers do not have any control over these allocated costs.

There are two methods for allocating common fixed expenses: benefit received or responsibility of incurrence. If neither approach is appropriate, some other reasonable, but arbitrary, basis (such as sales) is used. Assume the following information for Corvis Company:

Item		Basis for Allocation
General Expense	$10,000	Sales
Insurance Expense	20,000	Cost of Segment Assets
Maintenance Expense	15,000	Square Footage
Total Common Fixed Expenses	$45,000	

	Bamboo Division	Graphite Division	Repair Division	Total
Sales	$230,000	$190,000	$80,000	$500,000
Cost of Segment Plant Assets	50,000	30,000	20,000	100,000
Square Footage per Segment	8,000	10,000	12,000	30,000

The allocation of common fixed expenses would be as follows:

	Bamboo Division	Graphite Division	Repair Division	Total
General Expense	(a) $ 4,600	(b) $3,800	(c) $1,600	$10,000
Insurance Expense	(d) 10,000	(e) 6,000	(f) 4,000	20,000
Maintenance Expense	(g) 4,000	(h) 5,000	(i) 6,000	15,000
Total Common Fixed Expenses				$45,000

(a) $230,000/$500,000 × $10,000 = $4,600
(b) $190,000/$500,000 × $10,000 = $3,800
(c) $80,000/$500,000 × $10,000 = $1,600
(d) $50,000/$100,000 × $20,000 = $10,000
(e) $30,000/$100,000 × $20,000 = $6,000
(f) $20,000/$100,000 × $20,000 = $4,000
(g) $8,000/$30,000 × $15,000 = $4,000
(h) $10,000/$30,000 × $15,000 = $5,000
(i) $12,000/$30,000 × $15,000 = $6,000

Summarizing our discussion, the contribution approach for segment reporting and analysis includes the following information:

▬ *Contribution Margin:* sales minus variable costs

▬ *Segment Margin:* contribution margin minus direct fixed expenses. Direct fixed expenses are specifically traceable to a segment and include discretionary fixed expenses such as advertising and research development that would normally be eliminated if the segment were eliminated.

▬ *Net Income:* segment margin minus unallocated common fixed expenses. Unallocated common fixed expenses are those that are not directly traceable to a segment and include depreciation, property taxes, and insurance.

Evaluation Criteria for an Investment Center

Two evaluative criteria used with the investment center concept are *return on investment* and *residual income.*

Return on investment (ROI) calculates return (income) as a percentage of the assets utilized (investment) by a segment. The formula for ROI is:

$$\text{ROI} = \frac{\text{Income}}{\text{Investment}}$$

ROI, rather than absolute amounts of income, is used because a segment with a large dollar amount of assets usually has a greater amount of income than a segment with a small dollar amount of assets. ROI is a more useful measure of performance when the investment bases of segments differ.

The calculation of ROI is relatively simple. However, there is some disagreement as to the definition of *income* and *investment.* Possible definitions for income include net income, operating income, and segment income, while investment can be defined as total assets, operating assets, or controllable assets. After investment is defined, a choice needs to be whether to use cost, cost less accumulated depreciation, or replacement cost for the investment in assets. Whichever definitions and valuation bases are chosen must be used consistently for comparative purposes.

The ROI formula can be broken down into two components as follows:

$$\text{ROI} = \frac{\text{Income}}{\text{Sales}} \times \frac{\text{Sales}}{\text{Investment}}$$

This model was developed by financial analysts at E.I. DuPont de Nemours & Co. (hence its name, the DuPont model) in the late 1930s and was introduced briefly in our discussion of ratio analysis in chapter 11. The basic premise is that both profitability from sales and the efficient employment of assets in generating sales are factors that should be weighed in evaluating the profitability of a company.

The first factor, income/sales, or *margin,* is a measure of the percentage of each sales dollar resulting in income. The second factor, sales/investment, is called *turnover* and represents the efficiency with which a company uses its investment in assets to generate sales.

The point of separating the formula into two components is to emphasize the importance of efficient employment of a company's investment in assets as well as of earning a profit from sales. This can be underscored by an example. In 1990 the average ROI for American companies was approximately 15 percent. Suppose this ROI was achieved by a heavy equipment manufacturer and a grocery chain in the following manner:

	Margin	×	Turnover	=	ROI
Grocery Chain	1%	×	15 times	=	15%
Heavy Equipment Manufacturer	15%	×	1 time	=	15%

By focusing on either margin or turnover or both, management can create a plan to bolster ROI. Assume a company wants to increase ROI to 20 percent from the current 15 percent, computed as follows:

$$\text{ROI} = \frac{\$15,000}{\$200,000} \times \frac{\$200,000}{\$100,000} = 15\%$$

ROI can be increased by reducing expenses while holding turnover constant:

$$\text{ROI} = \frac{\$20,000}{\$200,000} \times \frac{\$200,000}{\$100,000} = 20\%$$

ROI can also be increased by increasing turnover by decreasing the company's investment in assets and holding margin constant.

$$\text{ROI} = \frac{\$15,000}{\$200,000} \times \frac{\$200,000}{\$75,000} = 20\%$$

ROI can be increased by actions that have the effect of increasing both margin and turnover. This can be accomplished by disposing of nonproductive assets. The investment in assets is reduced and income is increased through a reduction of depreciation expense.

$$\text{ROI} = \frac{\$19,000}{\$200,000} \times \frac{\$200,000}{\$95,000} = 20\%$$

This third example illustrates the point that excessive investments can have the same effect in terms of reducing ROI as excessive expenses.

If there is a problem with using ROI as a performance measure, it is the tendency of division managers who are evaluated on that basis to accept only those additional investments for which the rate of return exceeds that of the division's ROI. For example, assume a division is earning $20,000 per year on an investment in assets of $100,000. The division ROI is therefore 20 percent ($20,000/$100,000). This 20 percent ROI is above the company's minimum rate of return of 14 percent. If the division manager were presented with a project that would yield 17 percent on a $10,000 investment, the manager would not accept the proposal because it would reduce the division's ROI to 19.7 percent.

	Status Quo	Proposed Project	If Accepted
Income	$ 20,000	$ 1,700	$ 21,700
Investment	100,000	10,000	110,000
ROI ($20,000/$100,000)	20%		
ROI ($21,700/$110,000)			19.7%

In this instance, the division manager has taken an action that is in the manager's own best interest, but the action is not in the best interest of the company as a whole, because the 17 percent return on the project is above the company's minimum rate of return of 14 percent. This situation, called *suboptimization,* can occur when a company uses ROI as its sole criterion for evaluating the performance of a division.

To overcome suboptimization, companies sometimes use *residual income* to measure performance. Residual income is the amount of income that a segment earns on its investment in assets over a desired minimum ROI. Unlike ROI, RI is an absolute dollar amount, calculated as follows:

$$RI = Income - (Minimum\ ROI \times Investment\ in\ Assets)$$

The division's residual income from our previous example is:

$$\$20,000 - (14\% \times \$100,000) = \$6,000$$

Using RI, a division manager accepts investment proposals as long as the rate earned exceeds the division's minimum ROI, increasing the division's RI. Returning to our previous example, the proposed project provides a higher rate of return (17 percent) than the division's minimum rate of return (14 percent). Acceptance of the project increases RI by $300.

	Status Quo	Proposed Project	If Accepted
Investment in Assets	$100,000	$10,000	$110,000
Minimum Rate of Return 14%	(14,000)	(1,400)	(15,400)
Rate of Return 20%	20,000		20,000
Rate of Return 17%		1,700	1,700
Residual Income	$ 6,000	$ 300	$ 6,300

In conclusion, the use of RI focuses on the maximization of RI, not ROI. Some authorities consider RI to be a better measure of performance than ROI; They believe that the use of RI encourages division managers to accept investment projects that would be rejected if ROI were used. A disadvantage of RI is that it does favor larger divisions with larger investments in assets, making the comparison of segments or divisions of varying sizes very difficult.

CHAPTER PERSPECTIVE

Management's plans are implemented through the budgeting process. Monitoring the difference between actual results and budgeted amounts results in variances. Using the concept of management by exception, performance reports highlight these deviations from expectations, and managers deal only with situations in which a problem exists. Performance reports should be prepared on a timely basis so corrective action can be taken when necessary; employees should not be antagonistic toward performance reports, since they are prepared in an attempt to identify areas needing attention and not to assess blame. Finally, the performance report should focus on items under direct control of the department or individual being reported on.

Responsibility accounting seeks to provide information to evaluate a manager based upon the revenue, expense, or investment items over which he or she has control. Management establishes responsibility centers as part of a responsibility accounting system. Analysis of the performance of a responsibility center depends on the classification of the responsibility center. A center that produces no revenue and only incurs expenses is reported as a cost center and is evaluated on the basis of cost reduction or in relation to a budgeted amount. A profit center earns both revenues and expenses and is therefore evaluated on the basis of income, essentially the difference between the revenues and expenses under the control of the profit center manager. An investment center has revenues, expenses, and an investment base. Two different criteria exist for evaluating an investment center: ROI compares an income figure to an investment base, and RI evaluates performance in terms of how much of investment center income exceeds income based on a minimum rate of return.

Internal Audit Reports

INTRODUCTION AND MAIN POINTS

Auditors have traditionally examined records or accounts to check their accuracy. Today, auditors are responsible not only for checking the accuracy of accounting records but for checking and reporting on the results of business activities in all areas. We have seen (in Chapter 2) that external auditors express opinions on financial statements included in company annual reports. Internal auditors examine and report on efficiency, effectiveness, and goal attainment in all areas of operation.

In this chapter, we examine the role of internal auditors, the steps involved in an internal audit, and the reports issued by the internal auditor.

After studying the material in this chapter:

▬ You will know the difference between internal and external auditors.

▬ You will know the five aspects of company operations that concern internal auditors.

▬ You will understand the seven steps in the audit process and how the auditor relies on internal control in making the examination.

▬ You will understand the format of the report of the internal auditor and how it is used.

▬ You will see that the internal auditor tries to remain independent and objective even though an employee of the company is being audited.

KINDS OF AUDITORS

The original definition of *auditor* was one who listens; an audit in ancient Rome was called a "hearing of the accounts." While traditionally the role of the auditor has been to examine accounting records and check their accuracy, the role of the auditor is currently expanding; auditors are responsible not only for checking accounting records but for checking the results of business operating activities in all areas. Auditors issue two types of reports: external audit reports, discussed in Chapter 2, and internal audit reports.

External Auditors and Financial Statement Audits

The external auditor's audit opinion of published financial statements tells stockholders, creditors, and others outside a company how much they can rely on its financial statements as a basis for making business decisions, such as whether to buy or sell shares of a company's stock, make commercial loans, or extend trade credit necessary to do business with a company. To make these decision, financial-statement readers need the auditor's assurance of fairness and compliance with generally accepted accounting principles. The external audit report is addressed not to company management but to the stockholders of the company and is publicly circulated; the external auditor is responsible to third parties outside the firm who use the audited financial statements as a basis for making business decisions. External auditors are always certified public accountants (CPAs) and their function is much better known by the public than is that of internal auditors.

Internal Auditors and Operational Audits

If an external auditor acts as the agent of stockholders and creditors, internal auditors are the eyes and ears of a company's management inside the company. In fact, internal auditing is sometimes called *management auditing* or *operational auditing* because, in addition to accounting records, internal auditors check, monitor, and examine the operating activities that managers would check, monitor, and examine if they had the time (and audit skills). In an operational audit, the internal auditor examines business activities and creates reports on those activities to assist management in achieving efficient, effective, goal-directed operations.

The following has been proposed by the Institute of Internal Auditors as an official definition of internal auditing: Internal auditing is an independent and objective assurance and consulting activity that is guided by a philosophy of adding value to improve the operations of the organization. It assists an organization in accomplishing its objectives by bringing a systematic and disciplined approach to evaluate and improve the effectiveness of the organization's risk management, control, and governance processes. Professionalism and a commitment to excellence are facilitated by operating within a framework of professional practice established by the Institute of Internal Auditors.

External auditors are concerned only with the accuracy of the accounting records. Internal auditors are concerned with the same operating areas—efficiency, effectiveness, and goal attainment—that concern company managers. For example, an internal auditor might examine the operation of the purchasing department to see if bid procedures are being followed and if material is being purchased only from approved buyers and only in grades that meet engineering specifications. A credit department might be audited to see if it has established standards for granting credit and if controls are in place to help assure that those standards are being followed by employees. Sometimes internal auditors give opinions on what they observe, but frequently they report only what they see and express no opinion.

Unlike the CPA, the internal auditor is an employee of the company responsible to management and the board of directors and not to third party financial-statement users. Internal auditors are not required to be licensed, but many are certified internal auditors (CIAs) from the Institute of Internal Auditors (IIA). Internal auditors may also be CPAs or have other credentials as evidence of competence, particularly in data processing. Internal and external auditors are compared in Figure 17-1.

	Internal Auditor	External Auditor
Certification required?	no (CIA optional)	yes (CPA required)
Responsible to third parties?	no	yes
Reports to:	top management and the board	stockholders*
Report contains audit opinion?	sometimes	yes
Reports on fairness of financial statements?	no	yes
Reports on compliance with accounting rules and policies?	yes	yes
Reports on compliance with administrative rules and policies?	yes	no
Reports on efficiency and effectiveness of operations?	yes	no

*The firm's external auditor is selected and retained by the audit committee of the board of directors. The audit committee is composed of outside directors who are not managers of the company.

FIG. 17-1 *Internal Versus External Auditors*

CONDUCTING AN INTERNAL AUDIT

Internal auditors are concerned with five aspects of business operation. (Hereafter, internal auditors and internal audits will be referred to simply as "auditors" and "audits.") Auditors may seek to determine:

1. The reliability and integrity of information
2. The extent of management's compliance with company policies, plans, and procedures and government laws and regulations
3. How well assets are safeguarded
4. The effectiveness and efficiency of operations
5. The extent to which established objectives and goals are accomplished.

As a rule, a particular audit is concerned with only one or two of these aspects, rather than all five. A branch bank might be audited to determine if assets are safeguarded and if bank policies and government regulations are being followed, while a manufacturing plant might be audited to see if operations are effective and efficient and if company goals are being accomplished. Each audit seeks to address specific management concerns and has specific audit objectives.

An audit generally proceeds in seven steps, in the following general order:*

1. A preliminary survey is performed.
2. An audit program is developed.
3. Field work is performed.
4. Working papers are prepared to document the audit findings.
5. Deficiency findings (if any) are prepared.
6. The audit report is written and presented.
7. Any deficiencies found are monitored by the auditor until they are resolved.

Preliminary Survey

The internal auditor frequently begins the audit by making a preliminary survey of the operation to be audited, visiting the site, interviewing managers and operating personnel, inspecting operations, and attempting to become familiar with the activity to be audited. In this stage of the audit, the auditor generally tries to alleviate any fears

---

* The reference book perhaps most used by internal auditors is *Sawyer's Internal Auditing,* written by Lawrence B. Sawyer and published by the Institute of Internal Auditors. Our discussion of the internal audit report follows the discussion in the Sawyer text.

the auditees might have by explaining the scope of the audit—what will be examined and what will not—and explaining that in most cases the auditor is trying to help, rather than to police.

Overall, the internal audit profession is trying to enhance its image by focusing attention on the good that is done, rather than the culprits who are caught. The auditor's goal is to help managers do a better job; as a result, most auditors want to see operations improved, not employees disciplined. Usually, an auditor explains that if a problem is discovered, the manager of the problem area will be told immediately and will have the opportunity to correct or at least to begin correcting the problem before the audit report is issued. In that way, both the problem and the manager's action to correct it can be included in the audit report.

Objectives and Standards. An auditor, whether internal or external, must audit against some standard; when an auditor examines an account balance or an operating activity, the examination is meaningless if there is no standard with which to compare.

Financial-statement data are audited using generally accepted accounting principles as the standard for correct presentation; regulated activities in a bank are audited using federal and state requirements. These standards are readily available for auditors to use in examining financial statements and regulated activities. But what does the auditor do when no standards exist? In such cases, the auditor and the manager of the operation to be audited must establish and agree on standards to be used in the audit.

Sometimes the standards used in an audit are the policies and procedures already in existence for the operation. If there are no policies and procedures, or if they are outdated or incorrect, standards must be established before the audit can be performed. To develop standards against which to audit, the auditor looks first at the goals of the operation and then at the activities that should take place if the goals are to be achieved.

Suppose, for example, that an auditor has been asked to audit a personnel department that has no written policies and procedures (or has them but the auditor desires, as part of the audit, to confirm the adequacy of the policies and procedures followed). In either case, the auditor must determine what standards the personnel department should follow. First, the auditor considers what should be the goals of a personnel department. The auditor may decide (in discussion with the personnel department manager) that one goal is to hire qualified people; another goal may be to maintain employee files; still another may be to provide adequate training.

Limiting our discussion to the first of these goals, we can illustrate how the auditor might determine what procedures would result in hiring qualified people and hence serve as standards against which to audit. After consideration and discussion, the auditor may decide that, to hire qualified people, the personnel department must require applicants to complete application forms listing their qualifications and then must somehow verify that the qualifications are legitimate. Even before that, there must be a job description for each position to be filled; the qualifications necessary to perform the job must be determined. Once those determinations have been made, the auditor has operating standards that can be used to audit the performance of the personnel department in hiring qualified people:

- Each position should have a job description that includes the qualifications required for the job.
- Each applicant must complete an application form that includes a request for the applicant's qualifications.
- The qualifications of each potential new hire must be checked by the personnel department.
- The qualifications of each new hire must meet or exceed the qualifications listed in the job description.

Documents supporting the personnel department actions that satisfy each of these operating standards should be in the department files. The auditor does not determine what qualifications are required for a job or whether an applicant is qualified for a job (that is the responsibility of the personnel department), but the auditor *can* decide if the personnel department is following operating procedures that can reasonably be expected to accomplish department goals.

Internal Control. One goal of the preliminary survey is to examine the system of internal control, that is, any policy, procedure, or management action that provides assurance that company objectives will be met. In the example of the personnel department, files must be maintained on each new hire and their content reviewed by a supervisor to be sure that policies are followed. If no files are kept, the auditor cannot evaluate hiring activities; if files are not reviewed, the auditor cannot be certain that all files are complete unless he or she checks each file. Both the maintenance of the files and their regular review are internal control measures.

Some internal controls are designed to provide assurance that policies are followed; others are meant to safeguard assets. We discuss below several internal control measures and explain why they are important.

1. Prenumbered documents:

Many documents are used either to record important information or to authorize certain activities. All documents that management wishes to control should be prenumbered. When documents are prenumbered, management can control their use by requiring employees to account for all documents in their possession. Employees are reluctant to misuse prenumbered documents—by giving a special parking permit to a friend, for example—if they know they must account for all documents in their possession.

2. Separation of incompatible duties:

An error or an intentional fraud is less likely to occur if people must conspire to conceal it than if it can be committed by one person acting alone. To reduce the likelihood of such incidents, an asset such as cash or supplies should be held by one person and the accounting records maintained by another. When such related functions are separated, intentional misstatement of the accounts, either to commit theft or to conceal an error, requires collusion and is less likely to occur.

When incompatible duties are not separated, auditors must do much more checking to be sure that the operating results or account balances are not materially misstated. An auditor examining inventory records maintained by the person who also has custody of the inventory has to examine a bigger sample of the records—perhaps all of them—to be certain that fraud or errors have not caused the inventory account to be misstated. If these functions are separated, less checking is necessary.

Other incompatible functions include ordering and receiving materials, and issuing checks and reconciling the bank balance. In the first instance, the employee can create a bogus order, indicate receipt when no goods were received, and cause a payment to be made to a fictitious supplier. In the second, an employee might issue a check to a fictitious payee and conceal the check when it is returned with the bank statement.

3. Mandatory vacations:

Many fraudulent schemes require constant attention if they are to be concealed. Often, managers are shocked when a fraud is uncovered. "Why, Jane was so devoted to her job! She had not missed a day's work in ten years. She never took vacations and came in sick many times!" Why would Jane miss work? She could not miss work and let someone else do her job without risking exposure of her schemes. Mandatory vacations allow someone new to do each job, making it more difficult to conceal fraudulent activities. If employees must take a periodic vacation, the auditor can be more confident about the accuracy of account balances.

4. Limited access:

Many companies require cards or badges for access to the plant or offices on a "need to know" or "need to go" basis. Access may be limited by:

1. Something you know, such as a password
2. Something you have, such as a key or a "smart card" (as used in a bank machine) imprinted with an access code
3. Something you are, such as a body part (a retina, finger-, or handprint)

When Preliminary Surveys Are Not Needed. When a company has many essentially identical operations, such as branches of a bank or stores in a chain, a single audit program may be used for all operations and no preliminary survey is needed. Also, an audit may be begun without a preliminary visit when the auditor wishes the audit to be a surprise. Surprise counts of cash or audits of some types of records (especially records of cash receipts) are common.

Developing and Performing the Audit Program

The auditor develops a program for the audit based on the observations made and standards developed during the preliminary survey. The audit program includes a list of all tests the auditor wishes to perform; as each test is completed, the auditor documents the results in audit work papers.

An auditor seeking to determine the reliability of accounting information or the extent to which an operation meets certain standards could check every transaction or operating activity. Between audits, however, companies may accumulate millions of separate transactions or operating activities; checking each one is not feasible. Instead, the auditor looks for ways to report on a large volume of activities without checking each individual activity. This is accomplished by examining only a sample of the activities on which the auditor must report. The size of the sample is determined by judgment or statistics based on several factors, among them the kind of internal controls management has placed on the activity. For example, if the files of the personnel department discussed previously are reviewed by a supervisor after each new hire is processed and any errors or omissions are corrected, the auditor can be confident about the operation of the department after checking fewer files than if no supervisory review is made.

Deficiency Findings

A deficiency is anything that is not as it should be. Generally, deficiencies are required actions not taken, required actions taken improperly, or prohibited actions taken. Auditors classify deficiencies in three categories:

1. A *major deficiency* is one that can prevent the company from attaining a major goal. Failing to perform background checks of workers hired to work in sensitive areas is a major deficiency; a dishonest employee might steal information (or cash or whatever is sensitive).

2. A *minor deficiency* is one that is more than a random error but which would not prevent the company from attaining a major goal. Failing to file all the references of workers is a minor deficiency.

3. *Insignificant deviations* are random errors of the sort all people make occasionally. Filing a worker's references in the wrong file is an insignificant deviation.

For each deficiency discovered, the auditor completes a deficiency finding report that includes the items shown here and in Figure 17-2.

■ The *standard* the operation was supposed to meet
■ The actual *condition* of the operation (what was actually accomplished)
■ The *cause* of the departure from standard
■ The *effect* of the departure from standard
■ A *recommendation* as to how the correction might be made

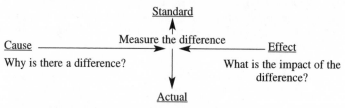

FIG. 17-2 *Components of a Deficiency Finding*

Auditors are careful to document deficiency findings because major and minor (but never insignificant) findings are probably included in the auditor's report and the person responsible for the problem frequently challenges the auditor's observation. When challenged, the auditor can then produce documentation in the deficiency finding report. The deficiency finding reports are not given to the auditee, but all major and minor findings are normally included in the final audit report.

The Audit Report

Internal auditors do not submit their reports to people outside the company; as a result, there is no standard report form as there is for a CPA report on published financial statements. The primary purpose of an internal auditor's report is to communicate the auditor's findings to the auditee and the auditee's manager and to make recommendations. The Institute of Internal Auditors recommend that an audit report contain the elements shown in Figure 17-3.

1. *Purpose.* The audit report should include the reason the audit was performed, such as "to determine the effectiveness of company policies on hiring new employees."

2. *Scope.* The auditor should explain what was covered by the audit and what was not. The auditor might explain, for instance, that the audit examined compliance with company policies for hiring factory workers but did not include an examination of the hiring policies for engineers.

3. *Audit findings.* The report should tell what was found. "Job descriptions specify the qualifications necessary for each position, but those qualifications were not met by 40 percent of the new hires during the last six months."

4. *Recommendations.* The report of a problem should be accompanied by a recommended course of action to correct any problem reported. Perhaps the auditor would recommend that "personnel department employees receive additional training and that supervisors monitor compliance with company policy and document their monitoring activity in the file of each new hire."

5. *Opinions and conclusions (where appropriate).* Audit opinions are the auditor's evaluation of the effects of any deficiencies found, such as: "Compliance with position qualification requirements is inadequate. Failure to hire qualified workers might result in significant cost to the company in excess scrap." Although many internal auditors avoid drawing a conclusion or stating their opinion on the activity they audit, managers are frequently curious.

FIG. 17-3 *Contents of an Internal Audit Report*

Generally, the auditor reviews a draft of the audit report with the manager of the activity audited. Since there is no standard language in an internal audit report (as there is in the audit report of a CPA), the auditor can often change any language in the report that offends the auditee, so long as the original meaning of the report is not altered. Responses of the auditee may be included in the audit report if there is disagreement over its content.

Copies of the final report are sent to the auditee, the auditee's superior, and any other person in the company responsible for seeing that the deficiencies found are corrected. Summaries of audit reports and audit findings are increasingly provided to the audit committee of the board of directors. (The audit committee of the board is composed of outside directors, not directors who are also company managers.)

After the audit report is submitted, the auditor monitors deficiencies until either the deficiency is corrected or upper management decides that no correction is necessary because it has decided to accept the risk of the deficiency. A decision to accept the risk of a continuing deficiency is usually based on a cost/benefit analysis that determines that the cost of correcting the problem is greater than the expected benefit from correcting the problem. Management, for instance, might decide not to place a guard at the plant entrance because the expected theft loss is less than the cost of a guard.

INDEPENDENCE

If people are to rely on the auditor's work, the auditor must be independent. Because auditors are employees of the company they audit, they cannot be independent in the same way that an external auditor is independent. An auditor who reports, for example, on the effectiveness of the person who controls the audit department salaries would not be seen as free of bias.

While the auditor cannot be independent of the company as a whole, the auditor can be made independent of the activities audited by having the internal audit department report directly to top management or to the board of directors. Frequently, auditors are protected from pressures because only the audit committee of the board of directors has the authority to dismiss the director of the internal audit department.

CHAPTER PERSPECTIVE

This chapter has discussed internal audit reports. Internal auditors are responsible not only for checking the accuracy of accounting records but for checking the results of business activities in all areas. Internal auditors perform operational audits and report on the efficiency and effectiveness of operations. An internal audit consists of seven steps: the preliminary survey, the audit plan, field work, work paper preparation, deficiency findings, audit reports, and follow-up. This chapter discussed the role of internal auditors in management audits and the format of the report the internal auditor issues. Internal auditors are kept independent of the activities on which they report by having the internal audit department report to a high management level or to the audit committee of the board of directors.

Reports of Governmental and Not-for-Profit Organizations

INTRODUCTION AND MAIN POINTS

While many people may have an interest in the accounting reports discussed in the preceding chapters, all people should be interested in the accounting reports of governmental and not-for-profit organizations. Churches, schools, charities, and federal, state, and local governments all use accounting reports based on the principles discussed in this chapter. We introduce the goals of governmental and not-for-profit accounting and reporting and explain how the methods used meet those goals. The chapter mentions different forms of not-for-profit accounting but concentrates on accounting and reporting for state and local governmental units, using as its model the material published by the Governmental Accounting Standards Board (GASB). Once you understand the accounting used by governmental units, you will be able to understand the accounting and reporting methods unique to each type of not-for-profit accounting.

After you have studied the material in this chapter:

▬ You will understand how and why governmental and not-for-profit accounting is different from that used by for-profit organizations.

▬ You will see how funds are structured and why they are used.

▬ You will recognize the different types of funds and how each is accounted for.

▬ You will understand the special nature of budgeting for governmental and not-for-profit organizations.

▬ You will see how budgets for governmental and not-for-profit organizations are recorded in the accounts.

▬ You will understand the special nature of encumbrances and how they are used.

▬ You will know the parts of a comprehensive annual financial report and how they fit in the governmental financial reporting pyramid.

NOT-FOR-PROFIT ACCOUNTING

Not-for-profit accounting is a separate form of accounting used by governmental units and other entities that do not seek to create a profit from their operations. Organizations of this type include the following:

1. Governmental units, including federal, state, and local governments
2. Schools, colleges, and universities, both public and private
3. Health and welfare organizations, including hospitals and nursing homes
4. Charitable organizations, such as the United Way, the Red Cross, or the Salvation Army
5. Religious organizations, including churches and church-related organizations
6. Private trusts and foundations

Governmental units and other not-for-profit organizations differ from profit-seeking organizations in ways that affect their accounting reports: They do not seek to generate profits and they do not have customers or stockholders to provide financial resources.

The Lack of a Profit Motive

When an organization is formed to create a profit, an annual measure of net income is a good measure of the organization's success in meeting its goals. But what of a not-for-profit organization? Consider these examples. The National Guard is a governmental unit. The National Guard meets, flies planes, drives tanks, and does other things, but it creates no profit. The United Way seeks to help children, battered women, and other people in need of assistance—but it creates no profit. How can an accounting report demonstrate that the National Guard or the United Way is meeting its goals?

Absence of Customers or Stockholders

A profit-oriented company such as Exxon or J. C. Penney obtains its operating funds ultimately from the investments of its owners and the revenues received from its customers; capital obtained from creditors must be repaid from these two sources. A governmental unit and a not-for-profit organization have no owners or customers in the traditional sense and obtain their resources instead from either taxes (paid involuntarily) or contributions (made voluntarily). In both cases (taxes and contributions), the resource provider does not receive, or expect to receive, a benefit in proportion to the amount of resource provided. Paying more taxes brings no more benefit than paying less (or no) taxes. An individual person cannot obtain more or less national defense by increasing or decreasing a personal tax payment; a contributor to the United Way does not expect to receive services in return nor a dividend from profits (of which there are none).

FOCUS ON GOVERNMENT ACCOUNTING REPORTS

All government and not-for-profit organizations have similar characteristics, but they are also all different in the manner in which their accounting reports are prepared. Our discussion focuses on the similarities among accounting reports for all government and not-for-profit organizations and will address in specifics only the accounting and reporting requirements of state and local governmental units. Once you understand governmental accounting reports, you will be better able to understand reports of other not-for-profit organizations and the federal government.

FISCAL RESPONSIBILITY

To understand the accounting reports of governmental units, you must first understand the fiscal responsibilities of governmental administrators. To accomplish this, let us pretend we are back in the days when Marshal Dillon was walking the streets of Dodge City. Let us pretend that the town council has just passed a law against wearing a gun in the saloon. If a cowboy wears a gun in the saloon, Marshal Dillon will fine him $10. All fines collected from gun-wearers are to be used to bury outlaws that Marshal Dillon is forced to shoot. Marshal Dillon carries his own money in his vest. To keep track of the money collected from fining gun-wearers and to avoid mingling it with his own, Marshal Dillon decides to keep the fine money in a cigar box in the bottom drawer of his desk.

Now suppose the town passes another law: Cowboys racing horses down Main Street in a reckless manner will be fined $20. The fines collected from reckless horseracers are to be used to pay the town drunk to remove the horse manure from Main Street. To keep track of the monies collected from fining horseracers, Marshal Dillon keeps that money in a second cigar box in the bottom drawer of his desk. He writes "Gun Fines" on one box and "Horse Fines" on the other and writes all amounts collected or spent on the top of each box.

Marshal Dillon now has fiscal responsibility. He receives money from specific sources that is designated for specific purposes. By law, he cannot spend the money received from horseracers to bury dead outlaws, nor can he use the money from gun-wearers to clean the streets. Marshal Dillon has established two cigar box *funds* to assist in keeping the monies from the two sources separate.

By putting all fines in the appropriate box rather than mingling fines with his own money, and by spending from the appropriate box when he cleans the street or buries an outlaw, Marshal Dillon is able to demonstrate two aspects of fiscal responsibility. He is able to account for all money entrusted to him, and he is able to demonstrate that money collected from each source is spent for the purpose intended by the town council.

These same responsibilities are thrust upon modern-day administrators. They must account for all money entrusted them and assure that money collected for specific purposes is, in fact, spent for those purposes. A gasoline tax may be intended for road maintenance; a sales tax may be levied to fund education; an assessment may be collected to pay for sewer construction. Money from each source is accounted for in a separate fund to assure that it is spent for its intended purpose and no other. (The actual money may well be commingled in one cash account.)

The Governmental Accounting Standards Board (GASB) Statement 1 says:

> A governmental accounting system must make it possible both: (a) to present fairly with full disclosure the financial position and results of financial operations . . . of the governmental unit in conformity with generally accepted accounting principles, and (b) to determine and demonstrate compliance with finance-related legal and contractual provisions.

Marshall Dillon's cigar boxes would enable him to accomplish the GASB Statement 1 goals in Dodge City. Fund accounting enables modern-day administrators to accomplish them in any other city.

FUND ACCOUNTING

The method of accounting used by Marshal Dillon in our hypothetical situation is called *fund accounting*. Fund accounting, like the accounting used in for-profit operations, is based on the different types of accounts and the way events are recorded. Try thinking of a government entity in terms of properties and property rights: All the economic resources of a governmental unit are owned by someone. The dollar amount of properties must equal the dollar amount of property rights. The basic accounting relationship (called, as in Chapter 2, the accounting equation) can be stated as:

$$\text{Properties} = \text{Property rights}$$

The accounting term for properties owned by the government is *assets*. The two types of claims against the assets of a governmental unit are *liabilities* (to the government's creditors) and any excess of funds over liabilities (which technically belongs to the taxpayers). The excess of assets over liabilities is called *fund balance*. The dollar amount of assets must equal the dollar amount of liabilities plus fund balance, as follows.

$$\text{Property Rights} = \text{Liabilities} + \text{Fund Balance}$$
$$\text{or}$$
$$\text{Assets} = \text{Liabilities} + \text{Fund Balance}$$

This equation shows the relationship of balance sheet accounts in each fund. Just as Marshal Dillon might have had two (or more) cigar boxes to keep separate monies from specific sources intended for specific expenditures, a governmental unit has a number of separate funds, each with a balance sheet structured as shown in the governmental accounting balance sheet equation. Understanding the governmental fund balance sheet equation is fundamental to understanding governmental fund accounting.

The construction of the fund balance sheet provides a system of checks on the accuracy of the fund accounting system for governments, just as accounting does in for-profit organizations. This system of checks is called the *double-entry system* (just as in for-profit accounting in Chapters 1–3), because each economic event must affect the fund balance sheet in two ways to keep the equation in balance. For instance, if a fund is formed with cash of $500,000, two components of the equation, the asset cash and fund balance, must be increased to show the effect of this transaction. If either assets or fund balance is not increased, the equation will not balance.

$$\text{Assets} = \text{Liabilities} + \text{Fund Balance}$$
$$+ \$500,000 = 0 \qquad + \$500,000$$

If the fund then borrows another $1,500,000, two more effects must be recorded: Assets are increased by the cash received and the property rights of the bank are recorded.

Assets	= Liabilities	+ Fund Balance
+ $500,000	= 0	+ $500,000
+ 1,500,000	= + 1,500,000	+ 0
$2,000,000 (total)	= $1,500,000	+ $500,000

If supplies are purchased for $4,000, cash must be decreased and the asset "supplies" increased. One asset is traded for another of equal value, and the equation still balances. When a loan is repaid, cash is decreased and a liability is decreased. Whenever one account is increased, another must be decreased to keep the equation in balance.

"Due from" and "Due to"

Fund balance sheets often have "Due from" and "Due to" accounts. These accounts are asset and liability accounts that designate receivables from and liabilities to other funds within the government or not-for-profit entity. Suppose a government fund established to receive and spend monies collected from a city transportation system temporarily lends money to the city's general revenue fund. "Due from the General Fund" in the transportation fund balance sheet is a receivable from the general fund. If instead the transportation fund borrows from the general revenue fund, the liability is shown in the transportation fund balance sheet as "Due to the General Fund." "Due from" and "Due to" amounts are different from other assets and liabilities because they do not represent claims from or obligations to entities outside the government. An amount due to the general fund from the transportation fund, for example, does not remove cash from the government; payment of this liability simply transfers cash from one fund to another.

Figure 18-1 shows a balance sheet for a Transportation Special Revenue Fund that contains a "Due to" liability to the general fund. This figure and all others which follow are taken from the 1988 edition of *Governmental Accounting, Auditing and Financial Reporting,* published by the Government Finance Officers Association, 180 N. Michigan Avenue, Suite 800, Chicago, Illinois 60601.

Revenues and Expenditures

The fees, taxes, and other charges collected by a government fund are called revenues, the same name used for similar items in a for-profit organization, but the outflows are called expenditures, rather than expenses. The expanded governmental balance sheet equation, including revenues and expenditures, is shown below.

$$\text{Assets} = \text{Liabilities} + \text{Fund Balance} + \text{Revenues} - \text{Expenditures}$$

Since government funds do not create net income, there is no income statement. Still, the relationship between resources received and expended is useful to both taxpayers and government administrators. As a result, instead of an income statement, funds publish a Statement of Revenues, Expenditures, and Changes in Fund Balance, as shown in Figure 18-1.

Name of Government
Transportation Special Revenue Fund
Comparative Balance Sheets
December 31, 19X8 and 19X7
(amounts expressed in thousands)

	19X8	19X7
Assets		
Cash	$ 65	$ 70
Investments	1,174	706
Interest receivable	1	6
Total assets	$1,240	$782
Liabilities and fund balances		
Liabilities:		
Vouchers payable	$ 332	—
Due to other funds—general fund	—	38
Total liabilities	332	38
Fund balances:		
Reserved for encumbrances	353	—
Unreserved, undesignated	555	$744
Total fund balances	908	744
Total liabilities and fund balances	$1,240	$782

Transportation Special Revenue Fund
Comparative Statements of Revenues, Expenditures, and
Changes in Fund Balances
For the fiscal years ended December 31, 19X8 and 19X7
(amounts expressed in thousands)

	19X8	19X7
Revenues:		
Motor fuel tax	$729	$355
Intergovernmental	100	—
Interest	77	44
Total revenues	906	399
Expenditures:		
Current:		
Highways and streets	742	—
Excess of revenues over expenditures	164	399
Fund balances, January 1	744	345
Fund balances, December 31	$908	$744

The notes to the financial statements are an integral part of this
statement.

FIG. 18-1 *Governmental Fund Type*
Source: Government Finance Officers Association

APPROPRIATIONS AND BUDGETARY ACCOUNTS

Another way administrators fulfill their fiduciary responsibilities is through a system of budgetary accounts unique to government and not-for-profit organizations. We saw in Chapters 13 to 15 that the budget and the budgeting process for profit-oriented organizations is an elaborate planning and controlling process. For a profit-oriented organization, budgets are only guidelines and are not recorded in the accounts. In governmental and not-for-profit accounting, budgets are not only guidelines; they are both an authorization to spend for some purpose and a legal maximum that can be spent. The budget amounts are recorded in the accounting system of government and not-for-profit organizations.

At the first of each year, both the estimated revenues to be received and the amounts appropriated to be spent are recorded in the accounting system. Estimated revenues are not assets, but they are recorded in the accounting system as though they are; appropriations are not liabilities, but they are recorded as though they are. Estimated revenues and appropriations are recorded in a self-balancing system of accounts separate from the actual assets and liabilities (shown previously in the governmental balance sheet equation).

If a governmental unit expects to receive estimated revenues greater than its appropriated expenditures, fund balance will increase; if estimated revenues are less than appropriated expenditures, fund balance will decrease. The self-balancing budgetary accounts interact as shown below (the governmental balance sheet equation is shown for contrast). The budgetary accounts show what inflows and outflows are authorized and expected. The balance sheet shows what assets, liabilities, and fund balance actually are.

Budgetary Account Equation
Estimated Revenues = Appropriations + Change in Fund Balance

Governmental Balance Sheet Equation
Assets = Liabilities + Fund Balance

Just as each fund is a separate balance sheet, each fund has separate self-balancing budgetary accounts showing the estimated revenues to be collected, appropriations to be spent, and the effect on fund balance. If a fund is expected to collect revenues of $100,000 and to have authorized appropriations of $80,000, the budgetary account equation appears as:

Estimated Revenues = Appropriations + Change in Fund Balance
$100,000 = $80,000 + $20,000

Figure 18-2 shows a Comparative Statement of Revenues, Expenditures, and Changes in Fund Balance—Budget and Actual for the Transportation Special Revenue Fund shown in Figure 18-1. This figure is also taken from the Government Finance Officers Association's *GAAFR*.

ENCUMBRANCES

Because the $80,000 appropriation above is both an authorization to spend and a maximum that can be legally spent, government administrators will likely want to spend the entire $80,000 but will be fearful of spending more than is authorized and violating their fiduciary responsibilities. As a result, many funds use a system of encumbrances to help assure that they do not overspend.

We illustrate the operation of an encumbrance system for the hypothetical fund above. Let us assume $55,000 is spent on operating activities and an order for $6,000 of supplies is placed, but the supplies are not yet received. How much more can the fund spend? An administrator examining the books sees only the appropriation of $80,000 and expenditures of $55,000 and may well assume that $25,000 of the budget is still available. But this is not true: $6,000 has been committed for the supplies ordered but not received.

To prevent the $6,000 order from being overlooked or forgotten, the amount of the order is "encumbered," that is, it is recorded in the *budgetary* accounts and acts like an expenditure in that it reduces the balance of appropriations available to be spent. Accountants periodically provide a report to administrations on the unencumbered balance of each appropriation. Such a report for the hypothetical fund in our illustration follows.

Hypothetical Fund
Schedule of Unencumbered
Appropriation
Balance
As of March 31, 2000

Appropriations	$80,000
Expenditures	55,000
Unexpended Balance	$25,000
Encumbrances	6,000
Unencumbered Balance	$19,000

Reserve for Encumbrances

Unlike expenditures, encumbrances are not shown as a deduction from revenues in a fund Statement of Revenues, Expenditures, and Changes in Fund Balance. Financial-statement readers are alerted to the presence of encumbrances by a Reserve for Encumbrances set aside in the fund balance sheet. The logic here is that fund balance is equal to assets minus liabilities and represents the unexpended, unrestricted funds available to be used. Since, in fact, a portion of the fund balance does not represent assets available to be expended, the amount of the fund balance needed to cover the encumbrance is shown in the Reserve for Encumbrances account. When the purchase order that caused the obligation to be created is processed and the purchased items are received, an expenditure is created, reducing fund balance, and the encumbrance removed. Our hypothetical fund balance sheet would show fund balance reduced by a $6,000 Reserve for Encumbrance because of the supply order not yet received and paid for.

Other Reserves of Fund Balance

In addition to the reserve for encumbrances, fund balance is reserved in several other cases in which the fund balance does not represent expendable resources. One example of this is the Reserve for Inventories, which designates the portion of fund balance not available to be expended because a portion of the assets are invested in inventories of supplies that will be consumed rather than converted to cash and expended in support of fund activities.

TYPES OF FUNDS

The funds we have discussed thus far focus on the collection and spending of financial resources and are unique to governmental and not-for-profit organizations. There are, in fact, three fund types: governmental, proprietary, and fiduciary funds. Two of these—governmental and fiduciary funds—are *spending-focus* funds, which function as we have explained in this chapter. The third fund type, proprietary funds, is used to account for profit activities of governments (such as water and sewer companies) and are accounted for just as profit-oriented companies account for their activities, as explained in Chapters 1 to 8.

Within each fund type, there are different fund categories.

Governmental Funds

Governmental funds are spending-focus funds that are concerned with the flow of current financial resources. There are four types of governmental funds:

1. *The general fund:* Used to account for all financial resources not accounted for in other funds.

2. *Special revenue funds:* Used to account for revenues received from specific sources and legally designated to be spent on specific purposes.

3. *Capital projects funds:* Used to account for monies to be spent on acquiring or constructing major capital projects, such as a civic center or new courthouse.

4. *Debt-service funds:* Used to account for the accumulation of resources to be used for the payment of general long-term debt.

5. *Permanent funds:* Used to account for legally restricted resources where earnings, but not principal, can be expended.

Figure 18-1, which shows financial statements for a special revenue fund for transportation, is an example of a governmental fund. All governmental funds have a statement showing revenues, expenditures, and change in fund balance and a balance sheet showing the resources (assets), obligations (liabilities), and fund balance.

Proprietary Funds

Proprietary funds are profit-focused funds that are concerned with the flow of economic resources, not just the spending of money. There are two categories of proprietary funds:

1. *Enterprise funds:* Used to account for operations involving external parties with operating goals similar to private, for-profit organizations. In these funds, unlike the governmental funds just discussed, a measure of profit (revenues versus expenses) is necessary for control.

2. *Internal service funds:* Used to account for a department that provides goods or services to another department on a cost or cost-plus-reimbursement basis such that the relationship between revenues and expenses is so important that for-profit accounting methods are used. A university, for example, may establish a motor pool with the idea that the motor pool will furnish cars and vans for faculty and students to use on university business and that the charges for vehicles will cover the cost of the motor pool. After an initial investment, the motor pool will operate as if it is a for-profit operation: user departments will be charged for vehicle use and these charges will cover the cost of motor pool operations. Because the motor pool must operate as if it is a for-profit operation, governmental accounting procedures that focus on spending and fiscal responsibility are not enough. Financial statements like those used by for-profit operations are necessary.

An example of proprietary fund financial statements is contained in Figure 18-2, which shows operating and cash flow statements for an internal service fund for a department supplying management information systems to other departments.

Fiduciary Funds and Similar Component Units

Fiduciary funds are either spending-focus or profit-focused funds. They are either concerned with the flow of current financial resources or with economic resources.

There are two basic types of fiduciary funds: agency funds and trust funds. Agency funds contain only assets and liabilities, with no fund balance. Trust funds may be either spendable or nonspendable.

The four fiduciary funds are:
1. Pension (and other employee benefit) trust funds.
2. Investment trust funds.
3. Private-purpose trust funds.
4. Agency funds.

Fixed Assets and Long-Term Debt

Long-term debt and fixed assets are accounted for in the financial statements of proprietary (for-profit) funds just as they are in for-profit organizations. But spending-focus governmental funds concentrate solely on expendable resources and do not include either general governmental long-term debt or fixed assets in their financial statements. Instead, these items are disclosed in two self-balancing account groups not considered to be funds: the *General Fixed Asset Account Group* and the *General Long-Term Debt Account Group*. An example of financial reporting for the General Fixed Asset Account Group is shown in Figure 18-4.

REQUIRED SUPPLEMENTARY INFORMATION (RSI)

The primary required supplementary information (RSI) requirement is Management's Discussion and Analysis (MD&A). MD&A is intended to be an objective and easily readable analysis of activities covered in the financial report. The analysis should cover the governments' overall financial position and results of operations. Management should discuss the relationship of the fund statements to each other and the different types of information they provide. The MD&A should also contain condensed financial information needed to support the analysis. The condensed financial statement information should contain, at a minimum, the following elements:[2]

---

[2]Statement No. 34 of the Governmental Accounting Standards Board, *Basic Financial Statements—and Managements Discussion and Analysis—For State and Local Governments, GASB*, No. 171-A, June 1999. Paragraphs 8–11.

Name of Government
Management Information Systems Internal Service Fund
Comparative Statements of Revenues, Expenses and Changes
in Retained Earnings
For the fiscal years ended December 31,19X8 and 19X7
(amounts expressed in thousands)

	19X8	19X7
Revenues:		
Charges for services	$593	$452
Operating expenses:		
Costs of services	374	341
Administration	64	58
Depreciation	92	83
Total operating expenses	530	482
Operating income (loss)	63	(30)
Nonoperating revenues:		
Interest	2	1
Net income (loss)	65	(29)
Retained earnings, January 1	296	325
Retained earnings, December 31	$361	$296

Name of Government
Management Information Systems Internal Service Fund
Comparative Statement of Changes in Financial Position
For the fiscal years ended December 31, 19X8 and 19X7
(amounts expressed in thousands)

	19X8	19X7
Cash flows from operating activities:		
Cash received from users	$643	$452
Cash paid to suppliers and employees	(506)	(385)
Interest received	2	1
Net cash provided by operating activities	139	68
Cash flows from investing activities:		
Purchase of investments	(33)	—
Purchase of fixed assets	(67)	(90)
Net cash used in investing activities	(100)	(90)
Cash flows from financing activities:		
Advance from other funds—general fund	20	—
Net cash provided by financing activities	20	—
Net increase (decrease) in cash	59	(22)
Cash, January 1	5	27
Cash, December 31	$(64)	$ 5

Reconciliation of Net Income to Net Cash Provided by
Operating Activities

	19X8	19X7
Net income (loss)	$ 65	$(29)
Adjustments to reconcile net income to net cash provided by operating activities:		
Depreciation expense	92	83
Decrease in due from general fund	41	—
Decrease in due from water and sewer fund	9	—
Increase in compensated absences	5	2
Increase (decrease) in accounts payable	(73)	12
Total adjustments	74	97
Net cash provided by operating activities	$139	$68

The notes to the financial statements are an integral part of this statement.

FIG. 18-2 *Proprietary fund*

Source: Government Finance Officers Association

Name of Government
Perpetual Care Nonexpendable Trust Fund
Comparative Balance Sheets
December 31, 19X8 and 19X7
(amounts expressed in thousands)

	19X8	19X7
Assets		
Cash	$ 231	$ 16
Investments	1,753	1,848
Interest receivable	82	41
Total assets	$2,066	$1,905
Liabilities and fund balances		
Liabilities:		
Accounts payable	$ 13	$ 18
Fund balances:		
Reserved for perpetual care	1,193	1,102
Unreserved, undesignated	860	785
Total fund balances	2,053	1,887
Total liabilities and fund balances	$2,066	$1,905

Name of Government
Perpetual Care Nonexpendable Trust Fund
Comparative Statements of Revenues, Expenses and
Changes in Fund Balances
For the fiscal years ended December 31, 19X8 and 19X7
(amounts expressed in thousands)

	19X8	19X7
Operating revenues:		
Interest	$ 41	$ 141
Operating expenses:		
Costs of sales and services	13	144
Operating income (loss)	28	(3)
Nonoperating revenues:		
Gain on the sale of investments	138	57
Net income	166	54
Fund balances, January 1	1,887	1,833
Fund balances, December 31	$2,053	$1,887

The notes to the financial statements are an integral part of this statement.

FIG. 18-3 *Fiduciary fund*

Source: Government Finance Officers Association

Name of Government
Comparative Schedules of General Fixed Assets
By Source
December 31, 19X8 and 19X7
(amounts expressed in thousands)

	19X8	19X7
General fixed assets:		
Land	$39,333	$38,775
Buildings	8,291	7,875
Improvements other than buildings	4,604	4,604
Machinery and equipment	4,376	7,401
Construction in progress	2,308	722
Total general fixed assets	$58,912	$59,377
Investment in general fixed assets by source:		
General fund	$ 8,801	$11,744
Special revenue funds	3,873	3,497
Capital projects funds	44,531	42,442
Donations	1,707	1,694
Total investment in general fixed assets	$58,912	$59,377

FIG. 18-4 *Fixed-asset account group*

Source: Government Finance Officers Association

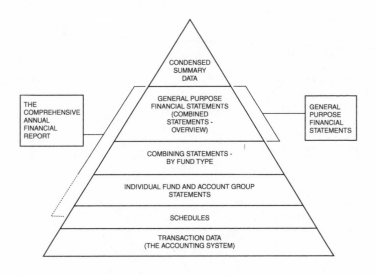

— Required
... May be necessary

FIG. 18-5 *The financial reporting "pyramid"*
Source: Government Finance Officers Association

1. Total assets, distinguishing between capital and other assets
2. Total liabilities, distinguishing between long-term liabilities and other liabilities
3. Total net assets, distinguishing among amounts invested in capital assets, net of related debt; restricted amounts; unrestricted amounts
4. Program revenues, by major source
5. General revenues, by major source
6. Total revenues
7. Program expenses, at a minimum by function
8. Total expenses
9. Excess (deficiency) before contributions to term and permanent endowments or permanent fund principal, special and extraordinary items, and transfers
10. Contributions
11. Special and extraordinary items
12. Transfers
13. Change in net assets
14. Ending net assets

GOVERNMENT-WIDE FINANCIAL STATEMENTS

A governmental annual report should contain government-wide financial statements that include the combined financial activities reported in the separate funds. The government-wide financial statements are prepared using accrual accounting (see Chapter 8), the method of accounting used by the for-profit sector. These statements are comprised of a statement of net assets and a statement of activities. Government-wide financial statements should:[3]

a. Report information about the overall government without displaying individual funds or fund types
b. Exclude information about fiduciary activities, including component units that are fiduciary in nature (such as certain public employee retirement systems)
c. Distinguish between the primary government and its discretely presented component units
d. Distinguish between governmental activities and business-type activities of the primary government
e. Measure and report all assets (both financial and capital), liabilities, revenues, expenses, gains, and losses using the economic resources measurement focus and accrual basis of accounting

The format for a Statement of Activities as prescribed in GASB Statement 3 is shown in Figure 18-6.

[3] Ibid., paragraphs 12–62.

Functions	Expenses	Program Revenues			Net (Expense) Revenue and Changes in Net Assets			
		Charges for Services	Operating Grants and Contributions	Capital Grants and Contributions	Primary Government			Component Units
					Governmental Activities	Business-type Activities	Total	
Primary government								
Governmental activities								
Function #1	XXX	XX	X	X	(XX)	—	(XX)	—
Function #2	XXX	XX	X	—	(XX)	—	(XX)	—
Function #3	XXX	XX	X	X	(X)	—	(X)	—
Total governmental activities	XXXX	XXX	XX	XX	(XX)	—	(XX)	—
Business-type activities								
BTA #1	XXXX	XXXX	—	X	—	XX	XX	—
BTA #2	XXXXX	XXXX	—	XX	—	XXX	XXX	—
Total business-type activities	XXXXXX	XXXX	XX	XXX	—	XXX	XXX	—
Total primary government	XXXXXXX	XXXXX	XX	XXX	(XXX)	XXX	(XX)	—
Component units								
CU #1	XXXX	XXXX	XX	XX	—	—	—	XX
General revenues—detailed					XXX	X	XXX	XX
Contributions to permanent hands					XX	—	XX	X
Special items					X	—	X	—
Transfers					XX	(XX)	—	—
Total general revenues, contributions, special items, and transfers					XXX	X	XXX	XXX
Change in net assets					X	XX	XX	XX
Net assets—beginning					XXXXX	XXXXX	XXXXXX	XXXXX
Net assets—ending					XXXXX	XXXXX	XXXXXX	XXXXX

FIG. 18-6 *Statement of Activities Format Taken from Governmental Accounting Board Statement No. 34*

COMPREHENSIVE ANNUAL FINANCIAL REPORT

Many governments are required to prepare a comprehensive annual financial report, identified by the acronym CAFR in the Government Finance Officers Association's *GAAFR*. The CAFR contains three sections:

1. Introduction
2. Financial
3. Statistical

This report is intended to provide the comprehensive information that might be needed by the most demanding reader of governmental financial reports. The CAFR contains the general purpose financial statements, in addition to other data. The financial reporting pyramid in Figure 18-5 is reproduced from the Government Finance Officers Association *GAAFR*.

CHAPTER PERSPECTIVE

This chapter introduced the goals of governmental and not-for-profit accounting and reporting and explained how the methods used meet those goals. The chapter concentrated on accounting and reporting for governmental units, using as its model the materials published by the Government Finance Officers Association and the Governmental Accounting Standards Board. Once you understand the accounting system used by governmental units, you are better able to understand the accounting and reporting methods unique to each type of not-for-profit accounting. The chapter explained how funds are structured and used, including the special nature of budgeting and budgetary accounts and encumbrances. Finally, the comprehensive annual financial report and the financial reporting pyramid was introduced.

Personal Financial Statements

INTRODUCTION AND MAIN POINTS

Personal financial statements may be prepared for an individual, a married couple, or a family and are used for financial planning, tax planning, obtaining credit, or complying with the disclosure requirements of a regulatory body (as many public officials must do).

Prior to 1968 many political candidates prepared their personal financial statements on either a cost or current value basis; there were no generally accepted accounting principles governing the preparation of those statements. Then, in 1968, the American Institute of Certified Public Accountants (AICPA) issued *Industry Audit Guide, Audits of Personal Financial Statements,* which required that these statements be prepared on a cost basis with supplementary disclosure of current values.[1] In 1982, the AICPA revised its position, asserting that because current values provide more relevant information than cost values, personal financial statements should be prepared on an estimated current value basis, with historical cost presented as optional supplementary information.[2] The latest AICPA publications on this topic, *Personal Financial Statements Guide*[3] discusses but does not change its recommendation.

After studying the material in this chapter:

▬ You will know where to find the sources of information used to prepare personal financial statements.

▬ You will understand the composition of personal financial statements.

▬ You will know the techniques that can be used to obtain the current values of the assets and liabilities included in personal financial statements.

▬ You will understand how personal financial statements are prepared.

▬ You will know what additional information should be disclosed in personal financial statements.

---

[1] *Industry Audit Guide, Audits of Personal Financial Statements* (New York: American Institute of Certified Public Accountants, 1968).

[2] *Amendment to AICPA Audit Guide, Audits of Personal Statements* (New York: American Institute of Certified Public Accountants, 1982).

[3] *Personal Financial Statements Guide* (New York: American Institute of Certified Public Accountants, 1999).

SOURCES OF INFORMATION FOR PERSONAL FINANCIAL STATEMENTS

The sources of information necessary to prepare personal financial statements include bank, brokerage, and property tax statements; tax returns; insurance policies; wills; prenuptial agreements; and decrees of divorce. If an individual has an ownership interest (investment in stocks or bonds) in a closely held entity (the stock of which is not actively traded), the financial statements and tax return of that entity may be a source of information. Other documents, such as titles to assets, may be found in an individual's safe deposit box. The individual, couple, or family is also a source of information for use in preparing the financial statements.

COMPOSITION OF PERSONAL FINANCIAL STATEMENTS

The focus of personal financial statements is on personal assets and liabilities at current value, not on the individual's net income. Personal financial statements consist of a *statement of financial condition* or a *balance sheet* at a point in time and an optional *statement of net worth* that presents the changes in net worth for a period of time. An income statement is not prepared because of the combination of business and personal revenue and expense items.

Statement of Financial Condition

The statement of financial condition presents the estimated current values of assets, the estimated current amounts of liabilities, the estimated income taxes on the differences between the estimated current values of assets and the estimated current amounts of liabilities and their tax bases, and net worth at a specified date. "Net worth" is the difference between total assets and total liabilities, including estimated income taxes on the differences between the estimated current values of assets and the estimated current amounts of liabilities and their tax bases. Generally, assets and liabilities are based on the accrual basis of accounting and are listed in order of liquidity and maturity, without classification as to current or noncurrent.

A statement of financial condition is shown in Figure 19-3 as part of the comprehensive illustration given later in this chapter.

Statement of Changes in Net Worth

The statement of changes in net worth, which is optional, presents the major sources of increases and decreases in net worth, such as income, expenses, changes in the estimated current value of assets, changes in liabilities, and changes in estimated income taxes on the differences between these amounts and their tax bases.

When the statement of changes is included in personal financial statements, it should be broken down into realized and unrealized sections. Realized increases in net worth are the tangible, liquid revenue and income items of the individual for whom the statement is being prepared. These sources include salaries, wages, interest, dividend revenue, rental income, and income from outside business interests. Realized decreases are expenses such as income taxes, interest, and personal expenditures.

Unrealized increases, which are potential, changeable amounts, arise from the increase in current values of assets, decreases in the current value of liabilities, and decreases in the estimated income taxes on the difference between the estimated current value of the assets and the current amounts of the liabilities and their tax bases. Unrealized decreases are caused by decreases in the estimated current values of assets, increases in the estimated current amounts of liabilities, and increases in the estimated income taxes on the differences in current value of assets and the amounts of liabilities and their tax bases.

Assume, for example, that an individual has a parcel of land originally purchased for $100,000. If the market value of the land today is $160,000, the statement of changes in net worth prepared today would include an unrealized increase in net worth of $60,000 relating to the land. If the tax rate is 30 percent, an unrealized decrease in net worth of $18,000 ($60,000 gain $\times$ 30 percent) would be included in the estimated income taxes on the difference between the estimated current value of the assets and their tax bases.

A statement of changes in net worth is shown in Figure 19-4 as part of the comprehensive illustration given later in this chapter.

Comparative Financial Statements: The presentation of comparative financial statements of the current period and one or more prior periods is optional; however, such a presentation is much more informative than financial statements for only a single period.

For instance, a stock investment may represent a significant portion of an individual's assets. If an external event such as the Iraqi invasion of Kuwait has an adverse effect on the stock market and the individual's investment, personal financial statements presented on that date might be misleading because, in this case, the statements provide only a picture at one point in time. Comparative financial statements would be more useful because the reader would be able to view each item separately and determine whether the item were growing or decreasing over time, as well as determining the proportion of the change to other items in the statement.

CALCULATING CURRENT VALUES

Theoretically, current value is the agreed-upon price at which an item would be exchanged between a willing buyer and a willing seller. However, when assets do not have a ready market value, determining a current value can be difficult. For instance, stock in a closely held corporation may not have a market value because the stock, which is owned by a small number of owners, such as a family, is not actively traded. This is why an assortment of techniques is necessary to estimate the current values of assets and liabilities.

The primary techniques for valuing assets and liabilities are based on available current market values, appraisals and valuations by specialists, and discounted (present value) future cash flows. Other, less frequently used methods include the use of liquidation values, price indexing using the historical cost of assets, and capitalization of past or prospective earnings.

The three primary evaluation techniques can be illustrated by considering a piece of land owned by an individual. Assume the individual paid $10,000 for the land, which is now appraised at $20,000. If developed and leased, the land is expected to create cash inflows of $3,000 for the next ten years. Assume also that the individual has been offered $21,000 for the land by a large industrial company. Assuming an 8 percent annual rate of interest, Figure 19-1 displays values that might be used in the preparation of the statement of financial condition.

Historical Cost	$10,000
Appraisal Value	20,000
Discounted (Present Value) Value of Future Cash Flows ($3,000 per Year for 10 years @ 8 percent)	20,130
Current Resale Value	21,000

FIG. 19-1 *Illustration of Valuation of Possible Current Values for Land in the Statement of Financial Condition*

Discounted Future Cash Flows

We touched on the concept of present value in Chapter 4 in our discussion of bonds. Recall that the present value of a bond is its cash value at a point in time. Discounted cash flow refers to the present value, at a point in time, of a stream of receipts or payments to be received or paid in the future. The receipts or payments pattern is called an *annuity*. The concept of present value is related to the application of compound interest. Earning interest on interest is referred to as compounding. For example, assume that we invest $1,000 in a savings account at a rate of 10 percent compounded annually. The balance in the account after five years would be $1,611 computed as follows:

Year	Principal at Beginning of Year	Interest at 10%	Principal at End of Year
	(a)	(b)	(a + b)
1	$1,000	$1,000 × 10% = $100	$1,100
2	$1,100	$1,100 × 10% = $110	$1,210
3	$1,210	$1,210 × 10% = $121	$1,331
4	$1,331	$1,331 × 10% = $133	$1,464
5	$1,464	$1,464 × 10% = $147	$1,611

The future value of a $1,000 deposit made today would grow to $1,611 at the end of five years. We can depict this sequence of deposits in the form of a time line as such:

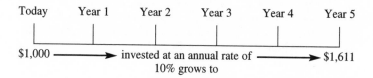

The present value of an amount views the compound interest concept in reverse. That is, the present value of $1,611 to be received in five periods is $1,000.

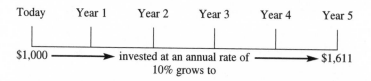

There are formulas for calculating future and present values. From these formulas factors can be derived and tables prepared. An example of a present value table is presented in Figure 19-2 for ten periods at various interest rates. Many calculators and computer programs include future and present value functions. From the table we can see that the present value factor for 5 periods at 10 percent is .621. Multiplying $1,611 by this factor results in a present value of $1,000 (rounded).

	Interest Rate							
No. of periods	1%	4%	5%	6%	8%	10%	12%	15%
1	.990	.962	.952	.943	.926	.909	.893	.870
2	.980	.925	.907	.890	.857	.826	.797	.756
3	.971	.890	.864	.840	.794	.751	.712	.658
4	.961	.855	.823	.792	.735	.683	.636	.572
5	.951	.822	.784	.747	.681	.621	.567	.497

FIG. 19-2 *Present Value of $1 Due in N Periods*

The present value of an annuity is simply the combined present values of the individual payments or receipts discounted back to today. Extending our previous example, suppose we wish to know whether we should accept a lump sum of $3,500 today, or five receipts of $1,000 each to be received at the end of each of the periods. The appropriate interest rate is 8 percent. Using the present value factors from Figure 19-2 we can calculate the present value of this annuity to be:

Payments	1	2	3	4	5

Present
Value
$ 926 = $1,000 × .926
   857 = ◄——— $1,000 × .857
   794 = ◄——————— $1,000 × .794
   735 = ◄——————————— $1,000 × .735
   681 = ◄——————————————— $1,000 × .681
$3,993

Because the present value of the receipts is greater than the lump sum, we would opt to receive the annuity rather than the lump sum.

There are also formulas for calculating the present value of annuities. These formulas can be used to derive factors for an annuity table. Such a table appears in Figure 19-3.

Interest Rate

No. of Periods	1%	4%	5%	6%	8%	10%	12%	15%
1	.990	.962	.952	.943	.926	.909	.893	.870
2	1.970	1.886	1.859	1.833	1.783	1.736	1.690	1.626
3	2.941	2.775	2.723	2.673	2.577	2.487	2.402	2.283
4	3.902	3.630	3.546	3.465	3.312	3.170	3.037	2.855
5	4.853	4.452	4.329	4.212	3.993	3.791	3.605	3.352
6	5.795	5.242	5.076	4.917	4.623	4.355	4.111	3.784
7	6.728	6.002	5.786	5.582	5.206	4.868	4.564	4.160
8	7.652	6.733	6.463	6.210	5.747	5.335	4.968	4.487
9	8.566	7.435	7.108	6.802	6.247	5.759	5.328	4.772
10	9.471	8.111	7.722	7.360	6.710	6.145	5.650	5.019

FIG. 19-3 *Present Value of $1 to Be Received Periodically for N Periods*

Remember we stated earlier that the present value of an annuity was the combined present values of the individual payments or receipts discounted back to today. If we sum the individual present value factors for five periods at 8 percent from the present value table in Figure 19-2, we get 3.993 (.926 + .857 + .794 + .735 + .681). This is the present value factor from the annuity table in Figure 19-3 for five periods at 8 percent.

Referring back to our illustration relating to the land in Figure 19-1, we can calculate the present value of the receipts to be received from renting the property. The rental amount is $3,000 for 10 years and the rate of interest is 8 percent. The present value is $20,130 ($3,000 × 6.710 factor, from Figure 19-3).

Determining Current Market Values

Marketable securities and stock options of publicly traded companies are reported at their market price on the date of the financial statement. If a stock is not actively traded in the open market, the bid price is used. (The bid is the price at which a securities dealer is willing to pay for the stock.) Investments in life insurance are shown at their cash surrender value less any outstanding loans. Intangible assets are shown at appraisal value, anticipated selling price, or the discounted value of future cash flows. If a current value cannot be objectively determinable, historical cost can be used. Real estate can be reported by using either appraisal value or, in some cases, discounted future cash flows. Accounts receivable are normally reported at the discounted value of future cash receipts (flows) using the current rate of interest at the statement date. Accounts receivable of $20,000 due in three months would be discounted as follows if the interest rate were 1 percent per month:

Accounts Receivable Balance × (factor for 1% interest for 3 months)
= Discounted Cash Flow
$20,000 × .971 = $19,420

Nonforfeitable rights such as vested pension and profit-sharing benefits, payables and other liabilities (excluding income taxes), and noncancellable commitments such as lease payments are also reported at their discounted future cash flows. Liabilities are presented at the discharge amount (amount needed to pay off or settle the debt) if this amount is lower than the discounted amount. Figure 19-4 summarizes how the values of sample personal financial statement items might be obtained.

Receivables	Discounted cash flow
Marketable securities, bonds, and stock options	Quoted market prices
Life insurance	Cash surrender value minus any outstanding loans
Investment in closely held companies	Liquidation value, earnings multiple, appraisal value, discounted value of future cash flow, replacement cost, or adjustment to the book value or cost
Investment in land or real estate	Current resale value based on sales of similar property, appraisal value, or discounted value of future cash flow
Intangible assets	Discounted value of future cash flow
Future interests (nonforfeitable rights)	Discounted value of future cash flow
Payables and other liabilities, including noncancelable commitments	Discounted value of future cash flow or discharge amount that amount is less than the discounted amount
Income taxes payable	Unpaid taxes from prior periods and the estimated taxes payable for the current period based on year-to-date taxable income reduced by withholdings and estimated tax payments to date

FIG. 19-4 *Determining the Current Values of Assets and Current Amounts of Liabilities*

"Income taxes payable" is the most complicated of the reported liabilities. In fact, three types of income taxes payable are possible in personal financial statements: income taxes payable for prior years (unpaid income taxes for completed tax years); income taxes estimated to be payable for the current year (estimated income tax for the expired portion of current tax year to the date of the financial statements); and an estimate of income taxes to be paid in the future based on the difference between (a) the estimated current value of an asset or the estimated current amount of a liability and (b) the tax base of the asset or liability at the statement date. The first two types of income taxes payable are reported as a single sum in the liability section of the statement; the third type is computed and reported as if the current value of the assets and liabilities had been realized or liquidated, taking into consideration current tax laws and regulations. The calculation of this component of income taxes payable will be demonstrated later.

Investments in closely held businesses are difficult to value because normally they lack a ready market value. Consequently, liquidation values, multiples of earnings, and replacement values are used. It is likely that the use of different estimating techniques will result in different estimated current values; the problem lies in determining which of the values is the best estimate of current value, which requires a subjective assessment.

PERSONAL FINANCIAL STATEMENTS: AN ILLUSTRATION

The following information was furnished by Joe and Ann Walka, who own Walka's Bookstore, as of September 30, 1999:

Assets

1. Mr. And Mrs. Walka's personal checking account had a balance of $26,000.
2. The Walkas held marketable securities of the Zee Company. The 100 shares had cost the Walkas $1,000 and currently had a market value of $55 a share.
3. Dividends receivable from the Zee Company totaled $1,000.
4. Mr. Walka had an IRA with contributions totaling $2,000. The current market value of the account was $2,500.
5. The value of vested pension benefits from Mr. Walka's previous employer was $25,000.
6. Based on several recent sales in their town, the Walkas estimate that the current value of their bookstore business was $75,000. The couple's initial investment in the bookstore was $45,000.
7. The couple purchased their home for $100,000. A recent appraisal valued the residence at $155,000.

8. Personal property had been insured for a replacement cost of $45,000. An estimate of selling price was $35,000. The personal property was purchased for $42,000.
9. The cash surrender value of life insurance was $75,000. Mrs. Walka had borrowed $20,000 against the policy.
10. Real estate had been purchased 2 years ago for $20,000. The market value of similar property was $30,000 on September 30, 1999.

Liabilities

1. Personal debts (including credit cards) totaled $11,000.
2. A personal loan for $5,000 could be extinguished for $4,400 on September 30, 1999. This means the Walkas could pay off the loan early for $4,400 and not have to incur additional interest.
3. The mortgage on the Walkas' home totaled $75,000. The discounted future cash flow of the mortgage is $68,000 based on a 10 percent interest rate.
4. Income taxes payable amounted to $14,000.

Based on this information, the statement of financial condition for Mr. And Mrs. Walka would be as shown in Figure 19-5. Each entry is based on the information items above; cash, for example, is from item 1, marketable securities are from item 2, and so on. Net worth is determined by subtracting the liabilities of $97,400 from the assets of $410,000. You should study this exhibit until you understand how each value was determined.

Assets	
Cash	$ 26,000
Marketable Securities (at Market Value $55 (100 shares)	5,500
Dividends Receivable	1,000
Individual Retirement Account (at Market Value)	2,500
Vested Pension Benefits	25,000
Investment in Closely Held Business, Bookstore (at Resale Value)	75,000
Home (at Appraisal Value)	155,000
Personal Property (at Market Value)	35,000
Cash Surrender Value of Life Insurance (Less Loan of $20,000)	55,000
Real Estate (at Market Value)	30,000
Total Assets	$410,000

Liabilities and Net Worth	
Personal Debts (Including Credit Cards)	$ 11,000
Personal Loan (at Cash Necessary to Extinguish the Loan	4,400
Mortgage Payable (at Discounted Cash Flow)	68,000
Income Taxes Payable	14,000
Total Liabilities	97,400
Estimated Income Taxes on the Difference Between the Estimated Current Values of Assets and the Estimated Current Amounts of Liabilities and Their Tax Bases	37,680
Net Worth	274,920
Total Liabilities and Net Worth	$ 410,000

FIG. 19-5 *Mr. And Mrs. J. Walka Statement of Financial Condition at September 30, 1999*

The estimated current value of the Walkas' total assets is $410,000. Some items are not taxable income nor are they deductible. Gains on the sale of a personal residence are only taxable to the extent that they exceed $125,000 for individuals over 55. If we assume that the Walkas are over age 55, the $55,000 increase in value is not taxable. Decreases in value in personal property such as automobiles and household items are not deductible for income tax purposes. Therefore, the decrease in value of the Walkas' personal property ($7,000) is not deductible. The total amount not subject to tax is $48,000 ($55,000 – $7,000).

The couple can pay off their debts for a total of $97,400. This is the current amount of their liabilities.

The tax bases and cost of the Walkas' assets are as follows:

Assets		Liabilities	
Checking Account	$ 26,000	Personal Debts	$ 14,000
IRA	-0-	Personal Loan	5,000
Marketable Securities	1,000	Mortgage Payable	75,000
Dividends	-0-	Income Taxes Payable	14,000
Pension Benefits	-0-		$108,000
Bookstore	45,000		
Home	100,000		
Cash Surrender Value of Life Insurance	55,000		
Real Estate	20,000		
	$247,000		

The calculation of the estimated income taxes on the difference between the estimated current values of assets and the estimated current amounts of liabilities and their tax bases would be as follows:

Assets:	
Current Value of Assets	$410,000
Less: Tax Base and Cost	247,000
Unrealized Increase in Value	163,000
Less: Net Amounts Not Subject to Tax	48,000
Unrealized Increase Subject to Tax	115,000
Liabilities:	
Tax Bases of Liabilities	108,000
Current Amounts	97,400
Unrealized Increase in Value	10,600
Total Appreciation from Increase	
in Assets and Decrease in Liabilities	125,600
Estimated Effective Tax Rate	30%
Estimated income taxes on the difference	
between the estimated current values of assets	
and the estimated current amounts of liabilities	
and their tax bases	$ 37,680

The optional statement of changes in net worth for Mr. and Mrs. Walka is shown in Figure 19-6 and is constructed from the information items in the statement of financial condition.

Realized Increases in Net Worth from:	
Bookstore Net Income	$ 30,000
Dividends	1,000
Total Realized Increases in Net Worth	31,000
Realized Decreases in Net Worth from:	
Personal Expenses	3,400
Interest Expense	9,750
Income Tax Expense	9,700
Property Tax Expense	3,250
Total Realized Decreases in Net Worth	26,100
Net Realized Increase in Net Worth	4,900
Unrealized Increases in Net Worth from:	
Mortgage Payable	7,000
Loan Payable	600
Bookstore	10,000
Home	23,100

Cash Surrender Value of Life Insurance	5,000
Property	12,350
Total Unrealized Increases in Net Worth	58,050
Unrealized Decreases in Net Worth from:	
Personal Property	3,000
Estimated Income Taxes on the Difference Between the Estimated Current Values of Assets and the Estimated Current Amounts of Liabilities over Their Tax Bases	17,400
Total Unrealized Decreases in Net Worth	20,400
Net Unrealized Increase in Net Worth	37,650
Net Increase in Net Worth	42,550
Beginning of Year Net Worth	232,370
End of Year Net Worth	$274,920

FIG. 19-6 *Mr. And Mrs. J. Walka Statement of Changes in Net Worth for the Year Ending September 30, 2000*

ADDITIONAL DISCLOSURES IN PERSONAL FINANCIAL STATEMENTS

Personal financial statements may require disclosure to augment and amplify other information contained in those statements, just as do corporate financial statements. The disclosures may be made in the body of the financial statements or in the notes and include:

▬ The names and relationships of the individuals covered by the statement

▬ The methods and assumptions used to determine the current values of assets and liabilities

▬ Any changes in methods and assumptions from those used in a prior year

▬ Maturities, interest rates, and other details of any receivables and debt

▬ Identification of all intangible assets, along with their useful lives

▬ The names and nature of companies in which the individual has major investments

▬ Material investments in closely held businesses, along with the percentage owned, nature of the business, basis of accounting, and summarized financial data for the most recent year

▬ Jointly owned assets, along with the nature of the joint ownership

▬ The face amount of the life insurance policies owned by the individual

▬ Methods and assumptions employed in computing estimated income taxes

■ Details as to vested rights in pension and stock ownership plans
■ Commitments of a noncancelable nature, such as long-term leases

CHAPTER PERSPECTIVE

Financial statements are prepared for individuals, couples, or family groups at a point in time (perhaps at year-end) on an accrual basis. Unlike those prepared for corporations, however, the statements are prepared using estimated current values for assets and liabilities.

Sources of information used to identify all of the assets and liabilities of the individual include bank statements, brokerage statements, life insurance policies, tax returns, and other documents. After identifying the individual's assets and liabilities, the estimated current values of the assets and amounts of the liabilities are determined based on recent transactions involving similar assets, appraisals, discounted cash flows, price indexing of historical cost, and liquidation values.

The resulting values for assets and liabilities are used to construct the personal financial statements. These statements consist of a statement of financial condition (not including an income statement) and an optional statement of changes in net worth. The statement of financial condition presents the estimated current value amounts of assets and liabilities in their order of liquidity and maturity. The cost or tax basis of the assets and liabilities may be presented as supplemental information; the presentation of comparative financial statements of the current period and one or more prior periods is optional but desirable.

To be complete, personal financial statements must include certain footnote disclosures. These disclosures may be made in the body of the financial statements or in notes accompanying the statements and include the individuals covered by the statements, methods used to determine estimated current values including estimated income taxes on unrealized gains and losses, identification of intangibles, and maturities, interest rates, and collateral for all receivables and debt.

The Mutual Fund Prospectus

INTRODUCTION AND MAIN POINTS

Mutual fund investors must always be given a prospectus before they invest. A prospectus is one of the most important pieces of information in the offering of a mutual fund for sale to the public. The information in a prospectus is so vital that the Securities and Exchange Commission (SEC) requires the prospectus to precede or accompany every offer for sale. Before a mutual fund can distribute its prospectus, the SEC examines both the document and more detailed information (called a "statement of additional information") to determine that all required information is included. After the legal requirements have been met, the commission notifies the company that it may offer its securities for sale. The statement of additional information is not normally sent to investors with the prospectus but can be obtained by communicating with the fund company directly or by contacting the SEC.

After studying this chapter:

■ You will be familiar with the contents of a prospectus.
■ You will know how to determine a mutual fund's investment objectives, strategies, and risks.
■ You will know where to find a fund's performance record so you can evaluate the fund's management.
■ You will understand how a fund's fees and expenses impact its performance record.
■ You will understand how to interpret a fund's per share data, ratios, and financial highlights.
■ You will learn how to find information on buying, selling, or exchanging a fund's shares.
■ You will see how a fund prospectus is used to alert investors to the potential tax consequences of their investment activities.

CONTENTS OF A PROSPECTUS

The prospectus provides information such as the fund's goals, objectives, and possible risks that generally cannot be found in the financial press. A prospectus is approximately 10 to 12 pages long. It contains no flashy photos, graphs, or advertising. The SEC's attitude is that the document should contain only pertinent information without any marketing hype. Although the SEC has more recently allowed funds to create a shorter, less technical "profile prospectus" the result is still a very dry, "just the facts" type of document that can be difficult to read unless you know what you're looking for.

For illustrative purposes, we will use selected information from the May 2, 1999, prospectus of the Fidelity Magellan Fund. This information is typical of what you would expect to find in the prospectuses of most mutual funds, although the level of detail can vary from one prospectus to another. Our purpose here is to focus on the most important categories of fund information found in a typical prospectus. These categories relate to 1) investment objectives, policies or strategies, and risks; 2) performance; 3) fees; 4) per-share data and ratios; and 5) shareholder information.

The Date

The date of the prospectus is normally displayed on the front of the prospectus. You can see from Figure 20-1 that the date of the Magellan Fund's prospectus is May 22, 1999. While the date of the prospectus might not seem important, you must remember that they are usually updated every six months or so. So you want to be sure that you have the most current copy. Additionally, companies also revise their prospectuses and insert these revisions directly into the document. Be sure to check inside the prospectus for any updated or revised information.

Single- or Multiple-Fund Prospectus

Many fund families group all their fund descriptions in one prospectus where all fund names appear on the front cover. You need to make sure that you carefully read and understand the descriptions and details that relate to the fund you are considering for investment. Objectives, strategies, and risks can differ significantly among funds in a given family of funds.

DESCRIPTION OF THE FUND'S INVESTMENT OBJECTIVES, POLICIES OR STRATEGIES, AND RISKS

In the first page or pages of the prospectus, a company indicates its investment objective, the policies or strategies needed to achieve that objective or objectives, and any associated risks that the fund might

Fidelity
Magellan®
Fund

(fund number 021, trading symbol FMAGX)

Prospectus
May 22, 1999

Fidelity Investments®

82 Devonshire Street, Boston, MA 02109

FIG. 20-1 *Front Page of Magellan Fund Prospectus*

be exposed to. The prospectus indicates that the Magellan Fund "seeks capital appreciation" as its investment objective. Understanding the fund's objective is important because if you don't agree with the investment objective using your own common sense, you probably should look for another investment. All of a fund's prospectuses indicate that there is no assurance that the fund will achieve its stated objective.

The prospectus normally indicates the principal types of investment securities that the fund will hold. For example, Magellan's prospectus indicates that the fund's principal investment strategies (used to achieve its objective) include "investing primarily in common stocks; investing in domestic and foreign issuers; investing in either 'growth' stocks or 'value' stocks or both; and using fundamental analysis of each issuer's financial condition and industry position and market and economic conditions to select investments."

Later in the body of the prospectus a more detailed discussion of these strategies is presented. This detailed discussion explains the various techniques that the fund might use to achieve its objective. For example, Magellan indicates that it may buy and sell futures contracts "to increase or decrease the fund's exposure to changing security prices or other factors that affect security values."

The prospectus indicates that another strategy may be to "lend the fund's securities to broker-dealers or other institutions to earn income for the fund." The discussion also notes that the fund's equity security holdings include common stocks, preferred stocks, convertible securities, and warrants and states that not more than 40 percent of the fund's assets may be invested in companies operating exclusively in any one foreign country.

Other types of strategies that might be included in a fund's prospectus might relate to the size of the companies that a fund might invest in (as small- and medium-sized companies) or the fund might seek undervalued stocks that are out of favor with investors and are currently trading at prices that the fund advisor feels are below what the stocks are worth relative to their earnings.

Like any investment, a mutual fund includes certain risks. Each fund prospectus lists the risk factors that may affect that fund's performance and cause stock prices to decline over some stipulated period of time. Magellan Fund's prospectus observes that the "fund's share price changes daily based on changes in market conditions and interest rates and in response to other economic, political, or financial developments. The fund's reaction to these developments will be affected by the types of the securities in which the fund invests, the financial condition, industry and economic sector, and geographic location of the issuer, and the fund's level of investment in the securities of that issuer. When you sell your shares of the fund, they could be worth more or less than what you paid for them."

The prospectus discusses other factors that may significantly affect the fund's performance. These include stock market volatility, foreign exposure, issuer-specific changes (such as changes in the issuer's financial, economic, or political conditions), and changes in general economic and political conditions that can affect the value of an issuers's securities.

FUND PERFORMANCE RECORD

Funds normally include performance results for some stipulated period of time, or sometimes for the lifetime of the fund. This allows you to see how money invested in the fund has fared in the past. In Figure 20.2, the year-by-year returns for Fidelity Magellan are presented for the previous ten years. Also, the fund presented its average annual returns for the past one-, five-, and ten-year period in comparison to the Standard & Poor's 500 Index (a market capitalization–weighted index of common stocks) and Lipper Growth Funds Average (reflecting the performance of mutual funds with similar objectives).

Note that the year-to-year returns are (1) on a calendar-year basis, (2) do not include the effect of Magellan's front-end sales charge, and (3) are not the same total returns presented in the financial highlights section of the prospectus (Figure 20.4). Those returns are presented for the period ending March 31, Magellan's fiscal year-end. This form of presentation is common in the prospectuses of most mutual funds. Keep in mind that the fund's past performance does not indicate how it will perform in the future. For Magellan, the average annual returns of the fund in Figure 20.2 do include the effect of the fund's 3.0 percent maximum applicable front-end sales charge. Total returns includes the reinvestment of both past dividend income plus net realized and unrealized capital appreciation (gains minus losses).

FEES OR FUND EXPENSES
Shareholder Fees

The prospectus contains information regarding all of the fees and expenses that a shareholder incurs when he or she buys, holds, or sells shares of the fund. Figure 20-3 illustrates the shareholders fees charged by Fidelity Magellan. Note that Magellan has a sales charge (load) on purchases unlike true no-load funds, which do not impose charges on purchases and reinvested dividends, or charge redemption or exchange fees.

Performance

The following information illustrates the changes in the fund's performance from year to year and compares the fund's performance to the performance of a market index and an average of the performance of similar funds over various periods of time. Returns are based on past results and are not an indication of future performance.

Year-by-Year Returns

The returns in the chart do not include the effect of Magellan's front-end sales charge. If the effect of the sales charge was reflected, returns would be lower than those shown.

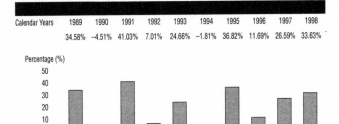

Calendar Years	1989	1990	1991	1992	1993	1994	1995	1996	1997	1998
	34.58%	−4.51%	41.03%	7.01%	24.66%	−1.81%	36.82%	11.69%	26.59%	33.63%

During the periods shown in the chart for Magellan, the highest return for a quarter was 27.22% (quarter ending December 31, 1998) and the lowest return for a quarter was – 16.48% (quarter ending September 30, 1990).

The year-to-date return as of March 31, 1999 for Magellan was 7.39%.

Average Annual Returns

The returns in the following table include the effect of the fund's 3.00% maximum applicable front-end sales charge.

For the periods ended December 31, 1998	Past 1 year	Past 5 years	Past 10 years
Magellan	29.62%	19.75%	19.53%
S&P 500	28.58%	24.06%	19.21%
Lipper Growth Funds Average	22.86%	18.63%	16.72%

Standard & Poor's 500 Index (S&P 500®) is a market capitalization-weighted index of common stocks.

Lipper Growth Funds Average reflects the performance (excluding sales charges) of mutual funds with similar objectives.

FIG. 20-2 *Fidelity Magellan Performance Record*

A redemption fee (sometimes called a "back-end load") is charged when you sell your shares while an exchange fee is imposed when you switch from one fund to another in the same fund family. From Figure 20-3 you can see that Magellan only imposes one shareholder fee, a sales charge of 3 percent on purchases. (The prospectus also indicates that a lower sales charge may apply to accounts greater than $250,000.)

Annual Operating Expenses

All mutual funds have operating expenses. These expenses, which are deducted from a fund's gross income each year, are expressed as a percentage of the net assets of the fund. You can see that Magellan's total expense ratio in fiscal year 1999 was 0.62%, or $6.20 per $1,000 of average net assets. Of the total fee, the management fee (0.43%) is normally the highest operating expense, most of which is paid to the investment advisors who make the day-to-day investment decisions for the fund.

Distribution fees that are passed on to investors are called 12b-1 fees (after the SEC rule that allows the charge). The fee consists of charges for marketing, advertising, mailing, and commissions paid to individuals who sell the fund's shares. Be careful! Over time these fees can add up and their effect on your return can be greater than that of a sales (load) charge. Figure 20-3 says that Fidelity Magellan does not impose this fee on its shareholders. However, even if a fund states that it does not charge a 12b-1 fee, it may simply pay these marketing and distribution costs out of the management fee. Either way, the fund is paying the fee.

The "other expenses" category includes office and operating expenses such as recordkeeping and transaction services to shareholders, state and local taxes, and legal and accounting fees. For Magellan, these fees were 0.19 percent.

A cost table is also provided in Figure 20-3. You should examine this table very carefully. The total dollar expenses are projected based on an investor's initial investment of $10,000, using the fund's current expense rate, and assuming that shares are held for one-, three-, five-, and ten-year periods. As the narrative accompanying the table indicates, this information can be helpful in comparing the cost of investing in different mutual funds.

The information is important because the cost of investing (operating expenses along with any transactions associated with the buying and selling of securities) can erode a substantial portion of the gross income or capital appreciation a fund achieves. Even small differences in expenses can have a dramatic effect on a fund's performance over time.

Fee Table

The following table describes the fees and expenses that are incurred when you buy, hold, or sell shares of the fund. The annual fund operating expenses provided below for the fund do not reflect the effect of any reduction of certain expenses during the period.

Shareholder Fees (paid by the investor directly)

Maximum sales charge (load) on purchases (as a % of offering price)	3.00%A
Sales charge (load on reinvested distributions	None
Deferred sales charge (load) on redemptions	None
Annual account maintenance fee (for accounts under $2,500)	$12.00

A*Lower sales charges may be available for accounts over $250,000.*

Annual fund operating expenses (paid from fund assets)

Management fee	0.43%
Distribution and Service (12b-1) fee	None
Other expenses	0.19%
Total annual fund operating expenses	0.62%

A portion of the brokerage commissions that the fund pays is used to reduce the fund's expenses. In addition, the fund has entered into arrangements with its custodian and transfer agent whereby credits realized as a result of uninvested cash balances are used to reduce custodian and transfer agent expenses. Including these reductions, the total fund operating expenses would have been 0.60%.

This **example** helps you compare the cost of investing in the fund with the cost of investing in other mutual funds.

Let's say, hypothetically, that the fund's annual return is 5% and that your shareholder fees and the fund's annual operating expenses are exactly as described in the fee table. This example illustrates the effect of fees and expenses, but is not meant to suggest actual or expected fees and expenses or returns, all of which may vary. For every $10,000 you invested, here's how much you would pay in total expenses if you close your account after the number of years indicated:

1 year	$ 361
3 years	$ 493
5 years	$ 635
10 years	$1,051

FIG. 20-3 *Fidelity Magellan Fee Table*

Also note that using an initial investment of only $10,000 can trivialize the costs of buying and holding a fund. Remember, the cost of holding a $100,000 investment will be 10 times as large as the cost indicated in Figure 20-3. As a potential investor you need to multiply your expected investment by the cost figures shown in the prospectus's fee table.

PER SHARE DATA AND RATIOS

Each fund's prospectus contains selected per-share data and ratios. Normally shown are: net asset values, investment income, expenses, and dividend and capital gain distributions, all presented on a per-share basis. You can use this data to determine the relative stability over time of the fund's income and expenses. The data also shows the extent to which realized gains (resulting from the fund selling securities) are passed on to shareholders as opposed to unrealized gains (increases in the market value of securities held by the fund) that remain part of the fund's net asset value. This information is normally presented for a five- or ten-year period. Magellan's table (called a "Financial Highlights Table") is presented in Figure 20-4. The information allows the user to compare the fund's operating activities during (in Magellan's case) the five-year period and is also presented with the fund's financial statements in its annual report. The total returns for Magellan represent the rate that an investor would have earned or lost each year on an investment in the fund (assuming reinvestment of all dividends and distributions) but do not include any front-end load (one-time sales charge).

Reading the Financial Highlights Table

Let's examine Fidelity Magellan's table. The table is broken down into two categories: selected per-share data and ratios and supplemental data.

Selected Per-Share Data. The Magellan Fund began the 1999 fiscal year with a price (net asset value) of $108.82 per share. During the year, the fund earned $.73 per share from investment income consisting of dividends from stocks and interest from bonds. The value of investments held or sold by the fund (net unrealized and realized gains) increased by $26.02 per share resulting in an increase of $26.75 per share from investment operations.

Magellan's shareholders received $5.82 per share in the form of dividend and capital gains distributions ($.67 in dividends passed on to shareholders plus $5.15 of realized capital gains earned by the fund and distributed to shareholders). Investment income from operations

Financial Highlights

The financial highlights table is intended to help you understand the fund's financial history for the past 5 years. Certain information reflects financial results for a single fund share. Total returns for each period include the reinvestment of all dividends and distributions. This information has been audited by PricewaterhouseCoopers LLP, independent accountants, whose report, along with the fund's financial highlights and financial statements, are included in the fund's annual report. A free copy of the annual report is available upon request.

Years ended March 31,	1999	1998	1997	1996	1995
Selected Per-Share Data					
Net asset value, beginning of period	$ 108.82	$ 80.20	$ 87.52	$ 72.44	$ 69.72
Income from Investment Operations					
Net investment income	.73^C	.73^C	1.38^C	.79	.27
Net realized and unrealized gain (loss)	26.02	34.35	5.25	19.57	5.22
Total from investment operations	26.75	35.08	6.63	20.36	5.49
Less Distributions					
From net investment income	(.67)	(1.25)	(1.10)	(.59)	(.14)
From net realized gain	(5.15)	(5.21)	(12.85)	(4.69)	(2.63)
Total distributions	(5.82)	(6.46)	(13.95)	(5.28)	(2.77)
Net asset value, end of period	$ 129.75	$ 108.82	$ 80.20	$ 87.52	$ 72.44
Total Return^{AB}	25.63%	45.41%	9.11%	28.43%	8.21%
Ratios and Supplemental Data					
Net assets, end of period (in millions)	$ 90.715	$ 71.968	$ 51.243	$ 56.179	$ 39.803
Ratio of expenses to average net assets	.62%	.62%	.66%	.95%	.99%
Ratio of expenses to average net assets after expense reductions	.60%^{D}	.61%^{D}	.64%^{D}	.92%^{D}	.96%^{D}
Ratio of net investment income to average net assets	.66%	.77%	1.75%	.95%	.39%
Portfolio turnover rate	37%	34%	67%	155%	120%

^{A} The total returns would have been lower had certain expenses not been reduced during the periods shown.

^{B} Total returns do not include the one-time sales charge.

^{C} Net investment income per share has been calculated based on average shares outstanding during the period.

^{D} FMR or the fund has entered into varying arrangements with third parties who either paid or reduced a portion of the fund's expenses.

FIG. 20-4 *Fidelity Magellan Financial Highlights Table*

($26.75) less distributions ($5.82) resulted in a share price of $129.75 at the end of the year, which is an increase of $20.93 (from $108.82 at the beginning of the year to $129.75 at the end of the year). Thus, a shareholder who elected to reinvest the distributions in the purchase of more of the fund's shares earned a total return of 25.63 percent for the year.

Ratio and Supplemental Data: The ratios and supplemental data show that as of March 31, 1999, the fund had net assets of $90,715 million. For 1999, the fund's expense ratio was 0.62% or $6.20 per $1,000 of net assets. The expense ratio (the ratio of expenses to average net assets) is an indicator of the efficiency of a fund's operating activities. A low expense ratio means more of your money remains in the fund to work for you.

Although the average expense ratio for an equity fund is approximately 1.4 percent, you should look for funds with a ratio of 1 percent or less, unless the higher costs to be incurred are justified by expectations of higher returns. Magellan notes that expenses of the fund were reduced to .60 percent of its net assets after adjusting for expenses paid or reduced by the fund's investment advisor and other third parties (custodian and transfer agent). Net investment income amounted to .66 percent of the fund's net assets and is often referred to as the dividend yield. For an income-oriented fund, you would expect a ratio of approximately 2 to 4 percent, and for an aggressive growth fund a ratio of 1 percent or less would be more common.

The portfolio turnover rate gives you an idea of the degree of annual trading within the fund's portfolio. The statistic is normally expressed as a percentage, e.g., a 100 percent turnover ratio means that a fund sold and replaced securities valued at 100 percent of its net assets within a one-year period.

The turnover rate is an important consideration in choosing a mutual fund because it can be an indicator of a fund's investment strategy. A low turnover rate may indicate a long-term orientation, while high turnover indicates a short-term strategy. In addition, turnover is directly related to transaction costs that affect the fund's future returns. Other things being equal, the higher the volume of buying and selling by the fund (turnover), the more transaction costs impact its return.

Also, funds with high turnover rates may be more likely to generate realized (and thus taxable) capital gains that must be distributed to its shareholders as income. Magellan sold and replaced securities valued at 37 percent of its net assets. A recent study by Morningstar,

Inc., indicated that the average turnover rate for all domestic stock funds was approximately 90 percent.

SHAREHOLDER INFORMATION

This section includes information on the specific procedures to follow when buying, selling, or exchanging shares. An exchange involves the redemption of all or a portion of the shares of one fund and the purchase of shares of another fund. The fund provides addresses, Web sites, and telephone numbers for use by shareholders and potential investors to conduct business. The fund lists the minimum amount necessary to open an account or to add to an existing account, and the minimum balance that must be maintained by an investor.

This section also includes information on the different ways that an investor can set up (register) an account, e.g., as an individual or joint tenant, Roth or simple IRA, 401(k) plan or 403(b) custodial accounts, trust, or business account. A fund will also include the features that are available to buy and sell shares in this section, which may include automatic investment and withdrawal programs, wire transfers, phone express transfers, and online trading.

The statements and reports that your fund will send you are also listed in this section of the prospectus. These documents include confirmation statements (after transactions affecting your account have occurred), monthly or quarterly statements, and financial reports.

Distributions. Funds distribute income (after expenses) and capital gains (less any losses) to shareholders at some time during the year. A fund prospectus will normally tell when distributions occur. Fidelity states that it normally pays dividends and capital gains in May and December. This means that you have distribution options. The fund's prospectus indicates what your options are which generally include:

1. reinvestment of both dividends and capital gains
2. dividends paid to you in cash and reinvestment of capital gains
3. all dividends and capital gains paid to you in cash.

Another option might be to have your dividends and capital gains directly invested in shares of another fund within your fund family.

Tax Consequences. Tax consequences of your investment are discussed in this section of the prospectus. Assuming your investment is not in a tax-advantaged retirement account, distributions are taxable to you at the federal, state, and local levels. Distributions in the form of dividends or short-term capital gains are taxed as ordinary income, while distributions of long-term capital gains are generally taxed as capital gains. Capital gains are realized whenever a fund sells securities for higher prices than it paid for them. The distinction between short- and long-term capital gains depends on whether a fund held the securities for less than or more than one year.

Fidelity's prospectus warns potential investors that if they buy shares when the fund has realized, but not yet distributed, income or capital gains, the investor will be "buying the dividend" by paying full price for the shares and then receiving a portion of the price back in the form of a taxable distribution. This is important because unless you are investing in a tax-advantaged retirement account, it is not advisable to buy shares of a fund before it makes a distribution, because doing so can cost you money in taxes.

As an example, assume that on December 28, you invest $10,000, buying 200 shares for $50 each. If the fund pays a distribution of $2 per share on December 31, its share price would drop to $48 (not counting market change). You still have only $10,000 (200 shares × $48 = $9,600 in share value, plus 200 shares × $2 = $400 in distributions), but you owe tax on the $400 distribution you received— even if you reinvest it in more shares. To avoid "buying the dividend," carefully read the fund's prospectus to determine the fund's distribution schedule before you invest.

STATEMENT OF ADDITIONAL INFORMATION

Additional detailed information about the fund can be obtained upon request directly from the company or from the Securities and Exchange Commission (SEC) (http://www.sec.gov) as the document is required to be filed with the SEC. This document is called the Statement of Additional Information (SAI). The SAI is legally a part of the prospectus (sometimes referred to as Part B). The SEC requires that only Part A be sent to the investor; Part B is sent only if specifically requested.

The SAI (written in a legal manner) contains biographies of the fund's directors and managers, and contains greater details on the agreement between the investment advisor and the fund, including the expense items charged to the fund, tax consequences of the fund's distributions, and investment objectives and restrictions. In addition to details of shareholders' voting rights and a statement of the independent auditors, there is other pertinent information that you might be interested in if you have decided that this fund is right for you.

CHAPTER PERSPECTIVE

This chapter has identified the major categories that should be examined by a potential investor. Reading the entire document from cover to cover is usually not realistic, but knowledge of the fund's objectives, policies, risks, past performance, costs, and pertinent shareholder information should be studied to allow you to "narrow the field" in your search for an investment target. Supplemental information, such as annual reports, investment advisory letters, statistical manuals (e.g., Morningstar Mutual Funds), and the financial press can also be useful for gathering information about potential mutual fund investments.

Glossary

Activity ratios a measure of management's effectiveness at using assets.

Administrative expenses costs associated with managing a company.

Audit report prepared by an accountant that attests to the accuracy and fairness of the presentation of data in the financial statements of a company in accordance with generally accepted accounting principles.

Balance sheet a report of resources owned and debts owed by a company at a particular point in time; includes assets, liabilities, and owners' equity.

Bonds a form of long-term debt, usually repaid in ten to 20 years.

Budget a formal, quantitative statement of management's expectations of future income, financial position, and cash flows. The master budget summarizes goals and objectives for all subunits of a company.

Business plan a comprehensive document that describes a company's past, current, and projected operatings and operating results.

Business resources those items of value that the business possesses and that can be used to produce a profit.

Common-size statements a variation of ratio analysis that converts items in a financial statement to percentages of the largest item in the statement.

Compilation a report by an accountant issued after checking a company's financial statements for proper form, appropriate disclosures, and accurate mathematics.

Consolidated statement the combined financial statements of a parent company and its subsidiaries.

Contingency a situation in which the company stands to gain or lose as the result of a past transaction or event.

Depreciation the assignment of historical cost of a long-lived productive asset to production periods. Land cannot be depreciated.

Earnings per share (EPS) company earnings divided by the number of shares of stock outstanding.

Encumbrance a budgeted amount of money that has been committed but not yet actually paid out.

Equity property rights.

Expenses decreases in owners' equity produced by outflows of assets.

Factory overhead total of all indirect costs of production, such as costs of supervisor labor, maintenance, equipment and factory depreciation, manufacturing supplies, energy, and insurance.

FIFO a method of recording inventory flow by listing First-In-First-Out; assumes the oldest units are sold first.

Fully diluted EPS includes in the denominator all items that could reasonably be converted to common stock.

Historical cost original cost of an asset.

Horizontal common-size analysis a variation of common size statements that uses the statements of a prior year as a base and expresses each component of a future year as a percentage of the corresponding component in the base year.

Income statement a report of the results of business activities for a period of time, typically one year. Includes revenues and expenses.

Intangible assets long-lived productive assets that do not have a physical existence. These include patents, copyrights, trademarks, franchises, organizational costs, purchased goodwill, and research-and-development costs.

Inventory current assets, carried in the balance sheet at historical cost or at the lower of cost or market value.

Liabilities accounting term for debts. Current liabilities are those expected to be paid within one year of the date on the balance sheet. Noncurrent liabilities are not expected to be paid within one year of the date on the balance sheet.

LIFO Last-In-First-Out method of inventory flow.

Liquidity ratios measure a company's ability to pay its short-term debt.

Matching principle requires that costs directly associated with producing a certain revenue be expected in the same period that the revenue is recorded.

Obligations amounts owed to nonowners.

Overall (debt and equity) ratios measure the relative size of claims of long-term creditors compared to the claims or property rights of owners.

Owners' equity accounting term for owners' investment; includes both owners' initial investment and reinvestment of company earnings not distributed to owners.

Period costs nonmanufacturing costs, such as selling and administration.
Periodicity the assumption that a company's life must be divided into periods of time in order to measure profit or loss.
Product costs manufacturing costs.
Profitability ratios measure of either management's operating efficiency or stock performance.
Prospectus a short booklet required by the SEC to be distributed to prospective mutual fund investors. The prospectus contains in part information about the fund's objectives, strategies, expenses, and performance.

Receivables all claims expected to be settled in cash, primarily as a result of the company's trade or business.
Responsibility center a company unit that has control over its costs, revenues, and/or investment and has its own budget. May be a cost center, a profit center, or an investment center.
Retained earnings profits earned by the business and not paid out as dividends to the owners.
Revenue increases in owners' equity produced by inflows of assets as a result of doing business.
Revenue recognition principle requires that revenue be recorded when the activities necessary to sell a good or provide a service have been completed, regardless of whether cash has been collected or a receivable created.
Review report issued by an accountant after reviewing a company's financial statements, but without performing the tests done for a full audit that guarantee compliance with generally accepted accounting principles.

Segment analysis assessment of performance of divisions, categories, sales territories, or product lines of a company.
Selling expenses costs associated with producing sales, including sales personnel salaries and commissions, office staff salaries, payroll taxes and pension expenses related to the sales staff, advertising, delivery and shipping costs, and telephone expense.
Short term one year or one company operating cycle, whichever is greater.
Statement of cash flows describes all of the changes that have occurred in the balance sheet during the fiscal year in terms of their effect on cash.
Stock a share in the company's ownership. May be preferred or common.
Stock option stock right issued to corporate employees and officers enti-

tling them to acquire common stock at a preset price within a specified period of time.

Stock warrant an entitlement that allows the holder to acquire shares of stock at a fixed price within a specified period of time.

Treasury stock stock issued by a company and later reacquired but neither canceled nor retired.

Trend analysis type of horizontal analysis that presents the current year's performance as a percent of the performance of a prior year.

Uncollectible account bad debt or doubtful account.

Weighted-average inventory inventory flow measure that charges both ending inventory and cost of goods sold with the weighted-average cost of all units available for sale.

Index